VISTA

Life and getting where you want to be

Elisabet Sahtouris
Evolution Biologist and Futurist

Elisabet Sahtouris

Vista:
Life and getting where you want to be

© Copyright 2023, Elisabet Sahtouris. All rights reserved.

Cover design: Elisabet Sahtouris
Interior book design: David Christel

No part of this book may be reproduced or transmitted in any form or by any means, electronic or mechanical, including photocopying, recording, or by any information storage and retrieval system, without permission from the author, except for the inclusion of brief quotations in review.

ISBN: 978-1-936965-42-7

Web Sites:
https://www.sahtouris.com
(my main website, with a wide selection of my articles, films, books, etc.)

https://ratical.org/sahtouris
(my older articles up to early 2004)

Images:

- Pg. 52 — Hunab-Ku / Maya Symbol für Gott by Anne Mathiasz, Adobe Stock: #45895729
- Pg. 52 — Yin Yang symbol by newbeginner, Adobe Stock: #39087695

Upaya house Publishing
9558 Hampton Reserve Drive
Brentwood, TN 37027

Made in the USA

"... real learning does notcome solely throughassimilating knowledge; it involves coming to hold one's conceptual framework sufficiently lightly to allow in experiences that don't fit well with existing frameworks. if our belief systems fundamentally change, through whatever process or experiences, our perceptions and everything else about our lives will change. That will be true individually and collectively."

– Willis Harman
Biology Revisioned
Co-authored w. Elisabet Sahtouris

"There is an ancient axiom that each of us human Earthriders encounters sooner or later, as he moves out, according to his sense of things, to be more of what he would like to be, or at least ought to be.... and the axiom is this: that no one ever finds human life much worth living, or the human world in which he finds himself much worth living in; he has to make them so.

It's a simple-sounding but terribly embarrassing little axiom, for it forces each of us, whether we like the idea or not, to accept responsibilities it is always so much more satisfying to unload on someone else, or an assortment of other people, provided, of course, that we can get away with it with good grace. But those who have been the most trustworthy guides and counselors to mankind down through the ages say that such evasion is utterly impossible, and that mankind's attempt to unload his responsibilities in the past as well as at the present time is responsible for virtually all the difficulties and woes in which we find ourselves today."

– J. Allen Boone
You Are the Adventure

Prologue

*V*ISTA *is my name for the Big Picture Worldview I evolved in the course of my life. The word VISTA is an overlap of two shorter words: Vita, which means Life, and Visa, what we need to get where we want to be.*

The cover photo is of myself on the peak of Waynu Picchu, right next to Machu Picchu in the Peruvian Andes. Just after a heavy rain, I went climbing the very steep and muddy trail to its top. As I passed a slower climber, he asked why I wore white when I would be covered in mud by the time I reached the top. While sitting on the very peak, I saw him approaching on the ledge below me and raised my arms calling "See? No mud!" In that very moment, he snapped the photo, which he then sent to me.

In Chapter 9 I speak of being given the Quechua name *Kuntur Ruyac* — White Condor — in ceremony. When I looked at the photo later, it seemed prescient, as if illustrating who I was to become. To create the human future well, I believe we all need good Vistas — consciously created belief systems comprised of worldviews, what we believe to be facts about ourselves, our world, the whole cosmos, and the values with which we steer our way among them.

This book is the story — or rather, a slew of stories — about the development of my own Vista, so that you, Dear Reader, can follow my trajectory in my hope it might help you in evolving your own Vista. *Why* I wrote this book in this way, is a story in its own right.

In 2012, while I was living on the Spanish island of Mallorca, I read the book *Presence*, a remarkable dialogue among Betty Sue Flowers, Otto Scharmer, Joseph Jaworski, and Peter Senge. I had met Otto in a workshop in England, and we had been published back-to-back in a

German magazine. I had also read Joseph's book *Synchronicity: The Inner Path of Leadership*. But it was Betty Sue Flowers, who had organized this book, Presence, that got most of my attention and admiration; so much so that I sent her an email. To my surprise, I got a quick and very positive response. We continued emailing, and then Skyping (Zoom not yet having been invented), finding our admiration mutual and growing quickly deeper. More on this story in Chapter 13.

When Betty Sue offered to help me with the book I was writing at the time, I was absolutely thrilled. I was calling it *Ecosophy: Co-creating the Wise Society*, but as we dialogued about it, she gently but firmly offered her opinion that it should not be another expositional book. Rather, she strongly suggested, I should tell the story of my intellectual/spiritual path such that my readers could follow the evolution of my thinking and discoveries — somewhat like the path onto which she had steered Joe Jaworski in midwifing his book *Synchronicity*.

And so, I started over, to tell that story of personal worldview development, and choosing the title *Vista*.

I often laughed happily, as my chapters for this book came back from her with edits. How I readily agreed with every suggestion she made! I'd been offered a few editors in the past, but quickly abandoned each in turn because I could not agree at all with their takes on my writing.

Here was a sister soul, if not an embodied angel, right at my side. Every conversation we had was delicious, and we found powerful common ground in our shared understanding that story shapes the whole human world. In her words, "mythology shapes current events;" in mine, "our stories create our realities."

Thus, this book is about my own conscious creation of my ever-evolving Vista — how I became aware of my beliefs, recognizing how I was creating my reality through them, identifying their sources, and questioning them in order to decide which ones served me well and which needed changing.

I came to see this process as gardening: planting beliefs, seeing whether they flourished, weeding out those that seemed not to do well for me any longer, planting new ones in place of them. My garden contains the two kinds of beliefs I mentioned above: the ones I think of as 'facts' and the value beliefs with which I steer my life through those 'facts' about How Things Are in my personally viewed world and cosmos — the only world and cosmos any of us can have.

While much of this book is autobiographical, only those events of my life that most influenced my evolving Vista are included, so it is not a normal autobiography. Further, there are many sections describing my actual beliefs as they developed — putting forth ideas that shifted my reality in expositional manner.

As I write in Chapter 12, "I'm aware that I devote far more energy to my global human family in my hopes for its evolution into mature cooperation, than I do to my own children and grandchildren — hoping they will one day understand and forgive me." I also mention there, my very first intention to write a book called *Vistas* — an expositional treatise on worldviews, rather than *this* story of my own.

In 2015, a spirit call got me to move from Mallorca across the globe to Hawai'i, as described in Chapter 14, and I abandoned the writing of this book for more than seven years before finally returning to it. I was so embarrassed after all Betty Sue's loving midwifery, that I did not dare ask her for more.

After all, I had to live this last phase of my life, in which my Vista continued to evolve, in order to see the new influences on it. Then, just as I was writing the last two chapters, David Christel appeared suddenly in my life as a new angel editor, taking over the tasks of seeing me through this book's completion as we also became friends. I am seeking no publisher, as my sole intention is to have it formatted as an eBook in order to give it away freely to any and all who might enjoy the ride and find some value in it.

Contents

Prologue v
Chapter 1: MidEarth Sea Reflections 1
    Science reconsidered 3
    First encounter with assumptions 9
    Freedom to ponder the bigger picture 10
Chapter 2: Lessons Learned in the MidEarth Sea 15
    The Epidaurus incident 16
    Greece as inspiration 18
    Lesson from the sea 19
    Paradigm shifting in science 21
    Thoughts on language 22
    Finding my voice 25
Chapter 3: Society as Political Economy 29
    Economics and the waging of war 30
    From nuclear darkness to art and science 32
    Political activism in Berkeley and beyond 33
    Museum reflections on human nature, science, and society 35
    Juvenile delinquents in Boston 38
    The view from China 39
    Re-entry and return to worldview explorations 46
Chapter 4: Science Meets the Sacred 49
    Paraphysics 49
    Encounters with past lives 53
    Beyond my body 55
    The best job ever 58
    Worldviews from Seth to Henry Miller 61
    Freedom from thing-glut 63
    The Delos vortex 64
Chapter 5: Trying My Wings 67
    A theatric cell 67

Competition to cooperation	69
A matter of maturation	71
Lovelock comes to call	72
Academia revisited in Catania	74
Deep-diving into the History of Science	77
Spirit calls me	81
Chapter 6: Spreading My Wings	**83**
Gaia Conferences – meeting scientists at the leading edge	83
Lovelock and life	84
New horizons on Hydra	88
Published	91
Worldwide Indigenous Science Network	91
Earth celebrations 2000 and Irini Papas	94
From rebirth in Egypt to Perestroika in Moscow	95
Costa Rica gold magic	99
Chapter 7: Indigenous Inspiration	**101**
From Findhorn to Hopiland	101
Florida: Hazel, the Great Spirit and dolphins	104
Andes adventure	106
Rio: Kari-Oca and Indigenous rights	108
Savages and politicians in Rio	110
Sapaim	112
From Kayapo to concert	116
A Guarana tree story	117
Concert under the moon	119
Chapter 8: Living in the Flow	**121**
Sufi summer	121
Washington, DC: The way up is down	123
From prayer vigil to prayer chapel	128
A matter of metaphor	130
J. Allen Boone	133
Chapter 9: The Call of the Andes	**137**
Peru calling	137
Cusco	

Journey to Hapu	141
Puma and the spirits of the Andes	144
Taking Puma north	147
Santa Barbara whale summer	151
Chapter 10: Weaving My Reality	**155**
Moon over Brazil	155
More reality-shifting stories	157
Revisioning biology	160
Views on consciousness	163
Writing *Biology Revisioned*	165
Seth at the Salk	169
My own magical reality	171
Chapter 11: Strands in the Tapestry	**173**
A walk through time … and space	173
Cross-cultural insights on religion	177
Chasing grand unified theories	178
Krista	184
Grounding cosmic love	186
Down to business	187
Dharamsala	190
More business world leader encounters	192
Chapter 12: Expanding Worldviews	**195**
(R)evolution in religion	195
Dissonance and resonance in Japan	198
Cultural creativity	201
Kauri Tree: New Zealand	204
Living systems in digital and business worlds	206
Heading for a Hot Age … and to Barcelona	208
Chapter 13: Return to the MidEarth Sea	**213**
Shoji and the symposia	213
Epiphany in Hokkaido	216
Kuala Lumpur without Shoji-san	218
Mallorca goes green	220
Paradise on Mallorca	221

Poison in paradise	225
From Istanbul to Oslo	226
Betty Sue Flowers	231
Storytelling in Findhorn	232
Chapter 14: Hawai'i	**237**
Settling in	237
My hanai Samoan family	239
Sister Saint Joan	241
Professor back to business	242
Making sense of a fast-changing world	245
Food	249
AI, an oxymoron	250
Chapter 15: Final Insights	**253**
Political economy and democracy in Nature	253
My own voice from the past	256
Dreaming and Waking Realities	268
Physical challenges become challenges to belief	260
Crisis as Opportunity; Celebrating Crises	263
Discussion vs Dialogue	263
The H2 Clipper	265
Peak experiences	266
Discoveries and contributions	267
Epilogue	**269**
References	**273**
About the Author	**283**

CHAPTER 1

MidEarth Sea Reflections

It was one of those intensely blue-sky fall days with billowing clouds beginning to hint of rain as weather cools down from summer — perfect for climbing up through the dense pine forest behind my whitewashed stone house. When the shady forest opened up to sun-bathed rocky heights, I clambered to the highest point where the sea came into view in almost every direction. Yes, I truly lived on a Greek island in that shimmering *MidEarth* Sea — my literal translation of Mediterranean.

My very first view of Greece from an airplane instantly brought to mind the whole Earth photo that may be the greatest thing science brought us in the past century. Silvery white clouds on such blue sea beneath me, broken by patches of pinkish-beige land, looked so like the space photo it was easy to imagine I was looking down on the entire planet — both Greece and Earth being around three-fourths sea and one-fourth pinkish-beige land masses. And surely Greece, culturally and geographically a link between East and West, as well as between North and South, qualified as MidEarth.

On these climbs through the forest to the top of my little island to look at that shimmering sea in all directions from on high, I never met anyone and so was free to dream of a world unmarred by my strange, still relatively new, two-legged species. Humans are that to me — a strange two-legged species I'm still trying to understand.

I became an evolution biologist to understand the human condition, but in Greece I became more of a Greek philosopher. I rather liked claiming that title; after all I was born in Athens — that is, Athens, New York, a small town in the US — and acquired Greek citizenship in marrying a Greek fisherman. It would've been fun if, when I was little and grownups patted me on the head asking what I wanted to be when I grew up, I'd looked them confidently in the eye and announced *"a Gweek philosopha!"* I have a photo of myself around age three, looking into the sky, blond curls highlighted by the sun, arms crossed almost defiantly with just that kind of confidence.

Actually, I came to Greece within a year after meeting the American author/philosopher Henry Miller and being inspired by him. I was in a relationship with the only one of his biographers Henry had approved, who took me to Henry's Santa Monica home and left me alone with him most days while doing library research for his next book. While he was out, Henry and I had the most delicious conversations.

Those conversations with Henry proved to be one of the greatest experiences of my life. His boundless good humor and intensely vivid memory — he complained of having no forgettery — led us to weave delightful strands of the past into adventurous musings on life and its meanings. His books, especially *The Colossus of Maroussi* and *The Time of the Assassins* and *The Air-Conditioned Nightmare*, along with many essays, qualify him as a great American philosopher. Pity the public had so focused on his breaking down sexual taboos that his marvelous philosophy of life — life itself as an affair of the heart, as a miracle — was overshadowed by his notoriety.

Anyway, I'd read his fascinating book *The Colossus of Maroussi* before meeting him, and he told me more stories of Greece in person. He'd left Greece in haste on the eve of World War II, and had left all his notes for the book with the Greek poet Seferis, not getting them back until long after the book was written and published in New York. I will never forget his telling me, in his thick Brooklyn accent and with laughter in his voice, *"So I hadda write da whole book widdout any notes in dis little alley acrosst from a synagogue in New Yawk."*

In another conversation, one about science, he said to me, *"I've always hated da straight line, don'cha know?"* And somehow that cut to the essence of my own problem with science and its strictures. Sadly, a year later, I heard his death announced on the radio as I was already in Greece, having abandoned science to write *my* first novel.

But my musings on Henry were suddenly interrupted as I walked back down from the heights of my little island through the long-needled pine trees, on the soft carpet of brown needles dotted with the first perky pink cyclamens beneath the feathery green branches overhead. I felt a plop on my arm as I reached out to push back a branch in my path. A large walking stick insect sat there, perched on my arm looking me straight in the eye.

I burst into tears! Happy tears. *Very* happy tears. For this was a long-lost friend I had not seen since childhood on the forested flanks of the Hudson River near Athens. As waves of nostalgia flooded me, I was a child again, extending my mind up into a hemlock pine far too tall to climb, to be right next to a woodpecker hammering away up there, in a world where science had not yet told me that was impossible — a world in which walking sticks were among my many friends.

As I looked into those tiny black eyes, my long-lost friend seemed to be trying to tell me something. Thrown back to childhood, I was recalling the empty, dried-out shells of locust grubs clinging to the bark of tall pines sheltering rabbit burrows. I had collected shoeboxes full of those translucent shells with their delicate hollow legs and the clean edges of the open slit down their backs that looked as if there must have been a loud crack when the shell burst open to release the locust into flight.

Back in the moment with my new-old friend on my arm, I realized that something in me still wanted to be released the way those locusts were released. I *had* released myself from my entire past life to get to my island paradise. But maybe that was just the stage at which a locust grub comes out of the ground after years of incubating in the dark earth, and now my shell had hardened to the next stage where its body quietly grew tightly furled wings, ready to come out and fly!

Here I was, a PhD-credentialed evolution biologist who had freed herself from science to write novels on a Greek island because *science* had felt like a suit too tight for comfort, or a lover who had constrained me until I had to burst free. Yet something about this lovable stick-with-legs being seemed to be telling me that I was not yet fully free, that I still needed to tell the story of evolution — the story of who we are and where we came from, in order to see where we can go from here. Could I split my shell now and fly free? Could I fly free *as a scientist*?

Science reconsidered

After that walk, I put away the two novels and several short stories I'd written to begin writing essays about various aspects of science. I loved science and wanted to analyze just where and how that suit was too tight for me — to discover how I would answer the questions I had, what I really did believe, what I wanted to research further. With no access to a library — even those in Athens I could get to with some effort would not have the material I sought — I began writing letters to scientists I admired, especially those at the leading edge, those who were pushing the boundaries as I wanted to. A Greek stamp proved to be magical in drawing replies from people I had no great hopes would respond; not only did I get letters, but books and articles were soon sent to me as well.

This project became more exciting than writing novels, and the more my essays piled up on my desk, the more my love of science flowed back into me. But this new venture also had me reflecting more on my whole life trajectory up to this point. If I wasn't going to continue writing the novels, was I off track?

All I had asked for in Greece while still new there had been said in a kind of prayer on the flat rooftop of my first house on the island of Aegina. Flinging my arms to the starry sky, not knowing whether there was any being or force that would hear me, I had simply said, each night as I stood there, "Use me!"

Now, thinking of Henry, who'd repeatedly pointed out that he had trouble with marriage to women because he'd always been married first and foremost to his work, I found myself wondering when it was that I first fell in love with *science*?

I was certainly born with insatiable curiosity and as a child spent most all my waking hours out in nature, with the good fortune to explore it freely almost from the time I rose up on my two legs to walk. We lived in the countryside on the Hudson River's shore, with a stream burbling through a cool forest of tall hemlocks, beech, and occasional oak trees. The squishy sun-soaked and snail-ridden mudflats along the river contrasted with the scurrying world of shady forest floor creatures while the nearby meadows were rife with grasses and fungi up to the great puffballs my brothers and I fought to stomp when dry and ready to release their spores in great clouds. Birds and insects in endless variety navigated between these domains and my mother was able to identify most of the flora and fauna by name (her father, a veterinarian who had died before I was born, having passed his own love of nature on to her).

From long hikes in the Catskill mountains to occasional camping on Adirondack mountain lake islands and regular weekly family food bartering excursions to friends' farms, my early childhood was rich with direct experience of nature. I was comfortable in that natural world, untainted by the ways of humanity in the world at large. But, too soon, I became aware that a terrible war was raging. Pearl Harbor was bombed when I was just 5 years old and in first grade. I knew enough of the ensuing war through radio, then newsreels at the movies, food rationing and victory gardens, scrap drives, and bomb drills to have nightmares about it.

Nature remained as ever my refuge. In my first year of high school, when I was twelve (I'd been skipped ahead in elementary school), I loved my biology class more than any other and often stayed after school to care for experiments in seed growth or work through an extra frog dissection. Our imposing but humorous teacher, Dr. DiCaprio, became the first adult to really *get* my deep love of and insatiable curiosity about nature to the point of encouraging me toward a future in the biological sciences as though reading my heart.

Outside of school, my education had been deliciously expanded by a sympathetic public librarian who broke the rules in allowing me, by the time I was nine or ten, into the adult stacks where I gorged on biology and archeology — especially of ancient Egyptians and Incas — as well as on swashbuckling Sabatini romances. By the time I met Dr. DiCaprio, whose PhD, we kids discovered, was actually in music, I knew I was slated to become an explorer. His encouragement got me thinking that the study of science, which was exactly the way to get to far-off unexplored jungles.

But my excitement was quickly squelched. My high school years straddled the transition from the '40s to the '50s, and my parents, despite having encouraged my love of nature, held science to be a profession only for boys. They steered me away from math, chemistry and physics into French, music and art. My teachers agreed with them, that my talent for drawing and painting surely meant I should study art after high school. They pointed out that if I still loved science, I could always become a medical illustrator, a suggestion that could not have been farther from what I had in mind — there would be no nigglingly detailed gut drawings for me!

Meanwhile, the minister of the Dutch Reformed Church in which I'd grown up had his own plans for me, pegging me to be "the next Mrs. Lindsey." Mrs. Lindsey was his role-model parishioner, a perfectly coiffed lady with perfect children, living in a perfect white house with picket fence & roses, making magazine picture casseroles for church suppers, fundraising and being on every other church committee — a pillar of the community, as was said. Straight out of the much later movie *Pleasantville*.

Mrs. Lindsey's life struck me as so excruciatingly boring I decided *that* future was *my* vision of hell. So, if I had to study art, I would throw myself headlong into the bohemian life I'd learned about in French class, where the only other PhD teacher in my high school whisked our small class quickly through the basics so we could read Andre Gide's explorations of freedom from constraining Puritanism along with other contemporary French writers by the time we were seniors.

Winning a four-year tuition, room and board scholarship to the state university of my choice at fifteen, I was off to the Art School at Syracuse University at sixteen. To prepare, I shopped the new post-war Army & Navy Store for army khakis with matching shirt to alternate with jeans (called 'dungarees' then) and long-sleeved black turtle-neck shirts. Fleeing my minister's church lady dream, I plunged myself into that art student getaway without ever looking back.

My parents *had* mentioned that a university would at least be a good place to find a suitable husband, so I lost no time at that, especially as being a married woman in those days catapulted me, still a teenager, from having to be safely in my dorm at considerably earlier evening hours than boys to being partnered with one of them to play house in our own apartment and qualify, as a married couple, to officially chaperone fraternity parties. Go figure!

Many of our friends were foreign students from Turkey, Pakistan, India and other exotic places, mostly studying political science and economics, which gave me windows onto a much larger world while broadening my culinary repertoire. Soon, I was not just an art student, wife, party chaperone and good international cook, reading up on the rest of the world, but, just after my graduation, the happy mother of a delightful baby girl, with the Indian/Turkish name Johara, meaning precious jewel.

Two years later, we had moved to Indiana, where the marriage dissolved, leaving me a single mom. It was then it dawned on me that I was also free to break the taboo on becoming a scientist. The revival of my dream so excited me I determined to try making up for lost time by pushing my way into the graduate school of sciences at Indiana University.

Without any of the requisite undergraduate background, but highly motivated, I spent a summer cramming enough to pass an entrance exam, learned statistics on my own to pass an additional required test, and convinced enough professors I was capable of doing graduate level work to be allowed into their classes one by one. I even got a teaching assistantship that pushed me to stay academically ahead of science undergrads while narrowly covering my food, rent and the gas for a motor scooter on which to go to classes, shopping, and get my daughter to nursery school. As an incipient scientist, I doffed the khakis, still the artist, however, by designing and sewing my own clothes. I made quite a splash going to the opera in heels and a barebacked dress on my white motor scooter — rather unusual behavior for a young woman before the end of the '50s.

At last, I felt, I was truly on my way! Plunged so suddenly into the almost entirely male world of microbiology, genetics, physiological psychology, perception neurology and philosophy of science, I found it an intensely challenging and amazing experience. Science was rife with world-shaking new discoveries. Jim Watson, Francis Crick's partner in the newly heralded discovery of DNA, came to visit his cousin who was a classmate of mine. Together we pushed his car out of an Indiana snow bank in the midst of a storm and I was thrilled, feeling myself to be part of the one human endeavor that could truly explain everything I wanted to explain about life and the human condition. Life couldn't have been better.

Science was brilliant! As I'd hoped, it offered the means to make sense of everything in the natural world, including humans. It was all so clear and logical. Theories were meticulously divided into various testable hypotheses; questions could be answered by carefully designed experiments. With the tools of microscopes, telescopes and recording devices, with statistical tests and other math tools, scientists built models of how things really are — from models of planetary orbits to the models of atoms with their orbiting electrons, from models of the brain to this new double helix model of DNA that gave cellular biology and genetics a new prominence in the world at large.

In art school I had foundered on the concept of abstraction, which no professor or fellow student could ever successfully explain to me. Suddenly the light dawned on me in — of all places — the world of science! Science built models of how things work in nature by identifying their measurable aspects. These measurable properties could, so to speak, be *lifted out* of whatever was under study, much as Picasso had *lifted out* certain aspects of war that he could assemble in brushstrokes to paint *Guernica*. Scientists were abstracting aspects of natural phenomena to build their models of them.

As humans got better at technology, more sophisticated scientific models of nature emerged. Freud's plumbing system model of the brain, with its pipes and valves that got blocked, had morphed into the telephone switchboard model of wires and junctions, which in turn was now replaced by the new computing devices. The better we got at technology, the closer we were to understanding natural mechanisms; the new fields of cybernetics and robotics began to be called 'artificial intelligence' (AI). What a heady time it was!

Fuzzy concepts, such as *God* and *mind* were rejected as unscientific; the murky conception of animal *instinct* was replaced by measurable 'fixed action patterns' of behavior. I enjoyed the whole process of thinking logically and clarifying things by defining them operationally.

Science was objective, not subjective. You measured what could be measured without reading into it. Thus, we were warned that in observing nature, we must never *identify* with animals as other living creatures in order to understand them. No truly objective scientist would commit the sin of *anthropomorphism*, the projection of human qualities onto other living beings.

And yet, it occurred to me — perhaps the first chink in the mental armor I was willingly constructing — that seeing creatures as complex mechanisms could be called *mechanomorphism*, which was actually, given that humans were the inventors of mechanisms, a kind of second-hand anthropomorphism. But I learned pretty quickly not to push forward such challenges as I loved being part of this insider world of science and wanted to fit in.

One of the exciting aspects of the mechanistic worldview of science was its application in technology, especially through the new development of computers. The Digital Electronics Corporation (DEC) was manufacturing computer 'chips' for laboratory equipment, which we graduate students learned to build for our own research projects. The chips were 3 by 5 or 6-inch printed circuit boards that we mounted in rows on tall standing metal racks, connecting them to each other with 'snap leads' we soldered by hand, attaching color-coded wire to metal snaps like those used in clothing, only larger. We were making circuit boards in their primitive iteration.

Complex connections among dozens of mounted chips permitted us to design experimental protocols to carry out using these digital relays, switches and timers, which we connected to sensors and recorders, lights, buzzers and electroshock delivery in mazes, runways, and other equipment for testing animals isolated from us in nearby rooms. Thus, we could measure animal behavior, or read and broadcast their neural activity via brain implants and record physiological biofeedback signals from test subjects including ourselves. I felt fortunate in learning how the guts of computers worked when they were such a mystery to almost everyone and drew on my younger brother's expertise in designing my experimental equipment as he knew much more about them than I did.

My favorite courses were in cellular microbiology and genetics, in no small measure due to the wonderful teaching style of Prof. Tracy Sonneborn, who conveyed his love of paramecia and fruit flies (never referring to them as *drosophila melanogaster* as other professors did) in his down-to-earth and yet exciting manner. He taught from the text of his English contemporary, C. H. Waddington (both were born in 1905) who introduced the terms *morphic field*[1] and *epigenesis*[2]. Sonneborn himself demonstrated acquired characteristics that were genetically inherited in paramecia, foreshadowing the vindication of Lamarck, still reviled at that time for proposing that acquired characteristics could be inherited. Sonneborn broke the ice by demonstrating what went counter to the genetic dogma of the time, and I thrilled to Sonneborn's audacity and perfectly valid research, while his own colleagues ignored it.

The more I learned about cells, the more awesome they were. Their elaborately constructed membranes and the complex arrays of interacting organelles inside them, with amazing networks of intricate scaffolding and transportation systems, housing uncountable molecular citizens in what amounted to busy microcities, run by the newly-elaborated DNA codes, as it then seemed. Epigenetics had been only very dimly foreshadowed by Sonneborn's work, and no one yet knew how DNA could be changed by an organism's life experience, much less the critical importance of the smart proteins that organized and then selected specific DNA sequences to carry out the cells' work. It was all so fascinating.

First encounter with assumptions

J. R. Kantor's Philosophy of Science course was also fascinating in the way it revealed the insides of science itself — something I had not yet even thought about! Kantor showed us that science was built on fundamental axioms — assumptions that were not provable but were formal statements of the most obvious characteristics of the natural universe science studies.

To make theories, and then testable hypotheses, this conceptual framework was needed because *it is impossible to make a theory in a vacuum*. How could you theorize about a universe if you had no concept whatever of that universe? I was fascinated by this — that the very foundations of science, without which it could not exist, were actually unprovable assumptions. It was a truly mindblowing revelation that would change my life.

These fundamental conceptions of the universe were formalized as axioms, such as: the universe is composed solely of matter and energy; the universe is non-living, devoid of meaning and purpose; the universe can be studied objectively (i.e., without interfering in it); natural phenomena arise by accident through the random collisions of fundamental particles; natural phenomena can be understood by analyzing the parts of which they are composed and natural laws operating on them; and things must be measurable to be real.

As part of the philosophy of science course requirements, we had to go through the process of writing out these assumptions and showing how they were reflected in particular theories based upon them. It was as though the 'guts' of science itself had become as visible to me as those of computers and cells, and still more amazing. For the first time, I became aware that there were certain kinds of questions I had about the world that could not be answered within the universe scientists had literally decreed. The scientific universe only had access to the measurable aspects of things — the aspects that could be abstracted into mathematical models.

Logical as this world science constructed and modeled was, it now became difficult for me to accept as unreal anything in my experience that was not measurable. Even the mind that made up all these concepts was held to be a mere 'construct.' Quantum physics, although well under way and producing heresies of its own by regarding the mind as consciousness and seeing it as critical to the formation of our physical world, was utterly unknown to, or disregarded, by my professors. Science like other human endeavors, had become fragmented. Again, I kept my budding heresies to myself, and focused on getting my PhD by doing as I was told.

Freedom to ponder the bigger picture

After a few years in Greece — much longer than I'd intended to stay to write novels — I read a review of the Hollywood film *Rich and Famous*. Apparently, one of the two women writers the story is about says to the other at the end that she's now had all the riches and fame but would like to find love on a Greek Island and marry a fisherman. That got a good laugh out of me, by illustrating the way I'd always seemed to do everything ass-backwards in life. Here I was, poor and unknown, but living on a beautiful Greek island — and I had married Arghiris, a fisherman fourteen years younger than I and very handsome at that!

We had met in a sweet shop one evening on the island of Aegina not very long after I arrived and had rented the small house on the roof top of which I prayed to 'be used.' He walked me home that fragrant dark evening and proposed marriage the next morning. I explained I had no such intention, but he stayed on until I fell in love.

After a year, I agreed to marry, committing myself to life in his world; to understanding and functioning happily in a very different culture without thought of ever leaving it behind. We soon moved into an old stone house we had rented on the beautifully forested neighboring island of Agistri. It was a 'fixer-upper' we renovated, part of a small hamlet of similar houses around a taverna, all set high up with a beautiful view of the sea below.

I'd come to Greece after my daughter Johara had gone off to med school and my son, Philip, born six years after her, graduated high school. My new husband had no interest in having children of his own as he was a fisherman from boyhood and had early on taken the role of caring for his mother, helping raise three younger siblings when his father died, too early, in an accident. Our life was simple, uncomplicated and good; he fished; I wrote; we cooked his fresh fish, mostly eating it with wild greens I gathered and local fresh daily bread.

Writing my first reflective essays on science, I had loads of time for writing my novels, then pursuing investigations into science as a human endeavor. This included my interest in those fundamental assumptions on which science rested. These characteristics of the universe, which the European founders of science had apparently found obvious, I realized were very much dependent on the culture and time in which they were 'identified.'

I began to understand that science as we know it was born into, and of, the European intellectual culture of recent centuries, much as it stood on knowledge gained in earlier sciences such as Arabic, Chinese, and Egyptian. In Europe, via the work of Galileo, Bacon, Newton, Descartes and other 'founding fathers,' their science was distinguished from, and considered superior to, these earlier sciences by the assumptions adopted about the nature of the universe, as well as in the development of more rigorous methodologies and the mathematics needed for building scientific models.

If courses such as Kantor's had continued to be taught in graduate science education, rather than being dropped in favor of more 'practical' matters, the trajectory of science and society might have been much different. Scientists trained in the understanding that science rested on unproven statements, on assumptions about the universe that appeared so obvious they needed no proof, might have paid closer attention to scientific findings that violated the fundamental assumptions. Quantum physicists, for example, had revealed a universe very different from the one 'obvious' in Newton's time — a new and different universe in which energetic relationships and even consciousness were at least as fundamental as matter, if not more so.

When Thomas Kuhn's seminal work, *The Structure of Scientific Revolutions*, was published in 1962, it revealed to the public at large, as well as to scientists, that the foundational assumptions of science had changed historically, and so it paved the way for yet another change to come. Indeed, it became the text for an evolving 'paradigm shift' in science — a shift in fundamental assumptions that would inevitably lead to a shift in theories and research on the part of the shifters and thus cause a significant rift in the world of science.

By 1962, when Kuhn's book came out, I had remarried and left Indiana University with a Master's Degree in Science. I typed and made diagrams for the doctorate thesis of my then husband, a brilliant mathematician from whom I learned quite a bit about the foundations of mathematics, and gave birth to my son the same year Kuhn's book emerged. I didn't return to my own studies of science for several more years, but when I did, I ended up with my own doctorate degree.

In beginning my writings on science and philosophy here on my small Greek island, I had only my son on whom to try out my ideas and essays. I had brought Philip to Greece, less than a year after I came, and he soon began fixing up another old stone house close by. Fortunately, he was actually interested and made a great sounding board.

In addition to my continuing interest in scientific assumptions, as well as the assumptions underlying mathematics, I was now developing a serious interest in *cultural* assumptions. My lasting interest in archeology and anthropology, born in childhood, was most helpful, as these 'soft' sciences also fostered awareness of the power of assumptions, reminding me to question my own assumptions in trying to understand another culture, whether ancient or contemporary.

As a simple example, the concept of 'a problem' in America is 'something gone wrong in need of fixing' while in Greece — at least in rural Greece — it is more likely seen simply as 'something gone wrong.' So rather than figuring out how to fix it, one waits for it to go away, as it often does with a little patience.

My fisherman was not only naturally intelligent, loving and good-looking, but a really good listener. Greeks love to tell and listen to stories, and problems invariably feature in their stories. Yet he never offered advice when I had problems, nor did it occur to him to 'fix' anything about me or any problems that arose for me, including, for example, a leaky roof. Assuming he would, I discovered, was futile. I was pretty much on my own as a 'fixer.'

Americans assume one should always be reasonably happy and on top of things, so when we aren't, we see it as problematic and seek solutions. Greeks tend to assume life is not a bowl of cherries, but more like a bowl of pits in which the occasional cherry turns up. As a result, I found Americans far more concerned about not being happy than Greeks, who are far happier because things are generally not as bad as expected.

Physical pain for example, seemed to me far better tolerated by Greeks than by Americans, who are quick to run for a painkiller pill or a doctor. Unless it really is an emergency, telling about it seems to pass the time in Greece until it goes away. I'm not saying that is a better way to live, just pointing out that different cultural assumptions lead to different feelings and behavior.

For a long time, it bothered me in Greece that adults often didn't keep promises made to children, nor were they at all consistent with rules and limits, letting the children negotiate them in each situation much like haggling the price in a market. After years of frustration, I *got* that the children were being trained for a world of adult behavior that resembles the vagaries of nature, as in the weather, not at all like my prediction and control-obsessed American society. Surprisingly, despite this cultural characteristic, businesses and transportation run on schedule in Greece.

One week, I watched my husband promise three different friends that we'd come for supper Friday night, and when I asked in private to which house we were actually going, he responded, "How do I know? It isn't Friday yet." He lived in the moment the way I thought only Zen masters could. One of my best lines in writing my essays was: *The Greeks, no sooner having invented logic, abandoned it because it did not fit the contradictions of daily life.*

No doubt it is a good thing that so much of the rest of the world *did* take up logical rationality, although linear logic, like Henry's straight line, was eventually exposed in science as *not*, after all, being up to describing life. Science moved on to circular or fuzzy logic[3], gradually expanding its range.

The strange thing about cultural worldviews is that you think they are just 'how things *are*,' not realizing that they are your own cultural scenarios until you encounter very different, yet equally valid ones. All this to say that unless we become aware of the assumptions on which we build both science *and* culture at large, we will fail to understand both the presumed certainties of science and the diversity of cultures. Studying such assumptions has greatly expanded my own worldview.

CHAPTER 2

Lessons Learned in the MidEarth Sea

Greece taught me many lessons, but perhaps one of the best was learning to undo my nagging Puritan ethic of keeping constantly busy. It had been very difficult for me, back on my first island, Aegina, to learn the fine Greek art of sitting and doing nothing but pass the time. Pistachio nuts and sunflower seeds in their shells are called by their Italian name of *passa tempos* in Greece as one cracks and nibbles them to pass the time.

Time, so scarce a commodity in America, apparently needed help to keep it going forward in the MidEarth Sea, where it often seemed happily stopped in the eternal Now. I squirmed through these lessons in the fine art of sitting for some time, but eventually I was actually able to spend actual hours doing nothing but thinking *without guilt*.

It came most easily at sea with fishermen for days at a time. I had bought us a larger fishing boat, a *kaiki*, to make sure I did not fritter away the remaining proceeds of selling my house in Boston. Occasionally, I accompanied my husband and his brother on trips lasting several days and nights. At first, I spent all my time aboard reading when I wasn't helping with the lines or nets or preparing food. Gradually, I discovered that inspiration comes best when the mind is completely lulled by the rocking waves, at peace with the endless sea and sky.

On star-studded nights at sea, I awoke and sat up to ponder things as my husband slept peacefully beside me on the deck of the kaiki. Despite the lulling motion of the boat, its planks were hard to my unaccustomed bones, which prevented steady sleep. I envied the easy catlike ability of the men — a brother and uncle were often with us — to drop into instantly sound sleep where they fell; yet I also found sleeplessness giving me a very special experience of being awake alone at night.

One of the amusements I enjoyed in such darkness lit only by stars was to stir the sea with a grappling hook or spear fork to check for bioluminescent plankton on the sea's surface — tiny glittering diamonds in the blackness of the sea, complementing the stars overhead. I have always been fascinated by the marvelous shapes of these microscopic creatures so beautifully modeled in handcrafted glass in New York's American Museum of Natural History. There, I had visited them as an awe-struck child and years later had gone back to them many times during my post-doctoral fellowship tenure at that very museum.

The tiny diatoms and the giant stars looked amazingly alike from my vantage point on the sea, so I loved contemplating my own size as 'halfway between the microcosm and the macrocosm' — words I repeated to myself like a mantra. I pushed my imagination from the smallest to the largest designs of the universe, visualizing the diatoms and stars as nodes in the Hindu image of Indra's Net — of jewels, each reflecting all the others, ourselves and our fishnets embedded within its great meshes. Indra symbolizes the cosmic design, Shiva its eternal dance.

Such musings expanded my sense of unity with time *and* space, knowing that I was seeing each star now as it was in a different point of time past from all the others. With a powerful enough telescope, I figured, I could look right then at the very oldest and most remote stars of the universe back when they were born.

All space and all time could thus be grasped in the here and now — all but the unknown, unfolding future, the future of this cosmos, of everything, including humanity. Always it came back to humanity. Where were we headed? To continued strife and confusion? To a doomsday almost upon us? To something brighter but as yet unseen? Where were the clues and who could read them? Why did I, an insignificant being halfway between the macrocosm and the microcosm, ask such questions?

Awareness of our position in the universe felt mystical, and yet, it was real. Science had given us the means to measure such things, and it turned out we humans really are halfway in size between the macrocosm and the microcosm — between the greatest and the smallest things we can measure. This gives one an interesting perspective, or location between the subatomic particles of which we are made and the greatest reaches of the universe we can imagine.

The Epidaurus incident

Inspired by Henry Miller's account of Epidaurus in *The Colossus of Maroussi*, I had been eager to follow in his footsteps on my very first late '80s trip to Greece, soon after which I decided to go back and live there.

Setting out on my own from Athens to Epidaurus, for my first visit to the great amphitheater and whatever else remained of this ancient healing center complex, I shunned package tours to work the trip out on my own, starting with a boat from Piraeus, the port of Athens, to Old Epidaurus on the coast, where I stayed overnight in a small family hotel to take a very early morning local bus up the long winding road to the ruins.

The driver dropped me off at the nearest point to the theater, indicating the direction in which I was to walk, though the thick early morning fog made it hard to see the road ahead at all. Only as the mist gradually lifted along what I later calculated as a full five kilometers to the gate, did fields carpeted in blood-red poppies beneath olive trees reveal themselves in all directions. Tears of joy ran down my cheeks at their sheer beauty as my heart overflowed in immense gratitude for being privileged to walk this ancient sacred ground.

When I finally arrived at the magnificent theater — the best preserved in all Greece — I was also grateful to have it all to myself, clambering over the tiers of stone benches, imagining all the olive pits that must have piled up during the day-long therapeutic performances, generally both a comedy and a tragedy on the playbill — talk about wide perspectives!

The theater's awesome acoustics made a pebble dropped on the stage floor audible in the great arc of its highest seats. Thus, some ten to twenty thousand people could gather in one place to learn about the human condition from highly entertaining actors speaking on a distant stage with no sound equipment other than a resonating tank of water buried underneath that stage and the open architecture of the theater itself.

Trekking through the rest of the ruins at Epidaurus, I gradually got a sense of what a magnificent spa this had been in its heyday. Amazing that these sun-whitened, scattered ruins of temples and hotels could still convey the original splendor of the grandness once all colorfully painted, just as in Egypt — seemingly endless stone-carved friezes of lion heads and flowers, fountains, statues and chariot racetracks, the gaiety of comedy played alongside tragedy for their deep psychological lessons about the actions of gods and mortals in a layered, or fractal, universe where everything affected everything else.

It seemed so clearly a celebration of life. No wonder people healed here — it was about so much more than sleeping with snakes on stone temple floors to inspire healing dreams. Well-being still seemed to ooze from these stones — bleached bones of their glorious past yet speaking to me of their original beauty. No wonder Henry Miller had sent postcards from here to three doctor and psychiatrist friends, telling them to come themselves, adding the biblical quote: *Physician heal thyself!* and then laughing when one proved to be deceased and the others unresponsive.

Preparing to continue from Epidaurus to Nauplion by bus for my next stop on this intended three-day tour, I went to the government pavilion and hotel next to the ruins intending to cash a Travelers check, only to find there was no place to do that, no way at all to get any cash. Banks had not been open before I'd set out from Piraeus the day before and I had only a few coins left in my pocket, not nearly enough even for the Nauplion bus.

Completely stymied by this unforeseen dilemma, with no means to go on and nowhere to sleep, I went into the hotel restaurant to think and spent my last coins on a Greek brandy, the only thing on the menu I could cover. As I sipped it, an agitated waiter suddenly ran up to me, grabbed my arm and pulled me rather roughly from my chair. I had no idea what I had done to offend him and get myself thrown out. He dragged me to the door and pointed into the road, as though to yell "Get lost!" at me.

Then I saw it — an official-looking vehicle like an RV with a side door, a step, and a clerk inside. Apparently, a little bank on wheels had pulled up! Sure enough, the clerk cashed my travelers check with a smile and I stepped back out into the road still dazed by the cash in my hands as I watched the vehicle pull away again without having attracted the attention of anyone else. Even the waiter still looked shocked himself as I regained the presence to thank him — at least I'd learned *that* word — and silently thanked Hermes the Trickster, the god of travels, for this magical good fortune.

In all my years in Greece when I returned to live there, I never saw another such bank on wheels. I did continue a habit begun after the incident at Epidaurus, of making daily gratitude offerings to Hermes, in the form of small coins given to beggars encountered wherever I went, and I did have many other delightful anomalous experiences after that one.

Greece as inspiration

Exploring Greece from mountains, islands or boats at sea, I was often confronted by vistas of color and composition reminding me again and again of that whole Earth photo that came to mind even from the plane before my first landing. To my delight, I found the uncanny intensity of the light here such that distant scenes seemed very close. Truly, it felt like the whole planet was in fingertip reach. The ancients had taken this MidEarth Sea to be the actual center of Earth, its navel at Delphi.

Poets and philosophers have perceived Greece as a centered and centering place for the human spirit or mind — for our *psyche*, born of this planet, still inextricably a part of it, likely the sole part of it which can reflect on the whole and determine its future course. Ezra Pound said no man should die without having sailed the Aegean; Henry Miller had felt the heartbeat of the world in Greece at Epidaurus. Psychic unity with Earth is felt even by foreigners in Greece, though it took native Greeks from Homer to Kazantzakis and other modern Greek poets to give it the fullest, most passionate expression.

Kazantzakis framed the human struggle for self-expression and self-transcendence in religious terms, but his religion was not that of the dogmatic and hypocritical Orthodox Church that excommunicated him and banned his books; rather it was religion in the true meaning of the Latin word *re-ligio*[4], the tying, or linking back to origins. His life was spent in a relentless search of our roots, of the meaning and expression of human nature in all its conflicts, of the cruel and painful inhumanities that are as much a part of us as our most splendid humanity. It was a Janus-faced God with whom he grappled, and not some falsely ideal patriarch.

I felt as fully engaged in life as he was, fully enjoying it and also sharing his pain, frustration and impatience with the human condition, with the persistence of hunger, inequity and hostility. I also shared his burning need to know why we are as we are and what our chances are of becoming something better. But I was neither a poet nor a novelist of his stature, and despite my criticisms of science, I turned back to it almost as if called by Nature herself to pursue *that* path toward understanding.

My personal path had led me to broaden my life beyond science to history, economics, politics and linguistics, as well as toward Eastern philosophies, mythology, and the esoteric world of mysticism. But it was what I sensed as a MidEarth perspective on Nature at large and human nature in particular — or perhaps more the possibility of gaining such perspective — that had made me eager to stay in a more settled way.

Lessons from the sea

Living on Greek islands took me back to childhood in more ways than one — by immersing myself in nature as in my actual childhood, when

I had not yet been burdened by analysis and theory, and also because my lack of language and meanings in a new culture often made for frustrating feelings of being a very small child again. Such feelings, however, were offset by the happier feelings of return to childhood — by the ability to escape to the forest, to the company of the wild again. After so many years in urban environments, I was free to commune with Nature and with my own mind again as I so loved. The more time I spent in reflection, the more Nature seemed to reflect back to me — not only myself and my experience of the world, but the depths of forest and sea, and the still vaster depths of sky.

The MidEarth Sea thus became a central part of my life in more ways than one. I fell in love with the sea, and then with my fisherman who was in love with it, too. When I was not actually out on the sea with him, I watched its changing moods from our tiny hamlet overlooking it through the window from my desk or bed. My fisherman told me endless tales of the sea. His forefathers had been pirates, divers and fishermen, one of them a famous pirate-become-admiral in the 1821 Greek war of liberation from the Turks — the one all Europe cheered, the one the English poet Lord Byron took part in, wearing a splendid admiral's uniform he had tailored for himself. Pirates, after all, were really good at sea battles, so drafting one as an admiral in that war made good sense. Wonderful adventures!

To my husband, the sea was mother, lover, goddess and guru, and out of these relationships with her came his easy, philosophic wisdom. If I had an emotional storm, he watched patiently without interfering or talking back to any accusations I made in anger. He treated me as he did the sea, neither turning his back on her storms nor arguing before the tempest died down so it was safe to return into her arms. It was a winning strategy that seemed to come to him naturally, forcing me to hear myself blustering and feel foolish as I simmered down. Flames go out when not fanned, rather the way many problems do disappear with patience.

He and the sea together taught me the first real silences I have ever known. The attempts I had made earlier at formal meditation had never succeeded in stopping the endless babble my mind engaged in when my mouth was shut. But as I spent more and more time on the sea, I began to experience a dissolving of mind wherein it seemed to become silently open to the universe at large. In this state, I, like all mystics describing such states, was content just to be a nameless pattern within an ever-changing greater pattern, blissfully free of thought, question or explanation, simply a seamless part of the cosmos.

But such states usually ended for me with the rise of some intuitively gifted thought *about* pattern in Nature or Cosmos, accompanied by that obsessive urge to understand from a relatively objective position. How did the patterns of nature, including our minds, arise? How were they interwoven and newly created in endless new ways? How could understanding the cosmos provide a coherent and meaningful way to comprehend humanity in all its complexities and contradictions?

Paradigm shifting in science

So many religions, histories, philosophies, *and* scientific theories I'd encountered were too dogmatic or idealistic to fit my sense of nature's boundless creativity. Science, purporting to explain nature, seemed to me to be farthest from it. Science had become a fragmented enterprise speaking a Babel of tongues, each specialty ever more refined and divided from the others — so much of science sequestered in sterile laboratories away from the others, away from the nature under study, away from matters of pressing human concern in the social context outside its ivory towers.

My fellow scientists had had no interest in what I cared most about — my burning desire to know where we humans came from and who we are beyond the descent from apelike creatures; who we are in our whole social and planetary context and where we can go next in this evolutionary process. Their noses were kept close to the grindstone in a fiercely competitive research world that permitted no more peripheral vision than to spot competitors for the Nobel Prize or at least a first in journal publication.

Now that I had distanced myself from all that, it began to feel like a good time, even a very exciting time, to reengage with science, to gain perspective on it within a broader view of life. Holistic views that seemed to be inspired by that unifying, iconic portrait of Earth from space were beginning to pave the way for a scientific transition from a mechanical to an organic worldview — from linear logic to fuzzy and circular logic, from a non-living Earth to a living Earth, from fragmentation to wholeness, as physicist David Bohm had put it.[5]

More books with broader perspectives were being published. A decade earlier, the few scientists who had dared question established paradigms and propose radically new ones had been written off as heretical mystics. Even the revered fathers of quantum physics, who publicly stated their interest in the Vedic science of a consciousness-based cosmos, were only given attention for their mathematical formulas. And even their very unmechanistic findings were dubbed Quantum Mechanics. Yet the mechanical view of the world and universe was slowly eroding in the eyes of paradigm shifters, most clearly through those quantum world findings that reduced the material world to pure energy, and even to pure consciousness.

Ever more organic views were emerging, including those of James Lovelock and Lynn Margulis with their Gaia hypothesis[6] and Erich Jantsch with his self-organizing universe[7]. These new contributions to science with their views of a self-organizing, living universe and planet were the antithesis of an accidental, mechanical view of nature and thrillingly rang true to my own experience of nature as alive and self-creative. They were a breath of fresh air, a joyous release from a cold cosmic machine running down relentlessly by entropy, dragging us with it, leaving us only the recourse of outwitting nature as best we can, exploiting and manipulating it as the doomsday machine ticks on.

I felt this budding conceptualization of evolution as one implying cooperative creativity inherent in nature, very different from ruthless competition against the odds. But if this proved a more accurate view of nature, why had we humans turned into such ruthless competitors with such enormous difficulties in cooperating? Had we always been like this, or had we distorted our own natures by projecting false images onto our universe and planet?

Darwinian evolution theory alone could not answer this question; I had to look back at our history within the perspective of this broader evolutionary context — look back to the dawn of our civilizations, to the formation of our languages and cultural expressions. I piled up books and papers, established communication with scientists, mythologers and historians who generously sent me materials I could not afford even had I access to them on my own. Having the luxury of time to reflect, hypothesize, and synthesize this ever-broader array of research and thought that came to my distant island outpost was frankly delicious.

Thoughts on language

As I gradually grew more proficient in Greek, I could also ask more questions and give more answers. I had brought a large single volume encyclopedia with me and my fisherman was amazed at how many answers I could produce by looking things up. He had never heard of such a magical book. We began to argue one day about whether skates lay eggs or bear live young, as I had found skate eggs on beaches, while he had seen them birth live young as a diver. The magical book made us both right in describing species of egg laying skates, as well as live young bearing ones.

One day, as I was trying to translate "I'm going to give a speech" into Greek, I tried out different versions that would translate literally as "I'm going to *tell* a speech, *say* a speech, or *give* a speech" and asked my husband which one was correct. He simply approved them all without making a choice and did not understand what I was after. Frustrated, I finally tried writing the sentence out in Greek with a blank for the verb I was seeking and, to my delight, found he could fill it in easily.

I was at the time reading Walter Ong's *Orality and Literacy*, which I had mail ordered. This helped me realize that my fill-in-the-blank prop had switched my fisherman, with his 6th grade education, into the literate mode he had experienced only during his brief schooling, while his everyday culture was an oral one in which grammar and sentence structure analyses were not on his radar.

Ong's historic analysis of literacy showed how it had separated the knower from the known and introduced objectivity and abstraction into the human world. It was fascinating to me that I lived with a real example of someone still far more in an oral culture than a literate one, one who had never actually read a whole book. As his first, I chose a Greek translation of Hemingway's *The Old Man and the Sea*, because its content would be familiar to my fisherman. The language was so simple I easily learned more Greek as we read it out loud together. It was a big hit with him.

Pondering the ways in which oral cultures differed from literate ones, I wondered how brains may have changed through literacy. Did ancient philosophers who, say, painted mandalas of the universe rather than writing books, have language centers as clearly in their left brains as ours?

Ever since 1956, when the book of Benjamin Lee Whorf's essays, called *Language, Thought and Reality*, had been published by MIT Press, it had been a seminal book in my library — one never left behind in a move. Whorf had arranged many human languages from all over the world on a continuum from those which sharply divided the world into things (nouns) and actions (verbs), as did the Indo-European languages, including English, to those at the opposite end of the spectrum which make no such divisions, seeing everything in the world as pure process. Somewhere over the years, I read that Einstein, on hearing Whorf describe this distinction and cite the Canadian Nootka language as a 'process' language, had commented that in Nootka the particle/wave problem in physics would never have arisen.

Remembering that intriguing insight in my new fascination with oral cultures, I wrote to a friend who, had grown up in an indigenous language and later learned English, with my questions about the differences in how the world is perceived through language. I also became more aware of my own changing ways of seeing my world through Greek as I became more proficient in it.

Looking into the roots of Greek language, I reflected on ancient cultures such as the Minoan, one of the earliest to develop the art, the technology, of writing. I thought about how written language brought in separation between transient spoken language, however repeatable even over centuries in poems and stories, and written, precisely reproducible words that were a kind of externalized, frozen thought. I wondered why written language, not only among the Minoans, but in other early written languages, was first used just to make accounting lists, say of temple donations, inventories, taxes paid in goods, and then later to write down laws, only lastly used to convey stories as songs, poetry, and narratives.

One day, musing on the longest Greek words I'd learned, my favorite one, *ornithoscalismata* came to mind, and suddenly brought new insight. The word means 'chicken scratches' and is commonly used by parents to make critical sport of their children's early efforts at writing. This led me to dreaming up a little story about the Minoans in which the old guardians of culture are sitting in a circle, with the young techies of the time who argue, "We've got this amazing new technology of writing that we've got to put our songs and stories into so people can read them for centuries to come without ever having to memorize them. Why just use writing for this boring business of accounting for temple stocks and stuff like that?"

The old guard is outraged, countering, "You want to do *what*? You want to reduce our stories to *chicken scratches* on clay? Where's the feeling? Where's the color? Where's the emotion? Where's the song? You can't do that! Writing is totally inadequate for songs and stories!" And they win, so all we have in Minoan writing is temple accounting.

My young techies were looking to the future, knowing their culture had produced an amazing technology, while the old guard wanted to preserve the songs and stories in all their richness for one generation at a time.

When I read that the physicist David Bohm, whom I'd long admired for his work with Einstein on quantum physics and eventually another kind of work with spiritual master Krishnamurti, had written an essay called *The Rheomode* — an exercise in 'verbifying' all English nouns — I wrote to him asking where I could find a copy. Bohm promptly sent me the essay, together with another on *Fragmentation and Wholeness* in a small, black, hardcover volume that had been published in Israel.[8]

The rheomode experiment failed. A natural process language, such as Whorf had described in various native cultures, evolves in people who conceive the world as undivided process, but it had proved impossibly awkward and futile to force existing nouns into verbs within a language based on their differences — their roles in an entirely different conceptualization of the world as a collection of things and actions. Worldviews and the languages in which they are shaped are chicken-and-egg matters in which it is impossible to say which comes first, yet clearly indicate their dependence on each other.

Finding my voice

As various threads wove themselves into some kind of coherent fabric in my mind, I set down my musings on paper. As I did so, a period of new frustrations set in — my writings seemed either too personal and rambling or too formally professorial and dully academic. I needed to get away from the male-dominated academic formalism I'd been taught to play out the more fluid dynamics in which I as a woman would naturally speak of an organic cosmos in telling its story to anyone interested in listening. Writing novels had been good practice, but my scientific ponderings were flipping me back to the academic mode.

I'd learned the voice and role of professor too well to abandon it easily. This voice that discredits and weakens free speculation was revived by the style of much of what I was now reading. The nameless, faceless academic professor looking over my shoulder would not disappear at my command or even polite request.

I sat at my desk trying to organize things coherently and logically, yet an ever-growing number of cats were climbing into my lap and prowling my desk. Outside my window and on my walks erratic wind and weather were playing with endlessly changing temperatures, colors, sounds, smells, and moods. These merged into cycles of seasons by a different kind of logic that began to imprint itself on me as it had long imprinted itself on the culture of the Greek people who surrounded me.

As my mind increasingly reflected these organic processes, I began to spin out whatever my mind had pondered in the night, as I felt myself becoming its secretary, its servant taking dictation, typing and retyping the same pages in endless new ways, letting new thoughts make new connections.

This often kept me from re-reading what I had written before. Rather than editing, I would start over on the same subjects, letting ideas flow as they came to me without looking back, and learning to trust that whatever had been of value would be preserved and integrated into the new writing. The pile of efforts leading up to the book I would eventually complete was growing much larger than the book itself could be and threatened to grow without end if I did not at some point say "this is the beginning of my book and from here on I will accept all that comes until it ends."

And so I began my chosen task of writing out a book of my reflections over a period of time on a deep evolutionary trajectory — a stream of ever-evolving thoughts; a chunk of them cut out of my ceaseless mental process. Still, it was difficult to integrate my natural woman's voice with my learned academic voice. It felt like shifting between speaking two languages — the languages of woman and man, of mythos and logos. The world needed both those languages, and perhaps they need never become one as long as we learn to make them mutually consistent in developing our picture of things, in telling our stories, and in explaining them.

Eventually I came to feel deeply that I could speak of science as logos only in the deeper context of the mythos from which it had itself emerged and been distinguished by humans. All science was a process of abstracting formalities from the flow of life itself. The shifting paradigm in science seemed to me more comprehensible in this broader context, as well as in the even broader and deeper context of natural evolution as it had rolled on for billions of years in linear time before we came along.

It was fun to think of myself as a Greek philosopher. I loved Jung's observation,

> *A philosophical statement is the product of a certain personality living at a certain time in a certain place, and not the outcome of a purely logical and impersonal procedure. To that extent it is chiefly subjective; whether it has an objective validity or not depends on whether there are few or many persons who argue in the same way.*[9]

The beginnings of the paradigm shift evident in an increasing number of published books, was revealing that many of us could reach agreement on essentials without saying things in the same way. We shared an understanding that science offers not truth but useful hypotheses, and that it must serve society at large, improve life for all, not just meet the concerns of a 'military-industrial complex,' as President Eisenhower had put it, or of a global consumer society.

We shifters knew there were no ultimate proofs, no ultimate truths, and so we were seeking to complement each other's work and ideas to produce useful hypotheses in mutual consistency and to keep open the friendly dialogue that encouraged us to seek further. That, at least, is how it looked from the outset, and that spurred my own reflections on nature, on self, on the work of others, on the long process of history and evolution that leaves us the clues to where we have come from and where we may yet go.

CHAPTER 3

Society as Political Economy

Despite the lack of modern conveniences in my Greek life, all food having to be prepared from scratch, laundry washed by hand and so on, the work involved still left me with more free time in Greece to think and write than I could have dreamed before quitting my job and selling my house and car in Boston to come there. One visiting couple went back to the US clearly baffled, reporting to a mutual friend that I was living in poverty and apparently loving it. As far as I was concerned, simplicity in lifestyle freed my mind to uncover riches in thought. Thoreau would have backed me.

Still, our marital economy was kept more frugal than it might have been because the fishing enterprise was not doing well. I'd bought that fishing *kaiki* because my husband and two of his brothers had fished from a smaller boat, not doing well enough to support themselves, a crippled brother, and an unmarried sister who looked after him as she raised her own young son. My aim had been to improve the family economy, and because, being American, I was determined to find solutions to fix such problems.

Unfortunately, the fraternal fishing operation was suffering from having added new debts by getting loans to buy big nets they were not used to, a large fridge for storing all the extra fish they imagined hauling in, a depth gauge to help identify what fish were likely near — none of this bringing in all those fish they envisioned.

There was also the weather. Sometimes it took days of watching the weather from an outdoor café, or *kafenion*, with tables overlooking the sea till it felt right, and then rounding up three men at once, which could take several more days, by which time the weather might have turned again. It also seemed necessary to give away most of the catch we didn't eat ourselves to help out other poor people. In short, the revenues were not enough to keep up with expenses.

My biggest effort to fix things was a total disaster. I'd organized — at least I thought I'd organized — a meeting to make better plans to increase revenues. It took me a long time to round everyone up around the crippled brother's bed — in the family house that had been inherited by the sister — as he was a key family member. In the fantasy that we could now at last have a real meeting, I began a process adapting *Roberts' Rules of Order* to the situation as best I could. But the meeting, rather than an orderly process, was more like Alice in Wonderland's croquet game with flamingos as mallets and hedgehogs as balls.

No sooner was everyone assembled and my opening speech concluded than one or another disappeared on some errand, the child jumping all over the bed, the new TV suddenly blaring, someone dropping by, a racket in the street they had to check out — the conversation a complete non-starter after my carefully planned introduction. None of them had a clue what to say, my own ideas clearly falling flat as pancakes until, eventually, I just started laughing at myself and they all joined in, happy to turn the 'meeting' into a party.

The only consequence for me was to feel a fool as a fixer and wonder whether the political economy of the world had not been easier for me to understand than something this local!

Economics and the waging of war

After that Alice in Wonderland gathering, I found myself musing on the rather remarkably successful local economy of my childhood — the weekend farm rounds in my father's Model-T Ford panel truck to exchange my mother's vegetables for chickens, eggs, milk, fruits, cider, honey and other food that kept rural Hudson River Valley folk (hard-working, grateful immigrants, on the whole) well fed at the cost of only their gladly shared labor throughout the lingering Great Depression and then through the Second World War. Nature's benevolence supplied the rest. We children played kick the can, chased animals in barnyards, and rolled in haylofts as the grownups traded food and news until we were called in for cake and cocoa.

The early childhood freedom to roam the fields and forest of the Hudson River's banks on my own or with my brothers was curtailed by the daily hours of sitting at desks in rows once I started school. I entered first grade at five, as there was no kindergarten then, having been sent a year early because my big brother had completed first and second grades, held in the same room, in one year.

My teacher was frustrated by my left-handedness, already noted as rebellion by my mother when I was six months old, as she wrote in a velvet-covered Baby Book I read only when it surfaced well into my adulthood. Mrs. Wood finally called a truce providing I slanted my paper the same way as the others so nothing looked out of line as she peered down our rows watching over us — a constant reminder that the life I'd been leading outdoors, free as a little Indian walking in the tracks of real Indians that had preceded me, was over on weekdays, though the long walk to and from school was through countryside and there were still weekends and whole summers for further exploration of nature.

Within a few months of starting school in 1941, my whole world changed as Pearl Harbor was bombed on Dec. 7th with Roosevelt declaring war on Japan the next day as every citizen in the country was plunged into a massive war effort. Every school began collecting scrap metal; cleaning, flattening and tying collected tin cans in bundles; whole classes bused into the countryside to pick milkweed pods for making military lifejackets from the fluff— synthetics not yet having made their appearance in the economy and little produced that could not be recycled.

Every child began saving pennies for war bond stamps, planting radishes and carrots dutifully in our Victory Gardens, and pondering what secrets we might harbor to be warned that LOOSE LIPS SINK SHIPS by a toothy Japanese character leering down at us from a big poster on the wall of the building facing the gas station. President Roosevelt got the entire US economy retooled for the war effort in a matter of weeks, an unprecedented feat that taught us all just how fast such enormous change could be made.

Soon after the war had officially begun in the Pacific, my brothers and I became aware that we were tainted as the children of German immigrants, sometimes openly taunted as Nazis. In early 1941, famous aviator Charles Lindbergh, was entreating our president to sign a peace pact with Hitler, while Churchill, no longer able to stall war by such means, was looking to the USA for support against Hitler.

Very quickly, my German immigrant parents were suffering suspicion and hatred from people outside our circle of friends, even receiving threatening midnight phone calls. In those childhood war years, I had a repeating nightmare of being forced down a tunnel under our driveway and confronted by a devil with a pitchfork and an evil leer, standing in flames I somehow had to get past however terrifying the prospect. I knew he was Hitler, whose voice I'd heard shouting on crackly short-wave radio.

Skipping the third grade, I was just eight years old entering fifth grade the year we moved into the larger town of Catskill. My mother started over on a big new vegetable garden as the weekend farm rounds continued. The war was still on and store-bought food, gasoline and shoes were rationed. My father resorted to driving down to New York City for black market sugar that ensured my mother's winter preserves and Sunday cakes, while we children whispered to each other as wide-eyed criminals huddled on blankets covering the large sugar sack in the back of the old Ford panel truck.

Our local economic self-sufficiency had brought us a good and healthy life, uncomplicated except for the war, and even that brought most people more closely together in caring and sharing. We were blissfully ignorant of the coming era of processed and packaged foods, along with other 'modern conveniences' soon to be brought about by the miracle of fossil fuels turned into farm chemicals, synthetic plastics soon made into clothing and countless other consumer goods, of the television that would turn us into evermore eager consumers, of the devastation and pollution this would wreak.

Our soils were still healthy and prodigiously grew food later to be called 'organic' after it had virtually disappeared in the onslaught of chemicals. We were awash in birdsong and the humming of bees as we drank from clear streams and soft rainwater. The truck, and later car windshields, were encrusted with dead insects after every Sunday farm food trip.

When the war finally ended, the terrible news of the Holocaust, along with the devastation and further mortal threat of atomic bombs, were a double shockwave to absorb. I now had to weave the thought of my own potential hideous death into my horror at these depths of human evil. My genetically German heritage made me feel responsible myself, and I mercilessly interrogated German exchange students crossing my path in my high school years to find out how they could have lived through such things without knowing they were happening or without stopping them. My researches into recent history to pry out how all this had come to pass was setting in as a fierce and lifelong determination to make a better world in which such terrible things could *not* happen again.

From nuclear darkness to art and science

Too soon, a new 'Cold War' began, a macabre nuclear race that kept us intimately locked in collective fear of nuclear holocaust. Our panic shifted from the 'Yellow Hordes' expected to cross the Pacific and take over our country to the Evil Empire of Soviet communism across the Atlantic that might any day beat us in the development of nuclear bombs and the missiles that would carry them fast and far, first and foremost to us.

In school we were shown movies of horrific nuclear attacks and put through endless drills of hiding under desks and handed literature on backyard bomb shelters. There was great concern with refugees from New York City who were expected to flee upriver to our towns and villages.

All this made for daily dark and fearful conversation among adults and children alike. Though still so far under age, my peers and I were recruited to canvas homes block by block, empowered to ask people personal questions about their income and space for housing refugees, as we filled out our forms and wondered whether there would be time to run home from school when notice of oncoming nukes was blared out by the sirens we'd been taught to recognize.

The bomb scares, if not the frantic fear of communism, faded out of my perception only when I left home; my four years in art school at Syracuse University were intellectually rich and enjoyable, marred only by the onset of the McCarthy Era. Hollywood — the biggest thing America had in its art world — was hit so hard we could not ignore it. My only female art professor, a stout but dignified lady, asked us, with some indignation, why our generation in the '50s was so apathetic that we had not held a single demonstration. Her words still ring out to me: *"I think I should have to be caught fornicating on the chapel steps on a Sunday morning to get a rise out of any of you!"*

She was right. We were naive and apathetic sheep in the '50s, quite unprepared for the responsibility of citizens in the fiercely proud democracy we were continually reminded was under threat by foreign enemies that had infiltrated us.

As it happened, my education in politics and economics was furthered in Berkeley, California, back when I was assisting my mathematician husband in developing a math teaching project, sponsored by Encyclopedia Brittanica, and birthing our son.

Political activism in Berkeley and beyond

November 1, 1961, just twenty years after my schooling began, I became a political activist in a nation-wide event that made waves. A loose-knit group calling themselves 'Women for Peace' had let it be known through amazingly effective telephone networks and a tiny handful of progressive radio stations on East and West Coasts, that women should give soapbox speeches on busy street corners that day in support of President Kennedy's speech calling for world peace at the UN. As I was pregnant, I was already counting as my own two children whose futures demanded I rally to this worthy and eminently reasonable call to action.

It wasn't long before Women for Peace was called before Senator McCarthy's HUAC — the House Un-American Activities Committee — where the women delegates caused confusion among the senators while acquitting themselves with style — bringing flowers to their glowering inquisitors. At that time, pirated copies of the movie *Salt of the Earth* — the only Hollywood film ever banned because it had caused riots in movie theaters — had filtered around our networks and inspired us to mimic the brave women who had carried on a copper miner's strike when their husbands were arrested. And so, when asked by the HUAC senators if there were communists in their ranks, the Women for Peace delegates responded that they had no membership lists and kept no records, but hoped they did have communists as they wanted *everyone* to be for peace. "Won't *you* please join us, Senator?" they asked McCarthy.

The bold KPFA radio station in Berkeley became my new university of choice, with its rich array of political and economic reporting and analysis. I devoured the books of interviewed authors, such as Paul Baran's *The Political Economy of Growth* and Andre Gunder Frank's *Capitalism and Underdevelopment in Latin America*. My interest in economics grew rapidly as the interconnectedness of the world economy became ever clearer and the nature of systematic underdevelopment for reasons of exploitation was revealed to me as a form of continued colonialism more insidious than the original.[10] What I learned from Baran, Frank and others, in short, was that colonialism had not died, but was stronger than ever, our comfortable lives in the US being heavily dependent upon the severe exploitation of people in far less fortunate countries far away from us.

Anna Louise Strong's book *Cash and Violence in Laos and Viet Nam*[11] explained the history leading up to US involvement in the Vietnam war, and her fascinating *Letters from China* impressed me with her gutsy courage and amazing accounts of life in revolutionary China as an elderly American woman, including personal meetings with Chairman Mao and participation in the Cultural Revolution. That led me to Edgar Snow's *Red Star over China* and *The Timely Rain* by

Stuart and Roma Gelder, about their travels in Chinese-occupied Tibet. I was getting an 'inside' view of southeast Asia and China from western reporters who were actually there and had views far from what I read in the mainstream press.

We were living just a few blocks from U Cal Berkeley's Sather Gate, so I was well aware of all the anti-racism, anti-war and pro-civil liberties demonstrations supporting the bus boycotts, voter registrations and sit-ins of the South that had been developing over the past few years. Opposing the war in Vietnam and other student causes on a campus with a long history of demonstrations added to the swelling protests. Though it was still a few years before the Free Speech Movement would be formalized, there was plenty going on and fire-hose crowd dispersal tactics had already been deployed. We were birthing something very big in Berkeley; it was to shake the whole nation and define the political character of the 1960s that would become historically iconic.

By the mid-'60s I was in Nova Scotia, my two children in school and in a nursery while I went back to studying science, now with a focus on evolution biology as a PhD candidate at Dalhousie University. An informal study group of graduate students who were political refugees from Cyprus, Israel, India and the US, along with a few South Americans, kept me learning more political economy on the side, and I led several peaceful anti-war demonstrations, even proudly getting Halifax's Mayor O'Brien to join me at the head of one parade through its streets, flanked by many a Mounted Policeman taking pictures for the US CIA as some of the onlookers taunted him as *"Ho Chi O'Brien."* That demonstration made it into newspapers as far as California, since only one US mayor had been as brave as ours!

Museum reflections on human nature, science, and society

By the time I got my PhD and a US government NIH (National Institute of Health, later the NIMH) post-doctoral fellowship in evolution biology at the American Museum of Natural History in New York City, I had come to see the materialist scientific worldview as fully compatible with the mostly Marxist economics I had learned in Berkeley during those politically dramatic early '60s. As an activist, it had been safer in Canada. Meanwhile, my elder brother had graduated from the US Naval Academy at Annapolis, switched over to the US Marines, and was in Vietnam, where he rose to the rank of Lt. Colonel in the US Marines. Politically, we could hardly have been farther apart.

Building compatibility of my scientific worldview with Marxist economics was a natural aspect of my lifelong need for coherence and consistency in my worldview. Consistent with my early intent to become an explorer were my explorations of the world from both scientific and sociopolitical perspectives, which I found no difficulty putting together, however much that integration in my personal worldview was soon enough going to cause me trouble.

During my post-doc fellowship in the animal behavior department on the top floor of the Museum of Natural History in New York City, I came to see my own and my colleagues' work there as 'trivia research' in a burning world. It was late '60s, and as I pursued my comparative brain/behavior research, the museum pioneered a major exhibit on pollution. How could I help but notice that the same museum's smokestacks were belching soot all over upper Manhattan? One or two of my colleagues would come with me to the roof of the museum, accessible from our labs by a spiral staircase, to get some air as we ate our lunch sandwiches. Too often, we were so sprinkled by the soot we were forced back downstairs. The nearby housewives, hanging their laundry from windows, had no choice but to take in severely grayed bed sheets.

The pollution exhibit was housed in an elaborate and expensive maze of elegant Japanese architecture erected within the Great Hall at the museum's entrance, weaving its winding walk-through tunnel among dinosaur skeletons. Inside, it was filled with sanitized plastic garbage heaps and other pollution displays, ending with a picture of Pogo over a mirror, saying "The enemy is Us!" while a speaker admonished, *"Don't drop that gum wrapper!"* The whole thing was blaming pollution problems on people who littered!

I was livid and made myself unpopular by pointing out the museum's own pollution cloud, and grew even more politically active after my work hours, demonstrating for poor people who were evicted from their homes, for better working conditions and for other causes with which the city abounded. It was a mystery to me how people could fail to understand the most basic economic relationships between wealth and poverty, cheap imported goods and the exploitation of foreign labor, corporate polluters, and laws protecting them.

I despaired at the dire situation of humanity in a win/lose local and global economy ever deeper in crises of poverty and other social injustices, warfare, nuclear threat, pollution, and desertification. Further, we scientists at the museum were finding that humans indeed were causing a Sixth Great Extinction — the first to be caused by one kind of Earth life, rather than a cosmic catastrophe — and that it was not just wiping out species but causing climate change. But none of this made headlines and would not until half a *century* later when stopping the runaway process would be so much harder, and virtually impossible.

I became convinced that economics and politics were more likely to answer my big questions of who we humans were and where we were headed than science. Political economy gave me some hope for understanding and improving the world while science did not. All evolution biology taught was that humans were large mammals with big brains that had come up through the ranks of other creatures by Darwinian struggles for survival in scarcity. Thus, we were doomed to continue in endless fierce competition and conflict by virtue of this 'natural' process giving rise to our own competitive 'human nature.'

This contradicted my childhood view of benign Nature and was no more inspiring than the broader scientific worldview of an accidental and meaningless universe running down to heat death by entropy. While I still pretty much accepted a universe without meaning, purpose or God, I felt deep down that evolution could not have had such splendid results if all Nature were no more than a survival struggle based on nasty hostilities.

Ethology (the study of animal behavior) was all the rage at the time, with one author after another writing popular books to explain our human aggressions as our evolutionary animal heritage. None of them seemed to have noticed that intra-species aggression almost never leads to killing; that, on the contrary, birds, fish and mammals were prevented from killing their kind by elaborate inborn rituals and limits that humans lacked.

This led me to an important insight that the sudden size increase of our brains on the evolutionary timeline, traded inborn behavioral limits for freedom of choice on how to behave. It follows from this insight that humans alone require ethical guidelines and have to devise them culturally along with forms of governance. If science persisted in its pretense to be value-free, how then could it offer any guidelines to society?

The clincher came one day when I was eating my brown-bag lunch with colleagues at the long table in the department library. One of the men was showing his new film footage on sexual behavior in rats as we ate. When it finished, another researcher commented, *"Wow, that reminds me I've now been studying the cat penis for eight years!"* I choked on my sandwich and looked at them both in horror. What was *I* doing *here*? Was *this* how I would be spending my life — watching rat and cat porn over lunch while slogging through my own 'trivia' research?

I was out of there very soon after that, fleeing as I'd fled my minister's vision of becoming a 'Mrs. Lindsey' — just short of completing the second year of my fellowship. Family circumstances had also become so impossible for me that I picked up my children and moved from New York City to Boston where one of my two closest girlfriends lived.

Juvenile delinquents in Boston

In Boston I worked on a scientific research grant at Mass General Hospital. It was not long, however, before I realized that a normal scientific career was impossible for me with all my disillusion and doubts, and the feeling of swimming upstream against an impossible tide when expressing them to colleagues. Taking a position as Juvenile Justice Planner for the Commonwealth of Massachusetts, I soon learned that mainstream politics were even more corrupt than the leftist political groups I had affiliated with over the years, both revealing in-house rivalries, hostilities, and elitist practices, which I'd also encountered in the world of science. Darwinian rivalry everywhere; nowhere I landed was capable of bringing about the better world for which I longed.

Serving on the Governor's Commission on Law Enforcement, I had fun with the Boston accent, answering my phone *"Committee Alarm Faucet"* with never a question or giggle in response. However, I came close to getting fired several times for standing on ethical principles. We did research in response to Federal Government Requests for Proposals, one of which concerned the effects of government subsidized low-income housing on juvenile crime. I had Harvard students as interns and sent them to interview mothers living in such housing on how their needs could better be met. For another study of street crime, I sent interns out to interview street kids who committed crimes to ask *them* how society was failing to meet their needs. The interns for both studies got very good information, on the basis of which I made recommendations, only to find I was in the doghouse for my approach.

I was roundly scolded, and my job threatened for asking people what they needed. It seemed the government was out to demonstrate that subsidized housing was no more a solution for social problems such as juvenile crime than was their funding of Head Start pre-kindergarten programs for children, as was claimed. Asking juvenile delinquents what *they* wanted, well ... let me just say it was considered to be *way* out of line.

Professionally, as a scientist *and* as a civil servant, I was the social misfit!

The best thing that happened while I had that job was that another maverick became Juvenile Justice Commissioner and single-handedly closed down all the Massachusetts juvenile jails (detention centers) after failing to talk the Legislature into doing it on the grounds that it cost more to warehouse kids in these detention centers than to send them to Harvard with ski holidays in Switzerland. The closed jails made it mandatory to set up some community programs judges could send convicted juveniles to, and that became my responsibility, with an annual federal allocation of three million dollars, no trivial sum at the time.

My favorite program was for turning purse-snatchers into escorts for the little old ladies they used to rob. A reading program I was developing for delinquents engendered a funny scene when the director of the Harvard Coop bookstore was aghast at my bringing a bunch of lanky young toughies in tight T-shirts with cigarette packs tucked into their turned-up sleeves into the bookshop and turning them loose in the aisles. He had forgotten his phone promise to let them each choose a free book. The idea was that they would figure out how to read something they themselves really wanted to read.

Unfortunately, this wave of positive activity in our criminal justice system was quickly curtailed as nepotism took over and my best intentions never saw the light of day, my funds being mysteriously allocated elsewhere before I could get at them. Teaching a couple of courses at MIT and the University of Massachusetts during this tenure, I avoided the full-time appointments that would have locked me into their 'publish or perish' tenure tracks. My fiercely independent spirit kept me away from traditional universities and government positions for many decades.

The one university I had interest in was the University for Peace founded by Rodrigo Carazo, president of Costa Rica.

The view from China

In mid-winter of early 1973, while still in the Juvenile Justice Planner position, I had a unique opportunity to travel to China with nine other scientists through an organization called Scientists and Engineers for

Social and Political Action. SESPA had been invited to send a delegation as official guests of the National Science Association of the People's Republic of China. Our journey was truly an adventure as the US, despite President Nixon's visit a year earlier, still had no diplomatic relations with China. We were advised to go to Canada for travel visas and on arrival in China the border guards had been instructed to admit us without stamping our passports so we'd have no trouble getting back into the US.

Our full month in China was awesome and life changing. Expecting things to be more formal and restricted than they proved to be, the great friendliness and variety of things we saw on request made China feel as open as it was welcoming. We visited a university, a psychiatric hospital, acupuncture research labs, schools, countryside development projects, a communal farm, and much more. The Chinese definition of science, however, puzzled us as they called science "the summation of the knowledge of the people" and they said, "science walks on two legs." These 'legs' turned out to be the knowledge of ordinary people and the work of professional scientists, as we were shown.

It was the tail end of the Cultural Revolution, during which many university buildings had been closed as professors, along with students, were sent to the countryside to learn from peasants. The Chinese told us that they were not sent into the countryside as punishment, but because poor peasants had rich scientific knowledge through their practical experience within Nature. Indeed, many ecologically sound techniques of natural pest control and soil management, for example, had come out of sending professors and students alike to learn from the peasants. Thus, we were assured, the universities were still alive and functioning, though mobile under these new circumstances.

Our group's request to meet with one such professor sent to learn from peasants on farms was fulfilled. As we sat in his hut on the farm, he told us enthusiastically of discoveries made by farmers, for example, in crossing different kinds of oil-bearing plants that scientists had held impossible to cross. His job, when he went back to his lab, would be to show scientifically why this *had* been possible, thus illustrating the Chinese definition of science.

Of course, we were all aware throughout this trip that we were being shown China's best side, as any country — or person, for that matter — would do with guests. It was also clear that revolutionary fervor was still very high — an intoxicating mood of celebrating all the new opportunities opened up by the revolution much in evidence. But we also often heard Mao's words, that a revolution is not a tea party; that "The tree would prefer calm but the wind will not subside" and we took that as an admission that the Cultural Revolution had its dark and stormy side.

In China I thought a lot about those pop ethology books describing human nature in biological evolutionary terms, such as Desmond Morris' *The Naked Ape* — books justifying human aggression as our animal heritage along with others bringing racism back into issues of intelligence just when our political activity had seemed to be ending racism.

This wave of literature had pushed me to question the very definition of intelligence, so I queried Chinese scientists for their views on it. The response was that they had determined motivation to be a better indicator of aptitude than intelligence tests, which had been abandoned in China on grounds they could not be standardized for urban and rural populations since children develop different kinds of intelligence under different circumstances. They were convinced that a young person seriously wanting to be a circus performer, or another as highly motivated to become a doctor, were likely willing and able to successfully do the work required to fulfill their respective dreams and should thus be given a chance to do so.

These conversations led me to formulate my own definition of intelligence. Rooting it in the old military definition of intelligence as the acquisition and use of information, I expanded it to include the embedded contexts and timespan taken into account when making decisions. For example, the *Haudenosaunee* (called Iroquois Indians by the white man) took the well-being of families, communities, and ecosystems over seven generations into account in all their deliberations, which is something of an intelligence record in my book of cultures. With such great cultural intelligence, they had made peace among six warring nations and devised a Great Law of Peace that became the basis for the US Constitution, largely through the efforts of Benjamin Franklin.[12]

Unfortunately, the participation of women, the importance of children, the pledge to peace and respect for Nature, along with the dignity of all human beings regardless of race, were all left out of the US Constitution, leaving it wanting as an equally intelligent agreement on governance.

My definition of intelligence as conscious inclusion of multiple levels of context and consideration of the future affected by decision-making seemed to me a valuable way of testing individuals, at least adults, as well as whole cultures. If the adults in a culture would not do well on such tests, one could hardly expect the children to do so.

China was rebuilding itself from the ground up on a policy of taking no foreign capital investments and refusing to tie their currency to the dollar — a policy that paid off handsomely when China became a strong and attractive enough economy in its own right to be able to negotiate terms with foreign investors as equals rather than as a needy nation. Such financial independence is surely an important lesson in development, as it has not happened in any other developing country since colonialism began.

For me, it was a big lesson to see how economies can be controlled by money, while they are not built by money, but by labor. As long as the labor is sustained by motivation, food, shelter and basic health care, all of which had obviously improved enormously in China — for huge numbers of people if not for its entire vast population — its economy could grow rapidly.

We did note that revolutionary fervor was sometimes clearly excessive to the point of danger, as when workers took pride in not wearing masks in factories where the air was filled with dust. We could not know the toll taken on people who died in the turmoil of the huge changes taking place among a people encouraged to strike out against oppression wherever they were and to endure all hardships encountered in making revolutionary progress.

But we did hear a great many clearly sincere stories of how much better life was now than in the past and it was obvious that work was available to everyone, while many starved routinely in the past from lack of employment opportunity or excessive taxation. China was rife with proud young women doing work such as driving huge bulldozers and other machinery, since Mao had insisted "Women hold up half the sky" and can do most anything men can do. That was enormously liberating for women in a country that had so undervalued them.

The most awesome project we visited was Red Flag Canal, recently finished and utterly spectacular. It was built to bring water to a great valley with hundreds of villages suffering such bad drought that old people drank kerosene to commit suicide so they wouldn't use up another drop of water.

A group of young people had proposed bringing water to this valley from a river seventy kilometers across the mountains flanking it. They did so at a time when the United States was threatening to bomb China back into the Stone Age, and China was responding by moving many urban factories from cities to the countryside and building communities and food production around them, while encouraging rural self-development projects and even teaching peasants how to smelt iron from red earth to make simple tools.

Central government engineers were sent out to trek the mountains to see if this irrigation project from such a great distance over such rough terrain would be possible. They declared it to be flat-out impossible and the young people were forbidden to waste their energy attempting it.

But as soon as those engineers left, the defiant and determined young people started anyway, with no resources whatsoever, building brick ovens for smelting iron from the dry, red ground of their valley floor to make pickaxes, shovels, hammers, and chisels. Mao's motivational insistence on self-sufficient initiative was clearly not lost on them; we repeatedly heard a story called *"The old man who removed a mountain"* — a man laughed at for the idea but getting more and more help as he motivated others to his seemingly impossible task.

Shortly before we visited, the first water had come down from the mountains through the canal, as we saw on a shaky black and white movie of the whole process in a village center where the old people were all crying tears of joy as they watched with us.[13] Swinging from sheer cliffs at the mountains' edge on homemade ropes, they chipped the first access pathways permitting them in time to build Roman-style aqueducts over valleys and blast tunnels through mountains while camping at night in a series of caves for years on end as they labored to build the seemingly impossible canal.

I interviewed the Iron Girls Dynamite Team that had blasted the tunnels with homemade dynamite as people in the villages chipped rocks with the homemade hammers and chisels, then transported them along chains of people up into the mountains along with food for the courageous youngsters building the canal year after year, kilometer by kilometer. Once the water poured down to the valley, small locally produced generators along its path harnessed its power to electrify the valley.

Li Shun Da, the village leader hosting us, had actually become a member of China's Central Committee. Sporting glowing gold teeth beneath his peasant's headdress of square white towel knotted at the corners, he was a broadly smiling Chinese 'Johnny Appleseed,' clearly much loved for planting apple and walnut trees by hand all over the newly watered valley when not traveling to his government job in Beijing. Children clung to him as to a grandfather, eager to hear his stories.

At a banquet he had ordered for us, Li Shun Da sat next to me, eagerly loading my plate. I saw a big platter of fat slimy sea slugs on the table, delicacies specially imported for us from the coast and sure to land on my plate shortly, among the more palatable inland peasant food. Wracking my brain on how to avoid them, I quickly asked through the interpreter whether he had been to other parts of China where food habits were very different from his. He nodded affirmatively with a look of disgust, telling me that Mongolians drink horses milk … cold! Milk was considered baby food in most of China and no adult would drink it; nor would they drink *any* beverage really cold. I mustered my most empathic look as I explained that sea slugs affected me the same way, and he understood immediately, assuring me there was lots more for me to eat.

I loved working at that kind of diplomacy and had another wonderful opportunity for it shortly before our trip was over. Our group had been taken to see everything on our request list except for one: I had put a prison on the list because of a wager. Before setting out for China, I'd arranged a meeting with Harvard Law professor Jerome Cohen, whom I'd identified as *the* US expert on Chinese Law, to get some background on the Chinese criminal justice system, given the interest I had in it because of my job. When I told him I intended to visit a prison in China, if possible, he responded that if I could get into one, I could come lecture to his law class upon my return. He had made it clear that I would fail — and I love a good challenge.

Thus, one evening near the end of our trip, I went down our hotel corridor to the room of our Chinese guides and asked them whether they could help me with a problem, knowing well that they would do anything they could for a guest. They listened attentively as I pointed out that they surely had a very good reason for not taking us to a prison as we had requested, but that I feared my colleagues back home would think it was because China was a closed society, so could they please help me with a better explanation.

The following morning their plans for us changed, and they took us to the Shanghai Municipal Prison, their largest, for a full tour. Built by the British, it was architecturally much like our own prisons, but each cell contained a stack of colorful folded quilts on a raised wooden floor for three inmates to sleep on together for more warmth, as it was winter and this was how most Chinese slept together in their homes.

There were huge rooms of sewing machines where men worked at making long underwear in bright red, blue, or yellow. We also saw the similar women's section, as well as recreation rooms where men and women came together for films and lectures, no doubt about reeducation or rehabilitation.

We met with staff, and I asked about recidivism rates, which clearly embarrassed them as they whispered to each other before answering that they did have some recidivism ... between 1 and 2 percent. Clearly, they thought that any failure to rehabilitate anyone would reflect badly on them and had no idea that the rate was over 70 percent in the US at the time.

I had also been called to a private meeting with three Central Committee members earlier in the trip, as Zhou Enlai, the peacekeeper Premier of China who was terminally ill by then, knew of my presence there through a friend of mine whom he'd invited to China two years earlier — a Black American well known in New York City as a peacemaker leader during the "hot summer" riots that had exploded there, though the courts and press had condemned him as a criminal communist terrorist.

The CC members asked me about my political work and, as our conversation developed, proved most interested in my sending Harvard students to interview low-income mothers and juvenile delinquents about their unmet needs in our society. They counseled strongly against any efforts of American radicals to import what they saw as Chinese communism, not only because they were still far from reaching that goal themselves, but because it was up to us to meet our own peoples' needs, not to copy them in any way. This may have come from their own failures in copying Soviet communism. But whatever lay behind their advice, it left a deep and positive impression on me.

Our group was also impressed by a national zero-waste campaign across China, the goal of which was to find ways to recycle absolutely all waste from the smallest homes to the largest industrial plants. Prizes were offered to anyone who could find a way to recycle any waste substance in industry for which such a process did not yet exist.

Empowering a whole generation of exuberant youths to go problem-solving across a vast society was perhaps the most daring move ever made by a nation's leader and their tactics, as we later discovered, were too often harsh. The severe abuse of people in the past was bound to play out in a new generation of abusers. Yet, overall, we were convinced that China was on an astonishingly successful path despite what shadow side came up in the process.

On the way home, I noticed things in my own culture with new eyes and feelings. The avoidance of eye contact, touch and conversation was newly apparent to me in airports, on conveyances, in elevators, and on the streets. I felt suddenly lonely even in a crowd after a month amidst jostling, laughing, touching people who were eager to look you in the eyes. On leaving China, we even hugged the border police.

Re-entry and return to worldview explorations

Back in Boston, I hastened to the Harvard Law School, to see Prof. Cohen. While gloating a bit, I reported politely enough for him to follow through on inviting me to tell my Chinese prison story to his students in class. They were happy to listen and a lively discussion ensued. It was probably as much fun as they'd had in the course.

While still a Juvenile Justice Planner, I also taught one course on social justice at MIT, where I had opportunity to converse quite a bit with other professors. I was also running some evening sessions on the same topic in a prison, where I found largely Black inmates understanding society better than the professors. While professors were focused on competitive theories of how things worked in less fortunate parts of their society, the inmates had been there and were still part of it, knowing their oppression firsthand, and understanding the social forces that kept them down.

Meanwhile, the Women's Liberation movement was in full force along with peaceful anti-war demonstrations in which I participated. I was shocked when we faced endless rows of fully armed and helmeted police looking distinctly hostile, with evident weapons and even fierce dogs, flanking us in the streets as if we were in some foreign occupied land. In one demonstration I was tear-gassed so severely that I was sure I was dying as the feeling of hot lead pouring into my lungs stopped me from breathing until I passed out. Obviously, I did recover.

Sometime after that, I was in Costa Rica, to meet with Rodrigo Carazo, its president and the founder of the University for Peace. I had met him at the UN, on a trip to New York while I was still living in Greece, where I'd heard of his U.P. and wanted to found a sister University for the Environment. This plan fell through when Greek colleagues supporting it fell away, but Rodrigo remained a treasured friend. And another treasured friend, Robert Mueller, former Secretary General of the UN (mentioned several times in Chapter 12) eventually became head of U.P.

While in Costa Rica, however, I found myself going from dancing Reggae with the natives of a coastal rainforest one evening to having cocktails with the president at his palace in the capitol next day, another example of my striving always to see things from very different perspectives. I eagerly sought such new perspectives, looking out for inconsistencies in my worldview and finding ways of eliminating or resolving them.

I never thought this unusual until I began to notice how often other people thought it so, and that became part of my learning how many people have inconsistent or one-sided worldviews because they apparently cannot take two sides of a situation into account. I had found it very strange that a fully committed materialist reductionist scientist could be equally committed to God on Sundays or that a concentration camp guard could torture his victims all day and bring flowers lovingly to his wife after work, or that a culture could tell its children not to take things from each other and then aggress on the people of sovereign nations to exploit their resources.

In my own life, I know others saw me as erratic, but I always felt true to my explorer's path and to my soul's deep yearning for wholeness and meaning. How could I act with integrity if I didn't know How Things Are in the great scheme of things — if I couldn't fit everything I encountered meaningfully into a larger perspective? In line with such questions, my years in Boston were also to take me into an exploration of cosmology and consciousness that would give me the largest contexts and perspectives I'd ever had.

CHAPTER 4

Science Meets the Sacred

Paraphysics

During our seven years in Boston, as my children grew to independence, before my move to Greece, I reflected a lot on how it had been drummed into me as a fledgling scientist that physics was the most fundamental and thus most important of all the sciences — the one looking into the nature of the universe itself, while biology studied the living things that had evolved within that physical universe.

To explain life, I was taught, one had to explain the physical universe with its inherent forces because the study of physics accounted for chemistry, which in turn accounted for life. But though I was finding science as it was taught to me to be suspiciously limited, I continued to believe that there must be better scientific explanations of the universe than this sequence, and beyond it to my whole world of experience — in short, better scientific ways of explaining *all* my experience. In particular, I felt there was something wrong with requiring biologists to fit themselves into that 'standard model' of physics.

In those Boston '70s years, I was drawn to a maverick field I hoped might actually be the leading edge of physics. It was generally called 'paraphysics' and was concerned with questions of how the universe works, but *not* according to the 'standard model.'[14] Rather than seeing consciousness as a late, emergent product of physically evolving brains, a good many of the paraphysicists were persuaded that consciousness was a fundamental aspect of the universe and even accounted for much more than what some of the quantum physicists allowed it. They held that phenomena such as telepathy, clairvoyance, and psychokinesis — easily demonstrable — were keys to the underlying reality they sought to reveal, however much they were denied as real by the 'standard model' physicists.

On delving into other literature on such matters, I discovered that in ancient ways of understanding the universe, such as in the Vedic tradition of India, consciousness was held to be more primary than matter. Indeed, matter was seen to arise *within* a primeval energy field of pure Cosmic Consciousness. This made sense to me as Einstein had, after all, showed the world that matter was a transformation of pure energy. Consciousness, it seemed to me, might well be a kind of pure energy of frequencies higher than science could measure with current instruments.

How fascinating that the fundamental beliefs of Vedic science and what I began calling 'western' science could be diametrically opposed: consciousness giving rise to matter in one science, matter giving rise to consciousness in the other! Were our western scientists right and the ancient Indians wrong? Or would the findings of twentieth century physics — that matter is not made of solid particles; that the most fundamental of physical particles were actually whirling bits of energy — prove the ancient Vedics correct after all?

In the early twentieth century, a handful of world-class physicists, including Niels Bohr, became convinced that human consciousness is intimately involved in our physical reality, causing a major rift in the world of physics that was not to go away. The fundamental axioms of science had declared the world of matter to be scientifically objective — independent of, and so unaffected by, human observation of it. So, while it was generally accepted that Einstein was correct in showing matter to be a transformation of pure energy — especially when the reverse transformation of energy *from* matter was proven in atomic bombs — it was still a big stretch to believe that consciousness is not only itself a kind of energy, but a kind that can interact with and transform the physical world.

Still, some academic physicists had adopted Bohr's 'Copenhagen interpretation' of quantum physics, and both Heisenberg and Schrödinger, co-founders of Quantum Theory had, like Bohr, looked to the Vedic model. In Bohr's view, physical events are the collapsing of pure, immaterial probability waves into matter at the very moment, and *because*, a conscious observer looks at some phenomenon. Most physicists were aghast at this new idea, being stuck with the fundamental axiom of objectivity that made it impossible. In short, they could not accept an interactive universe in which humans are co-creators.

This rift in the world of physics aroused my interest in the physicists on Bohr's side, including those farthest out but still scientifically credible.

I read moon-walking Apollo astronaut Edgar Mitchell's new book, *Psychic Exploration: from Outer Space to Inner Space*, published in 1974, the year after I went to China, and he founded the Institute of Noetic Sciences in California to foster scientific research on consciousness. I was thrilled that a physicist with a doctorate from MIT could walk on the moon and come back with a riveting account of how, on the journey back to Earth, he had a transformational experience of being an inextricable part of a living, conscious universe.

Then Fritjof Capra, a Viennese-born physicist in Berkeley, author of *The Tao of Physics*,[15] saw and wrote about the parallels between the discoveries of physics and the ancient cosmic models of Vedic and also Taoist traditions. He came to Boston, where I heard him speak, and we had a lengthy conversation through most of the night afterwards that further encouraged me in my own pursuits.

I also met Itzhak Bentov — known to his friends as 'Ben' — who was then writing the book to be published in 1977 with the title *Stalking the Wild Pendulum*. Bentov was the first paraphysicist I encountered who posited the 'doughnut' model of the universe, though it reflected a pre-Einsteinian theory that Lord Kelvin had introduced to the Royal Society of Scotland by blowing smoke rings into the air from a box. In demonstrating this floating geometric *torus* — the doughnut shape of a smoke ring — he argued that it was the only form able to hold its shape while floating in space and was apparently not contradicted as the Smoke Ring Universe theory became quite popular among British physicists until Einstein came along with *his* theory.

A smoke ring revolves on two axes: its polar axis, like an imaginary perpendicular stick through the center hole and the other like a fine circular thread embedded in the doughnut itself so that it would show as a dot at the center of any slice through it. As any 'slice' rotated around that center dot, the entire doughnut would be revolving as though turning itself inside out, one side expanding out from the hole while the other contracted into it.

Bentov showed how this simultaneous expansion/ contraction of the toroidal form through its hole could lead to the Big Bang theory. If an infinitely small doughnut hole were seen while standing on top of the doughnut as it revolved outward, it would appear to be spewing the doughnut's matter outward. And if one could not see the bottom of the doughnut, one would not see the hole sucking the matter of the doughnut back inward, so the matter would appear to come magically from the infinitely tiny hole.

Because smoke rings floating in air rotate on both axes, the expansion and the contraction are actually spiral flows in opposite directions, just as water spirals down drains in opposite directions in the northern and southern hemispheres of our planet. In Bentov's model, the inwardly spiraling side represents a cosmic black hole sucking matter inward, while the outwardly spiraling side represents the apparent Big Bang — actually a universal 'white hole' that spits out the whole universe continually, rather than only once, after the postulated Big Bang exploding out of nothingness.

I found this balanced universe of simultaneously recycling expansion and contraction, white hole and black hole as one, more appealing than a one-way universe originating in a single blast and running down ever since. And both the black/white *whole* yin-yang symbol of ancient Taoists in China and the remarkably similar black/white galactic Hunab Ku symbol of Mexican Mayans indicated to me that more than one ancient culture had come to understand the universe this way and beautifully abstract it into a 2-dimensional symbol.

Further, it turned out that Bentov was not the first to revive Kelvin's smoke ring version, as I later discovered the work of Walter Russell[16] showing a dually spiraling universal energy as early as the 1940s and I was eventually to find others, including David Ash in Australia and Nassim Haramein in the US, who worked out this model in exquisite detail.

The light of radiation is visible through telescopes and shows an expanding universe of stars and whole galaxies, but gravity is 'dark' in the sense of being invisible despite its clearly felt force, so the contracting aspect of the universe that keeps it together remains unseen, and thus mysterious.

Once the one-way model of the Big Bang universe took hold in physics and astronomy, the role of gravity became even more invisible and, despite eventual awareness of isolated black holes sucking in matter, the universal balance of radiation and gravity as already understood in ancient China and Mexico got no further attention except by a handful of paraphysicists who were marginalized.

My disappointment with the self-imposed limitations of science had led me to its explorative fringes, where I pursued credible — but still scientific from my own perspective — explanations of the world and humanity. I needed to know those who had broken the official taboos to find a bigger picture. And I needed a bigger picture to explain the human condition so I could see ways to improve it beyond what I perceived as the petty interests of both mainstream and radical politics, the confines of exploitative economics and beyond what religions had to offer.

Encounters with past lives

Working at my 'Committee Alarm Faucet' job while the kids were in school and spending evenings and weekends fixing and rebuilding various parts of my old house, I met a woman who told me of her exciting past lives reading by a psychic. She'd been told about a sequence of her very bold and adventurous past lives, and I listened somewhat spellbound despite my skepticism about the whole thing. A psychic? Past lives? As I continued to ponder her story, I realized I was truly intrigued and a bit jealous.

For the price of a concert ticket, I reasoned, I, too, could get — at least so I hoped — equally fascinating stories about myself. That might relieve the paper-shuffling boredom that had set in with the project-crippling nepotism at my job. I had no belief in reincarnation, but I booked a reading out of sheer curiosity and a sense of adventure.

My session was indeed fascinating, though not a single past life reported to me by Rosemary-the-psychic was anything like my friend's. What I got was romantic tragedies interspersed with intellectual pursuits, Himalayan monkhood, South American sacrificial ritual death, and some more mundane unpleasant demises. What most fascinated me was Rosemary's uncanny description of previous events in *this* life, about which she could not have known anything. Her accuracy about this life made me more open to the possibilities of others.

Soon after, a Lebanese-born friend who taught yoga and other esoteric practices did a past-life regression session with me, providing an opportunity to go more deeply into the most intriguing of the lives Rosemary had pulled up. Under his guidance, my light, self-induced hypnotism left me fully conscious and able to tell my experience as it happened. I found it easy to experience that life as my own, in full living color, sound, and emotion.

I was an unusually tall poor girl, in what is now Pakistan, wearing a sari, feeling rather free as I walked barefoot on dusty streets. Apparently,

I was happily but secretly in a love affair with a man of high rank, whose baby I had borne. Discovered by a traveling French artist, who saw me as the perfect model for the then popular in Europe *odalisque* paintings of reclining oriental nudes, I was taken suddenly off to Paris. When not posing, I was shown off at soirees, forced into tight corsets and pinching shoes that caused me great physical discomfort, thus exacerbating my mental anguish at losing my love, my child, and my freedom.

In a particularly vivid scene, I was looking down onto the equally forcibly pruned shrubs of the highly ordered Versailles palace gardens from a balcony, feeling only a dark bitterness. Soon after, I made a sudden exit from that life with a heart attack, suddenly shocked into a pure soaring joy at release from my body. I exploded in soundless laughter as I looked back, seeing my body all pent up in its pinched black clothing, so rigid it had not yet keeled over despite its stopped heart and my now soaring spirit.

In reflecting on that experience afterwards, I found myself — for the first time ever — in deep empathy with my mother. She and I had been trapped in an endless conflict of mutual disapproval from my first years on Earth to that moment, and I had been given a sudden healing insight into her own rigidity, by experiencing such anguishing rigidity in myself.

In her case, it was terror of being seen and judged as a bad mother if I were not the perfect daughter. She, as much as the minister, wanted me to be a perfect Mrs. Lindsey, a credit to my mother, my church, my community. All the while I had felt judged and blamed for my rebelliousness, she had been judging and blaming herself even harder for it. I could see her now as the victim of her own upbringing and forgave her absolutely. I could also — by accepting reincarnation as an interesting working hypothesis, if not as reality — try out taking responsibility for having chosen this life, this moment in history and this place, these parents, for my own soul's purpose. My blame game was thus over in a flash.

That kind of tolerance and forgiveness seemed so important that I decided to accept reincarnation as a useful scientific hypothesis, trying to live by it to see where else it might get me. In order to offer others such experiences, I learned the past-life regression technique — mildly inducing self-hypnosis that left the subject able, under my guidance, to report their experiences through past lives and deaths.

I opened all my sessions saying, *"Please don't worry about whether what happens is real or not, as that will only distract you and is not what's important. What matters is that the story you experience will come purely from your own deep consciousness and will therefore give you valuable insights into yourself."* That was honest on my part, and people found the sessions useful while I was fascinated by the stories they 'relived.' More and more, my worldview expanded to belief in these stories as realities, perhaps not all the particular stories, but the concept of having past lives made increasing sense.

Beyond my body

Such mobility of consciousness across time led me to exploring other investigations of consciousness. When Robert Monroe's 1971 book *Journeys Out of the Body* fell into my hands, I determined to figure out how to have my own OOBE's — out of body experiences — and made considerable effort, mostly using self-hypnosis techniques to follow the instructions of other books on the subject, but I failed repeatedly for quite some time.

It eventually occurred to me, drawing on my physiological understanding of brain waves and states of consciousness, that OOBEs might depend on an alignment between the frequencies of the powerful physical aortic heartbeat waves and slow brain waves, at a common frequency of around seven cycles per second. So I made a biofeedback device, such as I'd built in graduate school, to help me synchronize these frequencies. Whether it was that or some other factor, I finally succeeded.

It began with the feeling of growing vibrations throughout my body, followed by the sensation of being squeezed out through a small hole in the top of my head, like toothpaste out of a tube, then suddenly released from my body, zooming away from it to some non-material realm where I saw several people I knew were dead in seemingly good health and spirits, but it did not last and I was soon jolted back into my body.

I had no way of knowing whether I had really left my body behind through such physiological synchronies or whether these experiences had happened only in my mind, as a state of consciousness induced by those physiological events.

I was to wrestle with this enigma for years before realizing that *all* my experience is limited to what my consciousness can perceive — that all my experience is *within* my consciousness, as is *all* experience of *all* humans! It took this dive into esoteric experience and then years of contemplation of it for me to make this truly important observation, which had major implications for my scientific modeling of our universe.

In any case, the second time I managed an OOBE, I had determined to get out of my body but to stay in my room in order to test my capacities in a familiar environment. And so, as I lay on my bed, I felt the strong vibrations and then felt myself leaving via what I now understood to be the crown chakra at the top of my skull, I willed myself upright then and there. It worked. I felt myself standing beside my body and could see it. I was not a blob of light; I felt I had all my limbs and testing them I found I could put my hand through the wall, lightly feeling the plastering and laths inside it.

I tried jumping and found myself floating rather fast toward my hanging glass lamp and panicked for fear of breaking it. I should have known I would have gone through it as harmlessly as my hand had gone through the wall, but I was new at this and the panic sent me straight back into my body. I did not seem to need the silver cord described in the literature on OOBEs to get back to it, nor did I ever see one in any of my OOBEs.

With practice, I was able to leave my body, go through the roof or straight into tubes that shot me off to other places, some apparently in other dimensions. But most convincing that all this was not just my imagination was one rather trivial experience. I fell out of bed one night. Never having done that before, it truly surprised me, though the falling had caused no discomfort. Yet there I was, face down on the floor, my nose in the pile of my rug.

As I realized that 'I' was not my physical body, but only my astral self, as I'd learned to call it, which had somehow simply rolled out of my physical body in my sleep, I promptly returned into the face-up body on the bed with no effort. Why it was always easier getting back in than getting out remained a mystery.

The OOBEs were always distinctly different from dreams. Their beginnings were very vivid exits from the body and into journeys to wherever they took me on Earth or on other planes, while the ends of the experiences before the returns to my body were hard to recall. Dreams are just the opposite; one seems to have to work backwards from the ends that wake you up toward their vaguer beginnings.

My OOBEs continued into my early Greek years, but over time they took on a different and increasingly unpleasant character. Ben Bentov, in his *Stalking the Wild Pendulum* book, had warned of OOBEs for anyone who had not seriously trained their consciousness using practices such as meditation or yoga. He had written about cases of severe schizophrenia due to spontaneous unbridled kundalini energy releases and was adamant that no one should play around with their consciousness as I was. I protested to him, when we actually met, that I was too grounded to get into trouble. It turned out I was wrong.

The beginnings of my OOBE's shifted from intentional crown chakra exits to being dragged unintentionally out through my feet as soon as I began to fall asleep. At the same time, instead of feeling rather pleasant vibrations, I would hear a jagged whooshing in my ears — the image of a helicopter revving up with a broken off blade came to mind. The ensuing occasional experiences were negative and sometimes even terrifying, with gargoyle-like monsters harassing me.

On returning to my body with relief I would marvel at how much they were like medieval drawings and the gargoyle sculptures on cathedrals. Had people back then encountered such creatures in OOBEs as I now did? Did such creatures actually exist on the astral plane and was I getting stuck there?

When I got to Greece, I continued to work hard at preventing OOBEs by surrounding myself with protective white light the moment I heard those broken helicopter blades and felt the tugging at my feet, but to no avail. I leaped out of bed and paced the floor, but as soon as I lay down again the same thing happened. I got pretty desperate and only wanted a way out of the whole thing. I wanted nothing more than to never get out of my body again; to forget the whole thing.

At last, I remembered reading Robert Monroe's account of his own terror during an OOBE when he came up against a brick wall, seemingly endless in all directions, and could not get back to his body. It dissolved only when he finally surrendered utterly and found it dissolved instantly. The next time I was assaulted by gargoyles, hard as it was, I screwed up my courage to say, *"Do whatever you like with me; I surrender!"*

It worked. Instantly. Like Monroe's wall, they disappeared. And that ended my OOBEs as the involuntary ones stopped cold and I never had the inclination to try again for good ones. Had Bob Monroe and I produced these challenges in our minds? Had we created these terrifying situations out of our own fears?

In some sense that had to be an answer. And yet, it still seemed that OOBE world was another level of reality. The way my hand had gone into the wall of my room and the way I had repeatedly passed through my ceiling and roof, was something I had never experienced in dreams, though I had had dreams in which I flew. Could there really be another level of reality where physical things were permeable, far less dense?

The 1970s were a time of significant interest in UFOs and their associated aliens. I thought of one abduction report in which a woman insisted that aliens had come through the bedroom wall, taken her by the hand and led her out into a spaceship where she was placed on a cold metal table and subjected to some kind of painful procedure before being returned to her bed. Her husband said he had been up in the night and had seen neither spaceship nor aliens and that his wife slept soundly and never left their bed. It seemed that one of them must be wrong or lying.

My OOBE experiences enabled me to see how both the woman *and* her husband could be telling the truth! If the alien ship and the aliens themselves were in a less dense reality, the husband would not have seen them. Nor would the woman have seen any of this before she began having an OOBE when the aliens pulled her astral body out of her physical body — the way the gargoyles had pulled me out through my feet — to take her with them through the wall and to the ship.

I had noted myself that when out of body everything I encountered beyond the permeable physical world seemed as 'solid' as I felt my astral body to be. People who had died were solid to me in that state, while I could pass through physical walls and living people. Thus, the cold metal table in the spaceship would have felt real and solid to the woman's astral self, while she could pass through the walls of her house holding hands 'solidly' with the alien. Her husband would not have perceived the spaceship, the aliens, or her departure and return.

The astral plane is simply not visible to us in the physical world — at least not to most of us. Children who report seeing astral beings are usually socialized to believe that was "only their imagination."

The best job ever

Still in Boston, I began taking free-lance writing jobs to keep food on the table for my kids after leaving the Juvenile Justice job. I had had the awful task of firing my inherited secretary, who was truly incompetent and had been repeatedly warned her job was in danger. I wanted her to succeed because she was, like me, a single mother, but it became impossible to keep her. I vowed then and there never to have to fire anyone ever again.

In trying to find another position I went to a professional women's job bank and was offered a free employment counseling session. Taking up the offer I found myself across a desk from a pert young woman, perhaps half my age at best, and my hopes for a fruitful encounter sank. Somewhat defiantly, I explained that I was a hopeless case as I seemed to be unable to work for someone else and could also not stand to have employees under me. I apologized, telling her I would not waste her time, and got up to leave.

To my surprise, she gave me a big smile and told me that only meant I was a true independent. I sat back down and she asked what I was good at and liked doing. Eventually we settled on my trying freelance writing by joining a writers cooperative that had available jobs.

Soon, I was writing everything from medical implant research reports — one of which led to an offer to take a horrifyingly dull job — to science fiction stories I hoped would be interpolated into a book called *Cosmic Catastrophes* by an astronomer whose publisher sought a writer to make the book more interesting with illustrative stories. The three stories I submitted all ended up in the book.[17]

Eventually, I was hired by Boston's WGBH-TV to write the educational materials sent out to schools and colleges across the US for every episode of the popular science NOVA TV series, called HORIZON in Europe. Discovering that I already knew something about the science behind every program topic assigned, I realized how broad my science interests were and how many areas I had already explored in my ongoing search for a coherent worldview.

The NOVA materials had to be produced for each weekly show while the show itself was still in production, so I had great fun calling the inventor of the first manpowered airplane and various other research scientists on the phone, as well as talking to producers and guessing what would actually end up on the screen. I got so good at this that they had a difficult time replacing me when I left for Greece. I even thought I might become a producer myself, and applied for such a job when it opened up for application. I came very close to getting it; once again, nepotism reared its head and cut me out. But had I gotten that job, I would not likely have gone to Greece and life would have continued on a different trajectory.

Along the way, I'd also had a separate WGBH assignment to write a book to go with a film about the best public education programs in the US for physically and mentally challenged youth. I argued that programs got defunded and disappeared, but teachers tended to go from one to another in those cases, so it made more sense to find the best teachers in this field.

After the requisite research to find them, I set out across the US to interview these teachers, who proved in every case to be extraordinary people. Several of them were profoundly handicapped themselves, and each of these in turn impressed me as a highly evolved soul — a concept by then not only acceptable to me as further evidence of reincarnation, but as something inescapably obvious. These teachers' belief in their own abilities translated into instilling the same belief in their students.

I watched married quadriplegics in marvelously equipped wheelchairs come out of their house, enter their van, lock themselves in place, one as driver, and head to work as my driver followed them to our interview. He explained that neither could lift more than a finger or blink an eye to control their equipment.

On another visit, a young man hobbled with difficulty on crutches, his face so disfigured by not having closed into proper shape as an early embryo that I would have had difficulty looking straight at him, had he not shown me his soul in announcing to me what a wonderful person *I* was as he got into the car. I'd gotten out to take the back seat so he could be with his driver to help him and when I asked how he could know this before we met, he told me he'd seen my huge aura as he came down the path! His own sunny disposition belied his tragedy, having been crippled by several surgeries that went wrong in his childhood, adding to his challenges.

And then there was Shirley who worked at Houston NASA — born female, Black, a midget with no arms as a Thalidomide baby, and she had no prostheses. In her office she removed her shoes, then deftly did everything from using the phone and riffling through papers to showing me slides and writing a note, all with her feet and all the while joking to put me at ease as I sat on my hands resisting my urge to offer the help she clearly did not need.

By the end of this awesome interview, I was running late for a flight to my next stop and she could not get me a cab by phone so said she would drive me herself. Thrilled at having more time with her, I sat in amazement as she maneuvered through traffic with one shoulder stump in a cup mounted on the wheel and her feet on the rebuilt controls, raised to be in her short reach.

The ride was long enough to hear a lot of her life story, which included the challenging goals she set herself each year, this one having been to swim laps in a pool. Always in good humor, she recounted horrors of being taken advantage of by male predators, being sterilized without her permission while anaesthetized for a head injury when she had so wanted to have a baby, and more.

At last, I asked if she believed in reincarnation and she grinned, saying, *"Oh yes, and I know what I want to be in my next life."* I responded that I couldn't wait to hear and went wide-eyed at her response: *"I want to be born the same as in this life, but as a man, to get that perspective!"* I knew in that moment what an advanced soul she was. I recall her giving me a big hug when we parted like old girlfriends, though I cannot say how she did it.

We stayed in touch, and I learned she had been promoted from her position in an education program to being in charge of women's career advancement at NASA.[18] After I went off to Greece, Shirley wrote me long letters by foot and we made plans for her to visit — she wanted to ride a donkey.

These teachers were awesome role models, and through my experiences with them I understood why so many people working with profoundly challenged people so love their work. In conversations with the most severely challenged teachers, I saw more grit, more humor, more compassion, and more amazing grace than I had ever encountered. I was utterly humbled by this experience, seriously doubting I would ever be as good at life as any of them.

Worldviews from Seth to Henry Miller

My discovery that even the most challenged students tend to achieve whatever their teachers believe they can achieve might have been difficult to understand had it not been so consistent with what I was learning from the fascinating series of 'Seth books' Jane Roberts was writing and publishing.[19]

Seth was/is a discarnate entity dictating book after book, title by title, word by word, with even punctuation specified. He spoke through Jane, who was a rather frail, arthritic poet and fiction writer speaking as Seth in a booming voice far from her own. Her husband Rob wrote down every session by hand in his own shorthand. However long the breaks were between sessions, sometimes even months, Seth's first sentence always followed smoothly on the one ending the session before.

Always with good humor, Seth revealed a consciousness-based universe in which we humans create our realities individually and collectively from our beliefs. He spoke eloquently on cosmic physics, chemistry, psychology, biology, medicine, sociology, evolution, human history, religion, philosophy, politics, art and other subjects. Jane, who had little or no knowledge herself of any of these fields, never called her own dictations 'channeling' and, in Seth's own voice, consistently urged people to doubt the material he dictated and think things through on their own.

Though classed as esoteric or fictional literature because of its unusual origins, Seth's was the broadest, most coherent, internally consistent, and intellectually satisfying worldview I had yet encountered. I had delved deeply into esoteric literature of many hues, starting with Ouspensky, Gurdjieff, and Blavatsky; moved hungrily through Aurobindo and other easterners; anthroposophy, gnosticism, alchemy, magic, Kabala, Christian mysticism, Taoist and Vedic texts, Freemasonry, you name it! But nothing resonated with me as did those Seth books. They had the intellectual appeal to reach me, and not the slightest hint of my anathema: dogma.

By the time I met Henry Miller — all this reading, along with my personal experiences in this esoteric realm, had expanded my worldview dramatically. Sometimes, I had to hold alternative 'realities' like the proverbial physicist believing in waves on Mondays, Wednesdays and Fridays while believing in particles Tuesdays, Thursdays, and Saturdays. At other times, my alternate realities seemed to blend into a changed but coherent reality, mostly thanks to Seth.

Neither art nor science nor political economy had prepared me for this adventure, but the week I spent with Henry, taken to him by his favorite biographer, now my lover, gave me interesting opportunities to practice dwelling in my expanded psyche. I was eager to talk with Henry about his own mystical experiences and beliefs, having read of them in his writings, but, strangely, I found him on the opposite path. Anais Nin was arguably the deepest love of Henry's life, and her agonizing death had made Henry, as he told me, reject all his beliefs in the 'Beyond' — the meaningful, numinous world beyond our physical reality. And yet, in our conversations, he began calling me 'Blavatsky' or asking, *"So tell me, Isis, what's da meaning of da veil between woilds?"*

I truly enjoyed playing with answers to his questions, and that seemed to perk him up and catch his interest as his body was failing him. The distinct feeling grew in me that I was with him for a reason — that in some way I had been destined to play the role of restoring his faith before he went through his own death from this life.

Henry and his profound relationship with Greece were ever on my mind. And a new Jungian astrologer friend, Tony Joseph, who wrote the first astrological treatise on Chiron soon after that planetoid had been discovered, was also deeply involved with Greece, leading tours to its ancient healing centers. Under these parallel influences, I began to feel the tug in that direction — a tug that seemed to reach to my very soul. At my father's death in the late '70s, just nine months after my mother's, his small legacy financed my first foray to Greece, and while there, the soul call became so strong, I knew I had to come back to stay longer as quickly as possible.

The decision I was making was truly radical. I had read many intriguing books on consciousness and cosmology — on what was then called 'paraphysics,' including Erich Jantsch's *The Self-Organizing Universe* and David Bohm's *Causality and Chance in Modern Physics*. I had met David Peat, Bohm's co-author and later biographer, in Canada, along with Leroy Little Bear and (Pam) Apela Colorado, in our shared interest in indigenous science, which led to our forming the Worldwide Indigenous Science Network.

But now, in the late '70s, my children were grown, and inspired especially by Henry Miller's book *The Colossus of Maroussi*, I decided to follow in his footsteps, moving to Greece to write novels explaining the human condition to myself.

Freedom from thing-glut

Thus, as soon as I returned to Boston from that initial trip, I announced to Johara, now in med school and with a new partner, and to Philip, just graduating from high school, that I was going to sell the house and my car to go off to Greece to write for a few years. I offered Philip a year in Greece till he could decide what he wanted to do next as he'd shown me a college acceptance before tearing it up in front of me, saying he'd only applied to prove to me he could get in, but had no intention of going. Though he did not take up my offer then, it would not be long before he did.

To empty and leave the house I'd had such a great time rebuilding and redecorating, using skills I'd learned from my father in childhood, was not easy. More difficult than letting the house itself go, was the 'thing glut' with which it was filled — all the stuff of being a professional with an office and library, all the stuff of raising two children, the accoutrements of canoe, tent, and other camping equipment — made emptying the house a nightmare I determined never again to endure. Endless decisions had to be made about selling, giving away, and throwing away. Truly, I vowed never to suffer thing-glut again for the rest of my life.

The Delos vortex

One of the first fascinating experiences I had in Greece, very soon after my return, and before I met my fisherman, was on the island of Delos. The man who had taken me to meet Henry in California, had now visited me and we traveled to the tiny island of Delos from the nearby island of Mykonos, on a kaiki turned into a small day-trip ferry. Delos is famous as the birthplace of the mythological twins, Apollo and Artemis. Though it has far too few residents even to run a small hotel, it has a rich array of ancient Greek ruins, plus an Egyptian temple to Isis among them.

When we arrived, there were only a scattered handful of other tourists, leaving us blessedly free to explore on our own with no chattering tour groups herded about by loudly lecturing guides.

Not even a breeze stirred on that bright, clear day as we walked across the broad flat expanse of sandy ground toward the Temple of Zeus, visible on a hill in the distance. I picked up a seedpod in spiral form, and then a small snail shell, commenting on how both these plant and animal forms were such perfect spirals, marveling aloud at how many versions of this elegant design there are in nature. He seemed uninterested, and as we kept walking silently, I was drawn by this form into a dreamy reverie … as if pulled deep into the cosmos among great wheeling galaxies, all of them enormous spiraling vortices.

Suddenly, I was jolted out of my trance as the sand, some twenty or thirty meters directly ahead of us, whirled up before our eyes to form a perfect funnel, like a miniature tornado close to the ground. No sooner had it formed than it swept rapidly toward us in a long, graceful curve that brought it smacking right into us.

For a moment we stood paralyzed. Then, brushing sand from his trousers and apparently making the connection to my mention of spirals, he asked in amazement, *"How did you do that?"* Aware that he sometimes called me a witch, I responded defensively, *"I didn't!"* Then, on further reflection, I added tentatively, *"But ... I ... I wonder if I may have attracted it?"* He looked at me strangely, then asked, *"Well, what* is *it with a vortex like that? Does its energy spiral inwards or outwards?"* Without thinking about it for even a moment, I shot back "Both ways!"

In that moment I knew this with certainty — that it *had* to be spiraling inward and outward at once, both centripetal and centrifugal. I may never have taken a physics course, but I had intellectually grasped the black/white whole model of the Taoists and Mayans, revived by that tiny handful of scientists in my own culture, and here it was in my direct experience, on the island of the Twins. I *knew* in that moment that such vortices *had* to be the key to how the whole universe worked.

The incidents at Epidaurus and on Delos became more pieces of evidence to add to those I'd been accumulating — evidence that reality is far more malleable and mysterious than materialist science could ever explain.

CHAPTER 5

Trying My Wings

A theatric cell

The three streams of science, society and spirit were running through me with interesting meanderings, impeded at times by turbulence or obstacles that only the years of deep reflection upon the MidEarth Sea brought to a steady, coherent flow.

Certain events became markers. Just after I had become a Greek citizen in marrying my fisherman, Greece entered the European Union as the Socialists came to power under Prime Minister Andreas Papandreou, who had appointed Melina Mercouri, the popular Greek film star famous for her role as a prostitute in *Never on Sunday*, as Minister of Culture. Greece had another *prima donna* in Irini Papas — film star Irene Papas, as she was known worldwide, especially for her role as the widow in *Zorba the Greek*, with the title role played by Anthony Quinn.

I was among nearly twenty thousand people in that restored ancient theater at Epidaurus when Papas performed *Antigone* under a full moon. My Jungian astrologer friend Tony had brought a group of Americans to see the performance and I thoroughly enjoyed telling the visitors the basics of Antigone's story before the show.

The perfect disc of the moon was spectacular over the great amphitheater, the owls seemed to hoot in all the right moments of the play, and Papas had the magical ability to talk quietly in those perfect acoustics so that every member of her audience felt addressed personally.

I was fiercely proud as a new Greek citizen, in an uplifted political mood, delighted to show all this off to Tony's students. At the end of the play, as Papas took her bows in her stark black robes, Mercouri upstaged her by whirring into the theater by helicopter and stepping out of it in a gold lamé pant suit to embrace her rival. Such perfect Greek drama right in the Here and Now!

As I had watched the audience streaming into the theater from different directions that night, and then observed them streaming out again through various exits after the play, I saw the stage as the nucleus of a huge living cell with the crowd as its cytoplasm streaming toward and away from it as one sees that happen under the microscope in observing a single-celled amoeba's *pseudopodia* — 'fake feet' in Greek — alternately shrinking inward toward the nucleus or extending outward.[20]

Greek was such fun for me as a biologist. So many names I knew were suddenly transparent with meaning: *archeopteryx* was 'ancient-wings'; *pterydactyl*, 'feather-fingers'; *cephalopod*, 'head-foot'; and so on. Politics and economics, too, were rife with Greek words: *democracy* literally means 'rule by people'; *economics*, 'rule of the household'; *ecology*, 'design of the household.'

Seeing the populated theatre as a cell reminded me of how much whole cities looked like living cells from the air. I was seeing cells created by humanity at our scale just as it was becoming clear to me that cells — of vastly different sizes — were indeed the most important living entities in the natural world, far more important than the multi-celled creatures so obvious to us.

Lynn Margulis had shown how bacterial cells had evolved nucleated cells as giant cooperatives in what she called *endosymbiosis*, 'working-together-on-the-inside'[21] before she joined forces with James Lovelock in their joint Gaia Hypothesis, later a full-fledged theory.

Lewis Thomas, head of Yale Medical School, had written: *"I have been trying to think of the earth as a single organism, but ... I cannot think of it this way. It is too big, too complex, with too many working parts.... If not like an organism, then what is it most like? ...it is most like a single cell."*[22] Thomas understood that a single cell could be as complex as a large city, or even a whole planet. Cells, it seemed, came in *fractals* — those self-similar mathematical patterns revealed by Benoit Mandelbrot and quickly discovered by others everywhere in nature from cauliflowers to the meanderings of seacoasts.

So, I pondered: Lovelock was revealing a living Earth that Thomas declared a giant cell; Margulis was working out how ancient bacterial cells spent fully half of evolution evolving amazing complexity that resulted in huge, nucleated cell cooperatives. We ourselves, along with all fungi, plants and animals, were made of these nucleated cells and no other kind of cell had ever evolved on our Earth, which now seemed indeed a good candidate for being a cell in its own right. Earth, a giant cell populated by tiny bacterial and larger nucleated cells made such sense to me.

The elegance of this idea of cells as primary structures capable of immense complexity with their forms repeated at all size levels was very appealing. The cosmos may be a fractal array of cells within cells within cells!

Competition to cooperation

Thus, I began filling in the gap I perceived between Lovelock's planetary model and Margulis' microbial model — a kind of unification theory or model within biology. How then, I asked, had the evolution of creatures proceeded from the nucleated cell to us? Why had Darwin focused his theory on competition when those primeval bacteria had made what seemed to me the greatest leap in evolution through cooperation? What *had* made our remotest ancestral bacteria shift from clearly predatory behavior to that of such hugely important cooperation that the nucleated cell was never pushed to evolve into any other kind of cell — never had the evolutionary pressure to be 'reinvented'?

The answers to my questions about the 'gap story' began forming a children's book in my mind — not because I wanted to be a children's book author, but because it would force me to tell the story in the simplest, most coherent way. The 'archebacs' (short for *archebacteria*, as scientists had designated the ancient bacteria) had evolved three main types with unique lifestyles that I named *Bubblers*, those making their living by fermentation, then *Bluegreens*, making their living by photosynthesis and eventually *Breathers*, making their living using oxygen to produce food. Each had evolved into the next when some of them reinvented their energy producing technology — the metabolic processes by which they made their living.

Most interesting to me was that these 'technological' breakthroughs had apparently been spurred by crises created by the archebacs themselves.

So tiny they'd be invisible to the human eye, archebacs were so prolific they literally coated Earth, populating its waters, land, and atmosphere. The Bubblers, who were first, lived off free food — naturally occurring sugars and acids — but eventually did so faster than Earth could replenish them, thus causing a crisis of global hunger! Their solution, their amazing evolutionary adaptation, was to *make* food from the remaining resources of minerals, sunlight, and water. In short, they evolved photosynthesis, the metabolic technology that turned countless Bubblers into Bluegreens.

The immensely successful new Bluegreens, in their turn, caused another global crisis — this one of global pollution because photosynthesis produced enormous amounts of oxygen, which was a highly corrosive and deadly gas. Remaining Bubblers not killed by it were forced into swamps and other escape hatches.

Eventually, Breathers evolved through yet another metabolic invention that used the deadly oxygen as its energy input for breaking food molecules down into digestible bits — the metabolism of respiration we humans inherited. The huge numbers of mitochondria in every one of our own body cells, as Margulis showed, are the descendants of our hi-tech Breather ancestors.

It was amazing to ponder these matters of ancient evolution from my tiny village perch above the MidEarth Sea. Outside my window, the trees and shrubs and grasses were emitting oxygen breathed in by locusts, chickens, goats and people, who in their turn breathed out the very carbon dioxide needed by the plants.

I marveled at Nature's cooperative alliances, we creatures of all sizes and shapes feeding each other so easily on our waste gases without a thought or care, quietly recycling them in perfect harmony. All this because bunches of ancient bacteria had so cleverly solved such great crises, while we humans, embroiled in our own hunger and pollution crises, were too busy spending our energy on hostilities toward one another to solve them cooperatively.

But as my mind returned to those primeval times on Earth, I had to consider the horrendous hostilities engaged in by those hi-tech Breathers from which we descended. Things were as complex in that remote microbial world as they are in our own. Breathers, the hi-tech archebacs of that world, had invented electric motors — molecular motors that still exist in bacteria such as *E. coli* and in our own sperm cells. These biological motors comprise some forty kinds of protein molecules in arrangements of rotors, stators, cam shafts, even ball bearings. The sleek, motorized ancient Breathers had drilled their way into countless larger, sluggish Bubblers to smash the molecules inside them for food. They stayed inside the unfortunate Bubblers, reproducing themselves as they drained their hosts of life.

Always seeing parallels with us humans, I called this bacterial imperialism or colonialism, and tried such terms out on Lynn Margulis herself as I tested my children's version of evolution on her and on James Lovelock by mail. She rather liked my political/economic interpretation of her work and Lovelock, when I sent him the children's book manuscript, wrote, "While some scientists might quibble, this is just as I'd like to tell the story to my grandchildren."

The imperial Breathers surely had killed off Bubblers endless times in these predations. Margulis had surmised on good evidence that eventually some Bubblers took on Bluegreens to produce food for themselves *and* the invaders by photosynthesis, relegating the motorized Breathers to the function of attaching themselves to the outside of the colony and driving it into areas with enough light for the food production to work. This was the answer I sought to my question of how the nuclear cells evolved. They had, under survival pressure, creatively arranged divisions of labor that shifted them from hostile invasive competition to cooperation as viable colonies.

A matter of maturation

I felt this was getting me close to something important: the shift from competition to cooperation I was seeing as the greatest leap in all evolution was critical, as it evolved the only kind of cell other than bacterial cells within the confines of Earth. The timing of this great leap was interesting in occurring just about halfway through Earth's biological evolution from its start to the present.

More or less halfway through the second half of evolution — on the order of a billion years after the great leap to nucleated cells and a billion years before the present — another cooperative leap occurred. This time it was not a yet larger cell that formed, but an alliance of nucleated cells into multi-celled creatures.

Nucleated cells had, like their ancestral component bacteria and true to the Darwinian hypothesis, evolved their own vast diversity of lifestyles, many in hostile competition with each other. Yet they managed to form the multi-celled creatures we identify as sponges, corals, anemones, jellyfish, and primitive worms through their own divisions of labor and cooperation. Different kinds of cells performed different tasks, such as locomotion, digestion, sensing, outer coverings, and eventually skeletons, nervous systems, and so much more.

As I pondered how both types of cells — bacterial and nucleated — had evolved through hostilities to form cooperatives, there seemed to me two plausible explanations, both of which involved the evolutionary advantages of cooperation. Life forms live off energy, and cooperation is seriously energy efficient compared with hostilities. It may simply have gotten so much more expensive in energy terms to compete than to cooperate that the latter was a naturally advantageous adaptation to circumstance. The second alternative was a stronger version of the first: that they were forced into cooperation by severe crises that multiplied the energy efficiency advantages of cooperation — possibly even leaving no choice but to cooperate or die.

I felt this as an epiphany. It was a truly plausible explanation of how the greatest leaps in evolution had come about. I was literally *seeing* a very exciting non-Darwinian pattern emerge in the long process of biological evolution. These two great leaps had happened within the first three-fourths of evolution, which only saw the evolution of single, microscopic cells, and so had been virtually ignored in teaching evolution before Margulis' work except to refer to it dismissively as the 'primeval sludge' or 'molecular soup' stage from which everything that really mattered evolved! It was such unfamiliar territory that Margulis' brilliant work was itself dismissed for much of her career.

It was now dawning on me that this microbial world pattern of competition followed by cooperation might continue to play out in the evolution of the obvious multi-celled creatures of our plant and animal world. Were they, too, creative, competitive and expansive in multiplying rapidly as Darwin depicted them and then, in a subsequent phase, showing evidence of more stable, peaceful cooperation? Could the pattern be reflected even in individual humans as a maturation process from childhood to feisty adolescence to stable cooperation in community as adults? I could not help wondering why no one else seemed to have noticed something that suddenly seemed so obvious and important.

I abandoned the children's book project for an adult version and tentatively called it *The Brink of Maturity*. My son Philip, ever willing to let me sound out my ideas, strongly encouraged me to stay in the story-telling mode I'd taught myself in writing novels and when writing for children by 'telling' science, and not to fill my book with footnotes no one wanted to read. As he put it, *"If you believe it's true, stand on the courage of your convictions and just say it."*

Lovelock comes to call

It was clear to me that James Lovelock was getting traction on his Gaia

Hypothesis, so I'd asked him in a letter to please let me know if he were ever coming to Greece "to trace Gaia's roots" as I would so love to meet him. Not long after, he actually announced he would be coming and when I asked to what conference he was invited, and whether I could help him in any way, he replied that he was coming to see *me*. I could hardly believe it; I was over the moon about his visit! To think that he took me seriously enough to come to meet me was a huge validation of what I'd done on my own in the years since I'd abandoned academia.

Having been an inveterate smoker from my teen years, and unmoved by my occasionally visiting daughter Johara's pleas — she was now in residency after Med School and visiting on a badly needed rest break — I decided that if Jim Lovelock was not a smoker, I would give it up the minute he came as the wonderful distraction of his company would make that possible. Even if my fisherman did not join me in this, I would somehow manage.

Jim's company was wonderful indeed and I floated on air sitting, walking and talking with him morning to night between meals, but pretty much blowing a steady stream of smoke at him before I finally apologized the day before he left, confessing what my intent had been. Looking at me with that delightful twinkle he had in his eye, he said quietly, *"What a wonderful idea, because we really do need you, you know."* I looked back in amazement and found myself so deeply struck by his words that I stubbed out my cigarette and never lit another. No argument, no intention, had ever worked, but his simple, heartfelt response had.

Our talks had ranged from the macrocosm to the microcosm and to so much in between. His amazing trajectory of discovery was one of planetary science done by one maverick individual who, like myself, had shunned academia to work on his own. He proved that universities, laboratories, and grants were not necessary to doing good science.

In his countryside kitchen, on a very modest household budget, he had made his own lab equipment, inventing and engineering the Nuclear Capture Device that soon became a mainstay in environmental science and medicine, measuring trace substances in parts per million. He had hitch-hiked all the way to Antarctica on a research vessel to take ocean measurements with this device over a large portion of Earth to back up his scientific Gaia hypothesis.

Jim was the perfect person to validate my own pursuit of science on my small remote island. And when I told him my dream of owning a computer, he said he had more of them than he needed and would be happy to send me one if I could learn to use it on my own. I assured him that if he included the manual, I'd succeed, and in short order after his departure I received a notice that it had arrived at the Customs office in Piraeus.

I'd asked Jim not to use its original packing and to label it 'used goods' to avoid paying duty on it. When asked by the Customs officer what it was, I said it was a kind of calculating device used in English schools and that a friend had sent me one that was out of date. I'd really become a Greek storyteller! After hauling it home on two ferries, I strapped it to a borrowed donkey to bring it up the hill to my little hamlet, then installed the green-screened Epson QX-10 upon my desk with immense pride.

Writing on a computer was life changing. I had never learned to type properly, and all my novels, poems, letters, essays, and a handful of short stories had been typed with two fingers and a spacebar thumb. While I was fast, given these constraints, it was still very punishing to have to retype whole pages *and* maintain their length after changes to fit into the other document pages.

The sheer delight of easy deletion and retyping, cutting and pasting with impunity on this wondrous computer, however, was offset by something unexpectedly difficult. The very ease of making changes meant never being satisfied that something was finished. I had trained myself to produce finished copy on typewriters and now it had become impossible to read anything I'd written without seeing the need for and making further changes.

Academia revisited in Catania

One of the first things I wrote on my new computer was a nine, single-spaced, legal-size page speech to present at the Center for the Study of Human Science in Catania, Italy, where I had been invited because Steven Chorover, a very dear MIT professor friend, had recommended me as a speaker for this philosophical conference in 1986. It was utterly exciting to be taking my first trip out of Greece after seven years there, and in my capacity as a university professor in what by now seemed a past life in some long-ago age.

Before I knew it, I found myself standing in an Italian train station, luggage at my feet, looking helplessly around for the person who had promised to meet me there. The conference organizers at the University of Catania in Sicily had sent my air and train tickets, along with assurances that I would be met at this station. The evening was rapidly darkening and no one appeared, nor could I find anyone who spoke English.

Somehow, I got to a drab police station where lights glared and a grim-looking fleet of officers gathered rapidly, scowling at me as if I were some kind of vagrant, or perhaps something more sinister. I felt very uncomfortable, even guilty somehow. When the chief finally allowed me the telephone, and I reached a university person at home, they recognized my name and said they would send a car immediately. To my immense relief a limo quite quickly showed up, the driver bowing and addressing me as Dr. Sahtouris. Before he could whisk me away, the entire police fleet lined up to shake my hand, smiling and bowing to my magical transformation from Cinderella to princess.

The next morning, I found myself at the university, admiring a poster, a beautiful piece of graphic design advertising the conference — *Holistic Theories and Perspectives on Humanity* — in beautiful fonts, with an etching of the historic location as background and printed on thick but elegant gray paper that looked handmade.

Still feeling as if I were in a dream that had narrowly missed becoming a nightmare the previous evening, I noted that I was billed on the poster as coming from "the University of Metochi." I laughed, and in my lighter mood asked the conference hostess if I could have a few copies to take home for my students to eat. At her puzzled look, I explained that this fictitious credential had apparently been created from my mailing address, but that Metochi was the name of a tiny Greek Island hamlet where I lived with a goat lady, her family and a handful of others, while my mail actually had to be picked up in the nearest real village. I figured the goats were the only beings around me who would appreciate the posters as snacks.

Soon, I was standing at a podium, and, bursting with all the philosophy I'd read and cogitated on for years, began my printed-out speech with the Sixth Century BC 'Axial Period' when the philosophy of a newly literate world gave evidence of an intellectual turning point in human history across that ancient world. During that marvelous period, my favorite Greek philosopher, Anaximander, teacher of Pythagoras, was reputedly the first to put his words in writing. Though almost all of it was lost, I gave my translation from ancient Greek of the most verified fragment as: *Everything that forms in nature incurs a debt, which it must repay by dissolving so that other things may form.*

To me, this wonderful line encapsulated the first theory of evolution, and indicated how it happened through the recycling of creatures over time. Anaximander also warned that whatever disturbed the balance of nature would not last. I then worked my way through history up to the Lovelock and Margulis' Gaia Hypothesis and ended saying:

> *The potential health, rather than extinction, of humanity depends precisely — and not surprisingly — on our special species ability to conceptualize our relationships to our world and choose how to behave within it. Perceiving and conceptualizing entities as large as our Gaian planet and planet-wide humanity is very new, as are our attendant insights into evolution and ecology — into what it means to be part of a living planet, with no genetic insurance against self-destruction ....*
>
> *Like the rest of nature, we must constantly work at creative dynamic balance; for us, between individual autonomy and the holonomy of the collective, between integrity and evolutionary flexibility in our social organization. We have the freedom to inquire and discuss what may be most conducive to individual, species and planetary welfare, to find ways of limiting our territoriality and aggression to healthy ambition and cooperative dialogue, to find ways of ensuring that our chosen leaders do not undermine but promote wellbeing at all three of these levels.*
>
> *Our Gaian legacy is no more, no less, than to pursue understanding and act on it — to seek clues in nature and apply them in our effort to promote our healthy survival as every natural species does. The clues are there; the freedom to understand and act on them is ours.*

It was well received; I was treated as an honored colleague despite having abandoned academia for life among the goats. The Catania architecture, the sumptuous receptions and dinners with celebrities were as impressive as the conversations were stimulating. It was the first time I really got that *my* work, done *my* way as an independent maverick *could* be valued out in the greater world, and that was thrilling.

After the conference, I had a very special two-day tour of Sicily's most spectacular sites with a charming filmmaker looking for sites in which to film a new *Medea*. He took me to a valley with 40,000 year old tombs cut into stone cliffs, ruins of ancient Roman villas, and would have continued on to show me live lava high on Mt. Etna as he had a special press pass to drive there. Unfortunately, as he made a call to exchange his sports car for a four-wheeled drive vehicle to climb the mountain past the usual barriers, he was notified that he must go to Milan immediately to take over a TV filming for a colleague who had broken his leg.

Next day, I was off again myself, by train, plane and ferries, back to my tiny village, Metochi, clutching a couple of neatly rolled posters under my arm to remind myself this had really happened, if not to nourish my ravenous students, whose interest was hardly in my lecturing.

Deep-diving into the History of Science

Back at my typewriter, engrossed in writing essays, I was oblivious to the goats ripping ripe figs and leaves from my favorite tree, and often only remembered the big pots of cat food I concocted from yesterday's fishbones and rice or leftover bread when the smell of scorch reached my nostrils. I banged out essay after essay, trying to understand my world. The academic experience in Catania made me dig deeper into the history of science — into those aspects of science I had rejected. After all, they had so strongly influenced the course of humanity that I needed to understand them better in order to plot where science could go at its best.

Rudolf Clausius 'discovered' entropy in the same late 19th century decade that Darwin wrote *The Origin of Species*. Thus, science announced to the world that our universe is a blind mechanism running down and that life evolves by random accidents and fortuitous adaptations only along the way to its own doom. It did not take long for these two theories to be meshed seamlessly.

Once the Big Bang was hypothesized, it became the center of a universe governed by the Law of Entropy, miraculously exploding out of no-thing and then heading relentlessly back into no-thing-ness, as its battery-like energy was used up. Yet, this immense energy produced an impressive evolution of natural 'machinery,' including man himself, before it would exhaust itself. And so, life temporarily bucks the outgoing tide, though its fated doom is ensured by Natural Law.

This standard worldview of science, born of European scientists' love of mechanics, provided a framework in which the closed system steam engine experiments that brought us the concept of entropy was extrapolated to the whole universe by seeing it as this one-way process of explosion followed by deterioration. Yet the quantum physicists, digging deep into the presumed world of solid matter, broke through these material mechanics to discover subatomic particles made of pure energy — an inherently 'thing-less' world in which the patterns we experience as matter self-organize in a continuous and mutually creative dance wherein everything determines everything else and our own conscious observation within this dance literally creates our realities.

These entirely different and even antithetical basic assumptions in science (e.g., consciousness arising within matter vs matter arising within consciousness) had been living side by side, generating contests for unification theories that seemed to me elusive for the simple reason that a single theory could not be built on such opposing assumptions. But that barrier was never spoken about as far as I could see.

I felt Descartes, the founding architect of the standard scientific worldview, had come close to a consciousness-based universe in the famous meditation leading him to pronounce *Cogito ergo sum*, "I think therefore I am." Did this not imply that consciousness precedes material existence? Yet his great love for the practical translations of math into machinery led him instead to separate mind from matter, seeing God as a kind of Grand Engineer who put a piece of God-mind into his favorite engineered robot, man, so that he, too, could think and invent machinery that would eventually be as complex and lifelike as God's.

It seemed to me this was God in the image of man, rather than the other way around as claimed, and I wrote a poem called "The Other Way 'Round." Its relevant lines being:

> ... *Scientists have said Earth is inefficient*
> > *for using so little of available sunlight*
>
> *Scientists say a lot of strange things*
> *They say all nature is machinery*
> *Scientists invented God in their own image*
> > *saying it was the other way round*
>
> *Plato said He was always doing mathematics*
> > *centuries later Galileo agreed*
>
> *The founding fathers of science proclaimed that*
> > *math was the language of Nature*
>
> *(There were no founding mothers of science)*
> *Descartes gave Him new skills as the Grand Engineer*
> > *who invented the machinery*
> > *of birds and bugs and trees*

> *and you and me*
>
> *(except maybe you also have some God-mind given you,*
>
> *which I don't, being a woman, so said Descartes) ...*

Putting myself into the shoes of Europe's founding fathers of science, it was not difficult to imagine their excitement at the idea of nature as machinery. Machinery was perfectly understandable; it was built from parts and could be taken apart to discover its parts, in the case of natural machinery. Therefore, if all nature was mechanical, they could understand the whole of it — the dark mystery of nature as feminine would plague them no more.

True to the *hubris* of Greek myth, God the father had later been overthrown by his obstreperous, if inventive, human sons, who had determined that their fine minds were *not* God-given after all, but had arisen, like their bodies, from a long series of fortuitous accidents within an accidental, non-living universe. But from *my* perspective, tossing God out while maintaining a mechanical universe, they had painted themselves into a corner. Their universe *had* to be accidental to explain it without a purposeful inventor, without intelligence or purpose of any kind.

Descartes had understood that there can be no machine without a conscious and intelligent inventor, so his post-God followers had to explain the deepest mysteries of how life could emerge from non-life, consciousness from non-consciousness, and intelligence from non-intelligence in a mechanistic universe. It was done by invoking natural accident, and the task of science became the tracing of the series of accidents that led to these 'emerging' phenomena. In my perhaps strange feminine mind, without benefit of any parts of God-mind, it seemed to me that this accidental mechanics foundation for science was utterly illogical, and even magical hand waving.

Nevertheless, by the time I was studying science in the post-war economic boom of the 1950s, the machine models of everything studied by scientists were so ingrained that we were actually taught that enough Swiss watch or airplane parts blowing about in a long enough hurricane would assure the eventual assembly of the watch or airplane. In another version of the story, enough monkeys banging away at enough typewriters, would eventually turn up a Dostoevsky novel.

That one made me realize just how divorced the male world of science was from reality. As a woman, my mind went to men thinking up such stories in their ivory towers, ignoring the banana peels, monkey doo-doo, wasted paper and ribbons, damaged and rusted typewriters, and so on, piling up in this bizarre situation before it brought any literary results. And I wondered, back in my time at the Museum of Natural History and its pollution exhibit, if that was how pollution had come about — by simply ignoring our wastes as the industrial age proceeded.

Manmade machines, by dictionary definition, are purposive devices. They are invented by intelligent beings and assembled from parts to carry out specific tasks. They do *not* arise by accidental collisions of particles or atoms, and no saying they do will ever make it so. *If* nature is indeed mechanical, I reasoned, then logically it *must* have had an inventor as Descartes understood. If there was no inventor, there could be no machinery.

Historically, science, even well before dismissing God, had been seen as anathema by the Church for its violations of the biblical dogma, and the Church had great power over European society through its alliance with governing royalty. Heretics such as Giordano Bruno were burned at the stake, Galileo locked up and silenced. But society changed as the machinery of the Industrial Revolution brought new wealth and power. It became evident that the practical engineering applications of a mechanistic science had much to contribute to entrepreneurial wealth. Thus, a new power alliance was forged by the rising European industrial bourgeoisie and science, giving science the power to spread its materialist worldview throughout society.

New secular states born of the Enlightenment, both in Europe and the New World, kept religious power at bay by elevating science to a kind of secular priesthood empowered to tell the scientific creation story. Thus, the meaningless, purposeless, accidental universe in which life was a transient and ultimately doomed phenomenon, due to the Law of Entropy, became the *official* Creation Story in whole nations. The 1925 American Scopes trial, on the legality of teaching evolution in schools, made waves not only in America, but in Europe as well, squelching much of the religious opposition to evolution.

In this secular, scientific creation story, we humans are natural creatures descended from apelike ancestors and empowered by our biological natures to pursue competitive hostilities to gain advantage over our fellows, until life itself is washed away in the entropic slide. Small wonder we built a competitive world of business that brought us to lifestyles based on consumerism to make life bearable in such a bleak scenario.

The process was not framed that way; we were not consciously comforting ourselves in a bleak scenario. It takes hindsight to understand history and how much we human storytelling creatures actually do live by our stories, creating our realities from them.

Spirit calls me

Coming back to Metochi on the ferry from Aigina one day in 1987, I met a tourist whom I helped to find a hotel. In gratitude, she gave me a round-trip air ticket to Philadelphia that she could not use and was not refundable. Though my financial resources were long dried up, and fishing brought in only subsistence-level income, I had no thoughts of going back to the US when suddenly this ticket dropped out of the blue by way of a stranger on a boat.

A day or two later, my phone rang — a rare occurrence. It was a New York friend calling me from Athens, where she had flown on a sudden whim. When I told her about the ticket she asked for its dates and then I heard her say in surprise, *"Oh! You must be meant to go to the Harmonica Virgins!"* Wondering whether this was a concert by some feminist music group, I inquired who the Harmonica Virgins were. *"No, no,"* she laughed, *"the Harmonic Convergence, the fulfillment of the Mayan prophecy, the awakening of Quetzalcoatl!"*

Now Quetzalcoatl was a name I could relate to — I'd known about the feathered serpent god since childhood, having steeped myself early in Mayan culture through avid reading. I was so into it I had even named my teddy bear *Popocatepetl*, after the Mayan volcano.

No sooner had my friend said the god's name than goosebumps broke out all across my bare shoulders — I was shirtless in the summer heat. As we talked, they didn't go away, but seemed to move back and forth across my shoulders in waves. Brushing my hand over my tingling shoulder, off fell a huge centipede, squirming on the floor like a small-fringed snake. *"Elaine!"* I spouted out, *"I'll go — the feathered serpent has just appeared in person!"*

What a magical reality! The Harmonic Convergence, I learned, mostly after arriving at it *in Philadelphia*, had been called by a man named Jose Arguelles to celebrate an unusual configuration of planets on a significant Mayan Calendar date ending a long cycle of over a thousand years. It was about heralding a new world by creating a synchronized global peace meditation in various 'power center' locations, Philadelphia being considered one of the most important. Many interesting people had been brought together, including a number of indigenous leaders, and I gained several significant new friends there.

A highlight of the gathering for me was watching Chief Leon Shenandoah — *Tadadaho* (chief of chiefs) of the 'Six Nations' *Haudenosaunee* (whom the European settlers called Iroquois) — do a fire ceremony in a Philadelphia city park. As he prayed, a flock of wild geese flew over us, landed and walked circles around us. When I commented to him later how beautiful that was, he replied, *"When you speak to Nature correctly, She always answers."*

Oren Lyons, himself the Onondaga chief under him, was also there and we reminisced about being art students together at Syracuse University in the 1950s before I became a scientist and before he was appointed an Indian chief. He was fascinated by some of the things I shared about scientific evidence for Earth as a living planet, especially my stories of our microbial ancestors. Oren pointed out that even though Indians know Earth as alive, it is good to be able to use microscopes and scientific research to reveal these important stories.

CHAPTER 6

Spreading My Wings

Gaia Conferences — meeting scientists at the leading edge

Thanks to Jim Lovelock, I was invited in the late '80s to a series of three annual Gaia Conferences in Cornwall[23], organized there for Lovelock's convenience by Edward Goldsmith, founder of *The Ecologist*, a magazine mimicking the format of *The Economist*. 'Teddy,' as he was called by his friends, was the brother of Parisian Sir James Goldsmith, whom the press had nominated the richest man in the world.

The first time I saw Teddy was on my arrival in Cornwall in 1987. He was jumping up and down, looking like my image of the walrus in Alice in Wonderland, loudly announcing that his brother had done the first decent thing in his life by making the New York Stock market crash! Only by stopping the juggernaut of the global economy, he was shouting happily, could we stop the destruction of our planet.

Teddy had written a monograph called *Blueprint for Survival*[24] in 1972. It was prescient in its predictions of the consequences of our resource plunder, insane economic growth, contamination of our food chains, the failure of over-fertilized crops, overpopulation, and the destruction of our social networks.

He had also written a brilliant analysis of why the Entropy Law does *not* apply to Earth.[25] In essence, his argument was that the amazing complexity of the evolving Earth over billions of years was totally at odds with the law. To quote him: *"Indeed, either we are all mad and there has not been such a thing as evolution; and the biosphere with its myriad forms of life is an illusion; or else the Entropy Law does not apply to the behaviour of living things — only to that of hot air in a closed receptacle or steam in a locomotive."*

As I had found it extremely odd myself that a Law of Entropy derived from the study of mechanical steam engines could ever have been proposed to account for the universe as a whole, I was delighted by Teddy's work. British biologist Rupert Sheldrake, whom I met at the second Cornwall Gaia conference the following year, had come to the same conclusion about the illogic of this foundational belief of science. It seemed the emperor had no clothes, or at least had some very big holes in them!

Teddy Goldsmith hosted the Gaia conferences in great style, with wonderful food, some of it served to us on excursions to special restaurants along the Cornish coast. The luxury of his lifestyle, in a beautiful countryside mansion, as well as in London, like that of the Catania aristocracy I'd touched into, was a sharp contrast to my island life in Greece, thus adding yet another adventure to my store of experiences in seeing life from dramatically different perspectives.

Teddy and I quickly became friends. He was unquestionably brilliant, however quirky in his Luddite hatred of machinery, but then, I habitually gravitated toward clearly intelligent mavericks who questioned the *status quo*. He invited me to events in London and embarrassed me several times while introducing me, loudly blurting out things about me *he* considered colorful, but that I'd have kept to myself or shared only with close friends of the kind he had quickly become.

There were many interesting leading-edge scientists at the Gaia Conferences, among them evolution biologist Brian Goodwin, Mae-Wan Ho, who was working on light emissions from living cells with Fritz Popp in Germany, and Rupert Sheldrake, who was making waves with his work on morphic fields. All in all, for me, it was wonderful to be in a context of real scientific inquiry with so many like-minded biologists, more familiar to me, after all, than academic philosophers.

Lovelock and life

I also had the pleasure of visiting Jim Lovelock on his large Cornwall countryside property where, with the tireless help of his mentally challenged son, he had restored a devastated landscape by planting tens of thousands of trees. Within ten years, streams had begun forming again and foxes had returned to the barren landscape along with rabbits, proving that such an ecosystem could be restored. He was even having success with growing redwoods in Cornwall from California seedlings.

In his home, where he lived simply and frugally, Jim gave me a small paperback book that had been inscribed to him with the words *"Closet*

Gaia, love, Lynn." The book, *Traces of Bygone Biospheres*, was about the work of the Russian geologist Vladimir Vernadsky, who had seen life as a "transform of rock" — as slow geological activity transforming itself into the recognizably more rapid metabolic activity of living entities.[26]

I shouted the proverbial Greek *eureka!* on reading this, for Vernadsky gave me a seamless world of living geobiology, pointing out how rapidly soil could be transformed into cubic miles of locusts by way of grain grown from that soil and quickly consumed by the swarming insects, which as quickly died off and were dissolved back into soil. I began paraphrasing him by quipping, in my own writings, "Life is rock rearranging itself" — an appealing, but I thought very apt, pop music metaphor.

How I treasured that little paperback book Lynn Margulis had gifted him and he had passed on to me! There were some points in my conversations with Jim where we were not in complete agreement, and I wondered, when reading that little book at home, whether he had understood Vernadsky himself. One sticking point for me had been Jim's description of the living Earth — Gaia — as the cybernetic interaction between life and non-life. It seemed to me that Earth was either alive or not; that no other living entity would be described as an interaction of life and non-life.

I had had a similar reaction to Gregory Bateson's description of *mind*, also drawn from cybernetic mechanics such that he saw *mind* as an aggregate of interacting parts or components.[27] I understood the concept of feedback loops but did not feel it necessary to confine them to the mechanics of cybernetic systems.

More and more I was being pushed into deep contemplation on the distinctions between organism and that all pervasive metaphor in science: mechanism.

Jim pointed out that life had never been easy to define scientifically. The problem had been pushed around between chemists and biologist and physicists, but was mostly evaded by listing characteristics of life, such as the "irritability, motility, growth and reproduction," I recalled from my childhood 8th grade biology class. Thus, I thrilled in discovering the core definition of life named *autopoiesis* by Chilean biologists Humberto Maturana and Francisco Varela, working at MIT and the University of Paris respectively.

Autopoiesis — literally Greek for self-creation — stated that living systems and entities continually created and maintained themselves in relation to their surround.[28] If that were so, I reasoned, mechanical systems should be called *allopoietic,* meaning 'other created,' because they require external inventors and maintenance.[29]

This distinction of autopoietic and allopoietic entities became pervasive in the many essays I wrote at home on my Greek island to develop my thinking on this distinction. Of particular interest to me was that reproduction, so prominent on the old lists, was not part of this core definition and thus did not limit living entities to those that reproduced. That meant I could consider entities such as whirlpools, galaxies, even whirling atoms and particles, as self-organizing, form-maintaining living entities.

Even our planet Earth seemed to fit the definition as it continually renewed itself from the same materials in cycles of magma to crust to magma, water vapor to rain to rivers to oceans to water vapor, soil to creatures to soil, etc.

Erich Jantsch's work on the self-organizing universe, was also critical, along with Vernadsky's biospheres of rock rearranging itself — all these new propositions helping my own developing concepts as if they were tailor made for me to see how easily they all fit together.

It seemed so appropriate to apply the new definition of autopoiesis to Earth, so I wrote out my arguments for doing so in four pages of detail and sent them to Varela in Paris. Happily, he answered me, if only to say that while he found my arguments persuasive, he had never considered anything so large as Earth to be alive and believed that the fuzziness of its atmospheric boundary would disqualify it. I responded that if one could see single cells in the detail at which we see Earth, many of them would have far fuzzier boundaries. I received no argument back.

To develop a new, more accurate and more inspiring scientific model or worldview as a framework for the human journey, I *had* to think of the whole universe, Earth within it and humanity within Earth as a coherent living system with system dynamics. It was not a formal study of system dynamics that inspired me, but my own mental exercises in thinking holistically and systemically, far away from the academic culture that had separated scientific disciplines into ever smaller fragments and whose professors did not exactly encourage minds questioning the most basic assumptions on which their careers had been built.

Very helpful to this Big Picture thinking were two concepts. The first was my recognition that nothing is independent of context and that context is what gives meaning to things, to phenomena. While Gertrude Stein had written "A rose is a rose is a rose is a rose," a rose is actually very different to a bee, a donkey, a lover, a chemist, or an artist.

The other was Arthur Koestler's concept of *holons in holarchy*[30], a holon being any entity, and its contexts being the larger holons in which it is nested. In nature, we find particles exist in atoms, atoms in molecules, then on into cells, organs, bodies as a holarchy that continues with families, ecosystems and on to Earth, solar system, galaxy all the way to the universe. Everything is embedded in holarchy and holarchies intersect, as in the different holarchies in which a rose could be embedded.

The conferences in Italy and England led to my papers being published in conference proceedings, and were followed by new speaking opportunities in London and Amsterdam, then an invitation to speak at a major international peace conference in Costa Rica[31], which in turn led to speaking at a conference in Findhorn, a world renowned intentional community in Northern Scotland, then another trip to Costa Rica as a Greek delegate to the IUCN (International Union for the Conservation of Nature) conference, which felt like a huge honor.

All this convinced me that the intense thinking and writing I'd been doing on my own in Greece had the potential for real value in the world. My rooftop prayer of "Use me" seemed to have been answered. Dialogues with other thinkers by mail continued to flourish and my trips to Athens were no longer just with the fisherman to see our family and friends, but to develop more friendships on my own. This led to an invitation from Denis Simopoulis, director of the Athens Planetarium, to speak about my living Earth concept at an international conference of planetarium directors right there in Athens!

On the London trip, I gained the opportunity to help with organizing another spirit-based conference that was also to take place in Athens. I had been introduced to the "BKs" — the Brahma Kumaris, an international spiritual organization founded in the 1930s by a diamond merchant in India. In a vision of Krishna, he had been instructed to found a spiritual college for young women, taught by women teachers — a most unusual assignment for an Indian man at that time.

I was told his story personally by Dadi Janki, one of the young women he had chosen as the school's first teachers back then, now the elder head of the BKs outside India, supervising BK houses for both men and women in many countries.

We were sitting in a garden swing in the Swiss Cottage area of London, where she'd been sent to meet me by my absentee hostess, Elinor Detiger, who had sponsored me to speak at the Costa Rica peace conference. I was captivated, not only by the story of the BK's founder, but by the way she spoke of the BKs now, their beliefs, their work with the UN and more. I visited the London BK house at her invitation, and also went out to their countryside manor near Oxford. Soon we were talking about 'round table' events BKs were hosting in various professions to understand how cultural ideas and worldviews were changing, and I offered to help organize one for scientists to be held in Athens.

It was my contribution to make this event truly international by literally sticking pins in a global map to insure fair representation from all continents. There were BK houses enough around the globe to find the scientists easily, and we put together a truly impressive gathering, including a Nobel laureate. When we all met in Athens, I was especially delighted to have repaid my dear MIT professor friend, Steve Chorover, for the Catania invitation by bringing him to this event.

New horizons on Hydra

As all these wonderful things were happening and raising my self-esteem, I was growing frustrated by a collapsing patio and an increasingly leaky roof over my desk and in other places. My fisherman husband wouldn't let me fix them myself, insisting I would break roof tiles climbing around up there and that he would fix the leaks himself.

In fact, he no more fixed the roof than he provided firewood except when an elderly bouzouki player friend would come to stay overnight and needed the warmth. My own cold fingers at the computer didn't seem to count any more than my need for a dry desk. If the fisherman felt no discomfort himself, he didn't see why I should, perceiving me as a kind of extension of himself. No amount of pleading worked; I began seeing his selfless generosity toward others as lacking toward me.

When we met and courted, it was romantic to smoke a joint at sunset with his uncle or other friends, an old tradition in his culture. But as the years went by, the growing of marijuana plants became his obsession and the joints took up more and more time in our lives. They were made by mixing in tobacco and patching papers together to create what I called 'Churchill cigars' to pass around our social circles.

Having given up smoking, this was no fun for me, even though Jim Lovelock, who had inspired my abstinence had shown me I could soak weed in ouzo till it turned green and thus drink it. Somehow that never caught on with me and so I became a spectator watching the smokers. As a result, I was increasingly aware of the endless hours spent by my husband and his friends dreaming up projects to supplement our fishing income, which had dwindled along with the time actually spent fishing.

Some of the projects materialized briefly. I dubbed one 'the fish boutique' — a scheme for *buying* fish at the market in Aegina, twenty minutes away by ferry, to sell on Agistri from a booth constructed out of the prow of an old wreck of a rowboat and a male mannequin scrounged in Athens and dressed as a fisherman. It took artistry, to which I'd been recruited for the background mural, but the enterprise flopped.

Next, they designed fireplaces to build for people, which lasted no longer since disastrous smoke backed up into the first living room tackled and the project was hastily abandoned.

I encouraged smoking away from our house so I could stay at home to write as they filled rooms elsewhere with the smoke in which they dreamed up their projects. Eventually, I got tough and announced that I was going to find another place to live and would come home when the roof was fixed.

My fisherman was shocked, saying married people could not live apart. I pointed out that many an Athens wife had come out to the nearby islands to live, their husbands joining them for weekends. Pointing out we had no money, he assumed I was just dreaming myself. *"Watch me,"* I said, *"I'm American and that makes me resourceful!"*

It didn't take me long to find a house on Hydra owned by a London acquaintance who needed someone to keep it warm for the winter. I made it clear to the fisherman that he could visit on weekends, but only on weekends, lest he think that he, too, could abandon the leaky house while I feathered him a new nest.

Throughout the winter he came by ferry more often than not, alternately grumpy about the arrangement or sweet as could be — decidedly his more winning manner. I remained as unchanged in my determination while the roof at home remained equally unchanged.

On Hydra, I had not only a spectacular view of the harbor from high up the long stone stairways plied by people and donkeys alike but met interesting new people including ex-pat Londoners Robert and Audrey

Browning, who ran a kind of New Age retreat center in their lovely home even further uphill. Robert had been brought back from near death by a world renowned Greek Cypriot healer known as *Daskalos* ('teacher' in Greek).

Soon I had also spent a Sunday afternoon at Leonard Cohen's home, and more than one pleasant day with a new friend, Ina, who'd worked with Werner Herzog on one of my favorite movies, *Aguirre: The Wrath of God*.

In Hydra, I found a piece of technology that changed my life almost as much as having a computer — the fax machine down in the harbor in a lawyer's office where I got permission to send and receive faxes. This sped up communications so dramatically that I could have almost live conversations across the world. A dialogue with Willis 'Bill' Harman in California, president of the Institute of Noetic Sciences (IONS) founded by astronaut Edgar Mitchell, rapidly became the most important of these, and the fisherman marveled at what he referred to as my 'seven-meter letters' in watching me read through the joined fax sheets stretching across the floor.

Bill's most burning questions were about the paradigm shift in science. Were we 'shifters' developing a broader context for science, in which the old would remain embedded, or were we developing an entirely new science? I became deeply preoccupied with these questions.

At the same time, I was the foreign member of a reading group started by Fred Abraham in Vermont, who had been a fellow graduate student I'd lived with while at Indiana University, when I'd also met his brother Ralph, now a mathematician and dynamical systems theorist with an essay in one of my favorite books, called *Evolution and Consciousness*.[32]

That same book had an essay by Walter Pankow, called "Openness as Self-Transcendence," which made a huge impression on me in its carefully reasoned distinction between natural and formal languages, pointing out that formal languages, such as mathematics and logic, were artificially constructed languages — in a real sense, mechanical languages — *within* natural languages, and that they were not self-transcendent, while natural languages were.

As Pankow said, "Self-transcendence means the capability to change one's own point of view, and therefore the capability to view a situation in a new light," and, perhaps my favorite line: "It takes a living system to know a living system." This was profound — only life could *know* life, its description in formal languages would always miss its very essence.

Published

In my travels, I had met a book agent who offered to represent me, so I completed and sent off my manuscript about the human condition and history in the context of evolution biology and it was not long before we had an offer from Simon & Schuster, one of the best-known publishers in America. Only six months after my agent signed the contract, a letter arrived saying my book had been published — record speed for any publisher, especially such a large one.

I was unhappy with the cover picture (they had rejected my offering) and with the title they gave it — *Gaia: The Human Journey from Chaos to Cosmos*. It was clear they had seen *Gaia* as a newly hot topic and had jumped on the band wagon, but Gaia was not a human journey, nor had we humans come out of our *chaos* into *cosmos*, which meant 'order' in Greek. They had lifted the 'chaos to cosmos' phrase from the book but had used it inappropriately. Still, this was truly good news. Not only was my work worth publishing, but by a major publishing house in New York!

Worldwide Indigenous Science Network

The conclusion I had reached in my book was that we humans would have to learn very quickly to reorganize ourselves by the principles of living systems within the larger living system of our planet or do ourselves in as a species. I had recognized that indigenous cultures knew far more about this than western industrial culture did, and I had actively set out to learn all I could from them. This led to meeting Apela Colorado, an Oneida Indian who was founding a Worldwide Indigenous Science Network (WISN). She asked me to join this initial effort and got enough funding to bring me to meetings in Mexico and Canada. I became passionate about learning about and championing indigenous science.

On the Mexico trip, Apela and I cleaned out nasty toilets in our village accommodations and stuffed dry corncobs into a water heater fueled by them, alternating such mundane tasks with wonderful ceremonies, one of them at the huge pyramids of the sun and moon in Teotihuacan.

In Mexico City, our WISN group were invited guests at an amazing indigenous conference put on by and for indigenous people. It was held in a large park where there were workshops on Mayan mathematics and other cultural heritage topics while elders made paper birds on sticks for children. One elder taught children they could carry water from the fountains in their mouths even if they had no containers for watering new trees they were planting. Music and dancing provided endless joyful celebration. Aztec 'flyers' climbed a tall mast in fours, then, anchored at the top, rolled off their tiny platform to spiral outward as their ropes unfurled until they landed on the ground.

On my way back to Greece, I stopped off in Philadelphia for a scheduled week of six talks at universities and colleges, arranged by the Pennsylvania Council on the Environment. To my dismay, my throat glands became very swollen just as these talks began, and I was diagnosed with a roaring case of the mumps! Turned out I'd gotten them from a Mexican baby I'd played with on my lap and then bought a stroller for as his mom was heavily pregnant while having to carry him around on her arm.

I'd used my last dollars on that stroller, and spent a cold, uncomfortable flight-delay night on the airport floor coming from Mexico to Philadelphia as I had no money to buy greater comfort, yet I'd have bought that stroller even knowing what it would cost me.

I will never know how I managed to give all six talks through my painfully swollen throat, but I did, and by the time I got back to my home in Hydra, I was well into recovery. Soon, I learned that a fellow WISN member from Hawai'i, Puanani — whose name I now heard in my mind as *Poor Nani* — had also caught the mumps from the same baby. My daughter had by then produced my grandson, Nick, now a toddler old enough to laugh at Yiayia — Greek for Grandma — getting the mumps at *her* age.

On another WISN meeting trip to Banff National Park near Calgary, I was walking in the nearby town with Hopi elder Thomas Banyacya and stopped at a bakery to buy him a bag of bear claws — claw-shaped pastries with one end dipped in chocolate. A little way down the same street he stopped before a shop window with a full-sized mannequin dressed as an Indian chief with a large feather headdress that trailed all the way to the ground. Thomas seemed to be in deep thought as he pondered it, all the while munching a bear claw, looking it up and down from head to toe. Finally, he muttered, with a slight tone of contempt, "Chicken feathers!"

The morning we left Banff, I walked into the beautiful forest to say goodbye before heading to the airport. I had an intense desire to see a wild elk, but, feeling unreasonable, let go of it to close my eyes, sitting on a rock for a ten-minute meditation of appreciation for the mountain forest. When I opened my eyes, I was looking into the eyes of an elk, up close, directly in front of me.

Now, my meditations were never so deep that I would not hear a large animal approaching me. It was harder to believe that elk had approached in normal fashion than to believe it had simply appeared. Whatever had brought my wish into being, there it *was*, a real flesh-and-blood elk. I groped in my bag for an apple I'd taken from the breakfast table, and it ate the apple from my hand. I didn't wash its spit from my hand all day, nursing it happily, dried as it was, throughout the day's travel, like a woman in love who does not wash a kiss from her face.

When I later met and talked with David Abram, author of *The Spell of the Sensuous*, about his magical experiences with native people in Indonesia, I pressed him to tell me where he drew the line between magic and reality. *"I don't,"* he responded, *"because there is no such line. Nature, at heart, is profoundly magical."*

The western scientist in me wrestled with such concepts. Indeed, the whole of western culture is obsessed with drawing boundaries between fact and fiction, reason and fantasy, logic and magic. Letting go of such divisions was still new to me, despite the number of 'magical' experiences I'd already piled up in my own direct experience. I could go back and forth between holding the truths of western science and those of indigenous science, but I still needed to integrate them into a single science that I could believe. It had to be a science in which *all* of my experience could make sense.

Socrates, as story in Greece has it, was asked just before his death how he was able to see the road ahead of him, to follow the true path of his life. He replied that he never saw the way to go, but that he could always feel when he was *off* his true path and could thus follow it by correcting his steps again and again. This seemed an excellent advisory message to me as I did not see guiding visions either and was envious of people I met who claimed to have spirit guides showing them their way.

So, I liked this Socrates story that let me off the hook of desiring such visions. I *had* gotten as far as believing that our guts are somehow good 'shit detectors,' so why could they not warn us about being off course in our lives? I also knew that the pursuit of objective truth is illusory, and that we thus need this capacity to feel, somehow, what is good or bad for us. I just needed to understand the magical events of my own life, and I took comfort in reminding myself of Henry Miller's lovely repeated mantra: *Life is the miracle!*

Whether or not I could explain it, I was certainly witness to seeing nature listen and respond to native people's ceremonies, as well as to my own, sometimes very dramatically. What we call magical in our culture was normal in indigenous cultures — normal and natural dialogue between people and the rest of nature.

Earth celebrations 2000 and Irini Papas

While speaking at the remarkable intentional community of Findhorn in Scotland, I had offered to help plan another conference there on science — one bringing together western and indigenous scientists. That gave me the opportunity to invite my Oneida friend Apela and another WISN member, Mazatl Galindo, a fabulous Nahuatl musician, poet and artist, along with Jim Berenholz who often performed with him.

At that second Findhorn conference, I not only got to be with these friends, but met many other fascinating people, including a young man who was on the California planning committee for a 1990 event to be called Earth Celebrations 2000. As he described the plan, I suggested it could be more legitimately an *Earth* celebration if there were a parallel event in Greece and offered to put that together. With an official 'go' from the California committee, I got together a group of friends in Athens, along with my son Philip, who had moved to the city, to talk up the idea, secure their commitments and divide up the tasks.

Each of us agreed to take on one task, form our own committees and raise whatever funds and in-kind donations we would need to put on the event the following year. We had meetings throughout the winter, I secured a venue in the Athens park that had been built to cover the infamous scene of Junta tortures with a new amphitheater that could hold 2,000 people, and Philip designed and coordinated the entertainment program. Others worked on publicity, on donated hotel rooms for visiting guests, on food and wine to feed our projected multitudes, and on an art exhibit, while I continued to liaise with the California group, work with the city administration and coordinate my teams.

The event proved very successful as we filled the amphitheater and lavishly wined and dined the entire crowd afterwards in the park. MTV came to film the whole event and broadcast parts of the show Philip had produced brilliantly all over Europe, referring to me as "the Green Goddess." He had found dancers to perform a Gaia's Dance of creation and evolution, with beautiful slides shown on a large rear-projection screen and many acts followed, including two Aztec dancers in spectacular feathered headdresses.

Oscar and Miguel, the dancers, requested a meeting with Irene Papas, being fans of her film work in Mexico, and I was able to arrange it, having met her not long after I had seen her Epidaurus theatre performance. She told me she was too depressed for more than a very brief meeting — no more than ten minutes — agreeing to this brief meeting in her in-town apartment, not at her main home, a villa on one of Athens' famed hills.

At this meeting, and within those allotted ten minutes, Oscar literally ordered the famous actress to change her black blouse to something lighter, which she did, and then got her to agree to a weeklong series of rituals he guaranteed would lift her depression. She was utterly taken by these golden-brown-skinned Aztec men and their theatrics, as she ended up agreeing and spent the following days obeying their every command, including walking into the sea one morning, as though they were directing her in a film.

On the last day they staged a special ceremony, now invited to her villa, with a few of her invited guests in addition to myself and the Aztecs. It was staged on the large patio next to her swimming pool and surrounded by gardenia bushes in full bloom. Irini was dressed in flowing lacy white with her long hair undone like a young bride as they enthroned her in a tall, ornately carved black chair at the center of a white satin sheet spread over the tiles. Pots of incense were lit as all the gardenia blossoms were picked to throw over her, and all through the ceremony, it was whispered, her current lover hid sulking in the parlor across the patio.

The ceremony over, we were all invited into the kitchen overlooking the patio to have lunch at a long trestle table in Mediterranean villa style. Irini quickly changed into a simple dress, put the finishing touches on the food, then suddenly stopped and stared out the picture window at the gardenia hedges, saying, *"Paedia, den mazepsoume olla afta ta louloudia?"* — "Guys, didn't we just pick all of those flowers?" Indeed, we had, and all of us now stared speechlessly with her in disbelief at seeing them again in full bloom so impossibly quickly. Oscar and Miguel smiled like cats in cream.

From rebirth in Egypt to Perestroika in Moscow

When I had left the house on Hydra, I'd kept warm all winter, and the roof at home had still not been patched, I decided to find my own rental. A few paid talks — one to address a Women in Management Conference in Rotterdam, of all things, and several more in London, left me with just enough money to feed myself, fund my frequent Athens trips and find my own rental a beautiful walk away from the Hydra harbor and right on the sea. It was a small ground-level apartment just steps across a green area with big eucalyptus trees to a private pebble beach no one else seemed to use.

I reveled in gorgeous walks along the cliffs of Hydra to the harbor and back, and to a well in the other direction from which I backpacked its local drinking water in preference to that barged into Hydra and flowing through its pipes. I lay in bed at night listening to the beautiful *phlisvos* sound of pebbles rolling in the lapping water on my little beach.

One night — in the middle of the night — I received a phone call from Apela, calling excitedly from Calgary with no idea what time it was in Greece. She was asking me to meet her in Cairo the following evening! *"Cairo?"* I asked. *"Cairo, Egypt??"* *"Yes,"* she pleaded, *"I'm on my way to a UN 'prep com' — a regional conference to plan a big deal Earth Summit that will happen in Rio in 1992 and I'll have a big hotel room you can share. I'm looking at a map right now and you are only an inch away from Cairo, so pleeeeeze come!"*

I laughed so hard about the inch-long trip that I decided I would do this crazy thing if I could. In the morning, I knocked on my landlord's door and he actually lent me the money for the Athens-Cairo flight in dollar cash, so off I went to the Athens airport!

After paying the Egyptian entry fee in Cairo, I had just ten dollars left in my pocket. With no choice but to go the rest of the way, I jumped into a taxi and sat back as we whizzed over the dry land toward the Hilton Pyramids Hotel. When we arrived, I grabbed my carryon bag, handed the driver my ten-dollar bill and fled to the door with him on my heels. Somehow I managed to shake him and duck into an elevator to call Apela from an in-house phone on another floor, praying she would be there. She was, and moments later we were both laughing and crying happily in a huge room with two enormous beds — a far cry from our Mexican village accommodations.

With carry-outs from the breakfast buffets we were set through lunch and her daily allowance got us suppers and adventures including a camel ride to the Sakkara pyramids, where Apela did a renaming ceremony for me in the depths of one of them, because I had suddenly realized that my very first journey in this life had been from the hospital in Cairo, NY, where I was born, to our home in Athens, NY, and in a few days I would again be traveling from Cairo to Athens!

When Apela asked me what was the first nickname I could recall, I responded immediately that my mother had called me a Crow Mother because I ignored my dolls in favor of live animals. *"Crow mothers,"* she had said, *"abandon their babies!"*

"Perfect," Apela said. *"The Lakota call Crow Mother — Kanghi Ina — the Keeper of Sacred Law."* I was delighted at the huge upgrade and loved the honoring, powerful name.

Back at the other pyramids, we easily bribed the camel boys to get us into the Sphinx enclosure by moonlight that night. Apela insisted she would never ever forget me flapping over the fence in my black coat like a crow under the full moon.

Back on Hydra, I had been doing my own ceremonies of gratitude, particularly during walks in the Hydra hills behind my house by bright moonlight that lit up the limestone landscape left by myriad sea creatures that had built shiny calcium carbonate into their miniscule shells such eons ago. Those walks were like mini vision quests for me, and I learned that when I did ceremony with total focus on my embeddedness in nature and my gratitude, nature invariably responded with some signal of recognition, such as the sudden appearance of a gecko, or an eagle overhead. Each time it happened, I recalled Leon Shenandoah's words, "When you speak to Nature correctly, she always answers."

I was learning to 'live in the flow' — to trust that the universe was alive and intelligent; that I was indeed being used as I'd prayed to the starry night sky on my roof in Aigina; that everything would keep coming to me as needed. All I had to do was to stay in an attitude of gratitude, and to express it. Life could not get better than that.

Still the late '80s, I had several articles published and was invited to speak in rapid succession at an International Institute for Advanced Studies in Cybernetics and Information Systems conference in Baden Baden, Germany, then for the Turning Points Programme in London. My Philadelphia friends working on intercultural peace brought me to speak at a conference in Moscow called the Seventh Generation Conference on Environment and Education. It was amazing to me that my ideas on biological evolution and its meaning for humanity at this time of transition were of interest to such diverse audiences.

Perestroika in Moscow! Amazing that I had been living as close to Moscow as that flight indicated; it had seemed a world away. Now I was meeting not only many Russian schoolteachers, but a sizeable delegation of indigenous people from Siberia and other parts of the Soviet Union.

The mood was very positive and hopeful despite considerable deprivation, with Moscow's food shops having little more than lard, black tea, storage potatoes, cabbages, apples, and onions to offer. But the Russian people were resourceful and most had countryside garden plots or relatives with such, to grow both veggies and chickens. We were hosted lavishly by ordinary people who made it look easy when we knew it was not.

Our group of foreigners was the first ever to visit Zelenograd, just an hour's ride from Moscow — an amazing walled city where IT engineers were kept as pampered pets since the space race began, never leaving the self-contained city once there; raising their families within its walls. The whole city was heated from a central plant, the grocery stores were stocked lavishly like those in America, the opera house foyer was lined with huge bouquets of fresh roses, an underground disco flashed strobe lights and belted out pop music — a veritable fairyland in a drab landscape. No wonder the Soviet Union had competed so well in space!

Impressive as Zelenograd was, my most memorable experience on the whole trip was an evening with the poet, novelist, screenwriter and actor Yevgeny Yevtushenko, who had become known in the West for his gripping poem on Jewish martyrdom, "Babi Yar."

One of our group of Americans, Mark DuBois, a 6'6"-tall environmental activist, had met Yevtushenko on a previous trip to Lake Baikal with musician Paul Winter and had been invited to his country cabin *dacha* outside Moscow. As Mark and I had become instant friends — a very karmic feeling between us — he invited me to come with him. As we left our modest hotel and climbed into the poet's old car, he greeted us, saying, *"Just before you came out, two drunk men vomited into the gutter in unison."* How could one forget such a line?

We sat eating supper and drinking wine on benches at a long narrow wooden table lit by the glow of candlelight, the rest of the room dark. Yevtushenko spoke of how uncomfortable he felt as a member of Parliament, a position he had not sought.

As soon as we finished eating, he brought out the proofs of a book of his collected poems in English, just sent to him from London, and asked me to read one of them to him as he had never heard them in English. He listened enraptured, then asked me to read another one, then another. I could not believe what was happening to me — that I could be sitting there, reading this great poet's work to him. Back home in Greece, I was inspired to write poem after poem myself between travels.

Costa Rica gold magic

Two more trips to Costa Rica had manifested since my first to the peace conference, to which I had taken my fisherman, making three in all, and all from different sources. Did I have some special karma there? On the third, I visited the underground gold museum owned by a bank and approached by an elevator that took people beneath the central square of the capitol, San Jose. The atmosphere in the gold museum was dreamy, with dim lighting and small spotlights on the golden objects in glass cases, many of them representing spirit guardians to the ancient Tairona people who had made them.

Walking among them in a kind of reverie, I mentally addressed a query to Quetzalcoatl — whether he had ever appeared to his people as a humble centipede. No sooner had I formed the question in my mind than something caught my eye at the far end of the very large room, something glinting, moving. I walked straight to it and found a golden centipede swinging from a thread inside a glass case. Nothing else moved, and as I continued through the museum, I found no other such image, nor anything in motion.

The live centipede falling onto and from my shoulder to signal the Harmonic Convergence and the swinging gold one in the case seemed meaningful messages coming to me — not as visions, but as real, if surprising, events in the physical world. They seemed connected to my growing work with indigenous people — people who had not lost their natural relationships within all of nature — their richly intelligent world apparently still spoke to anyone who would acknowledge it in gratitude and listen.

One evening on TV in Greece, I saw Alan Ereira's BBC film on the Kogi Indians of Colombia, *Message from the Heart of the World: The Elder Brother Speaks*.[33] It had such a profound effect on me, that the next time I was in London, I looked him up and we spent a fascinating evening together. At the end of the film, Alan had made it clear that the Kogi did not welcome visitors as they wished to protect the isolation they had nurtured for centuries since the devastation of the Conquest.

Not long after that, however, I actually got an invitation to visit the Kogi with a herpetologist friend in New York who, I discovered, had gotten to know them when he happened upon one of their villages while collecting snakes in the Andes and, always carrying remedies, saved a Kogi from death by snake bite. Though I could not take up his invitation, I soon *did* respond to my almost lifelong and dearest friend Audrey's invitation to come live with her in Tucson, Arizona, for a while — to figure out what to do next with my life.

Deep inside, I felt it unlikely I would return as my work was clearly taking precedence over my marriage. My fisherman would be a fish out of water, were I to try to take him with me, and I had to leave my tiny island life to do my world work well. I could see the roof would not get fixed, as had been my condition for coming home to him, so he, too, was making his own choice. I could not bear to make a final decision, however. I needed to go back to the US, to see how he did without me, to buy some time.

CHAPTER 7

Indigenous Inspiration

From Findhorn to Hopiland

At the Findhorn conference in Scotland to which I'd taken my indigenous friends, I had cut one of the sessions to relax in a hot bath. Pondering my work with indigenous people, and my cosmic plea of "Use me!" it hit me like a flash that *this* was how I was to be used from then on: to continue learning from native people and to assist them in reviving and teaching their traditional values, scientific knowledge and practices, through my work with WISN and in other ways.

That was the first time I was aware of a spirit call to do something specific. From then I've been living not only by the intent and goals of my everyday consciousness, but by inner inspirations and guidance, whenever they surface, as did the Findhorn tub message. I try to be sensitive to such messages, to pay attention whenever something deeper wants to get through the chatter of my active mind. And, as it turned out, much of my activity back in the US has been on learning from and serving indigenous people (and peoples) as best I can.

Having accepted my almost lifelong friend Audrey's invitation to come back from Greece and live with her in Tucson, Arizona, while working on my re-entry to so-called 'civilization,' I had once again reduced my possessions to a small number of boxes. To make packing a lighter task, my last ceremony in Greece was to burn piles of my writings, including two of the three novels I'd written before going back to science and before I had a computer to stash paperless writings. I regarded those novels simply as practice in developing a storytelling voice to replace the scientific voice I'd been taught.

Unfortunately, as they went up in flames, I suddenly remembered I had stuck twenty-three pages of 'dictation' from Henry, just after he died, into one of the books I burned. As *I* almost cried, I could hear *him* laughing!

Those pages had come to me when I heard the English language radio announcement of his death while at my desk typing away on my first novel less than a year after arriving in Greece. I had asked Henry to come back to me when he died, to tell me what it was like. He had lost all faith in such things, and I had tried to revive it.

So I had quickly pulled out the page I was typing when the announcement came on, put in a fresh one, closed my eyes with my fingers poised on the keyboard and had simply typed out everything that came into my mind. Now it had all gone up in smoke, long enough afterwards to recall only that all was very well with him and that he'd been verbose enough about it to cover twenty-three whole pages!

All I could do was shrug it off and return to my packing. My 'potlatch' goal was to again reduce my possessions to what would fit into one cubic meter of space as I had in Boston. Being a very good packer, I could fit many things into such a small space, and I actually enjoyed the challenge.

The shock of reentry to the US was more severe than I'd anticipated, much harder than had been the entry into Greek culture. I had missed the entire decade of the 1980s, and much had changed. The ebullient '60s and '70s spirit of abandoning nine-to-five jobs in favor of building a whole new world was gone; young people seemed only to think of climbing the corporate ladder.

My dear astrologer friend Tony had died of AIDS, and there were now a number of other new auto-immune system diseases afflicting people I knew, along with other apparent social stresses. Americans did not suffer as well as Greeks and people seemed more unhappy in general than what I'd become used to.

An inflated consumer culture had made huge supermarkets, giant drugstores and other 'big box' stores ubiquitous in my thirteen-year absence, and they became symbols of my difficult readjustment. The food markets were almost terrifying in their vastness and stultifying number of different products; their gigantic carts unwieldly, unnatural lighting preventing me from telling whether the tomatoes were really that red. Huge drugstores hurt my nose with scary chemical smells, especially in their new clothing sections, making my eyes water till I had to flee outdoors. I felt like the proverbial frog cast into boiling water while my fellows had had time to adapt as the water heated up.

During my first four months, staying with Audrey in Tucson's lovely Sonora desert, when not feeling like a frog in boiling water, I felt like a fish out of water — sometimes literally in my hunger for the sea. As I continued the work I'd begun with Hopi elders during the WISN trips from Greece, I often noticed how much their villages in Hopiland were like my island hamlet in Greece, with outdoor brick baking ovens, yellow gas bottles on doorsteps and women still in long full hand-woven skirts. Entering one stone house in Hopiland at dusk, a kerosene lantern lighting the wattle ceiling and a bent figure weaving at a large loom, I thought for a moment I *was* back in Greece. All that was missing, in looking off the mesa by day, was the sea. In my imagination, I could easily fill it in, turning the mesa into an island to complete the similarity. It was like discovering a whole other country within my native land.

For one of my trips to Hopiland, I recruited a young builder to drive me up from Tucson in his truck, loaded with materials for repairing the home of a Hopi elder known as *Honan*, meaning Badger. Her caved-in ceiling had given me an opportunity to offer some help in return for what I was learning. I was working especially with Hopi elder Thomas Banyacya, whom Id met at the Banff WISN meeting, intending to help him tell the Hopi Prophecy in the U.N. General Assembly.

The prophecy — of the destruction the white man's inventions and lifestyle would bring to the world — had been given decades before to four young Hopi men and was to be told in the "Great House of Mica on the Eastern Shore." This had been identified as the glass-clad UN building in New York. Thomas was the only one of the four still alive and despite a series of helpers from the white world over the course of forty-three years, the efforts remained unsuccessful.

Thomas had spent a few years as a young man working on prison chain gangs as a conscientious objector, the Hopi identity being People of Peace. After World War II, hundreds of uranium mines were opened in Hopi and Navajo territory, worked by Indian laborers who carried water from the mines home to their families, and soon people began getting ill from their radiation-poisoned water and dust in the air. Even as I visited, dust and water were still spreading the poisonous radiation among these peoples, with little cleanup or compensation because of slow-moving federal courts. Actually, the largest nuclear accident in the US[34], almost unreported, had happened on their lands just as I had gone to live in Greece.

I carry a lasting image of walking in on Thomas at home, glued to his TV set, watching a Mr. Magoo cartoon with great delight. As we worked together, I also brought him down to Tucson for hearing tests and a hearing aid, which were facilitated by Audrey as she was head of the

Hearing and Speech Sciences Department at the University of Arizona and ran its clinic. But the important work was to find new UN contacts to get that Hopi prophecy heard as intended.

The best I could do for him was to arrange, by letters and phone calls from Arizona, a meeting with John Washburn in the Secretary General's office in October, 1991, so that Thomas could deliver a formal letter and a sacred prayer feather into his hands.

That in itself was not easy. While I had arranged it with John Washburn, and had called him from Arizona as soon as I was notified that Thomas was approaching the delegates door in the UN Plaza, Mr. Washburn told me sternly on the phone, "He cannot come in that door. He must go in through the visitors' entrance."

I held my breath for a moment and said slowly into the phone, mustering the strongest energy I could while remaining very calm: "Mr. Washburn, you and I have come this far, and now Thomas is there; I cannot reach him right now, so, *please*, Sir, get up and go downstairs to the delegates door and receive him." He was silent; so was I. Then I heard him say, "All right; I will." I cried tears of immense relief and gratitude as I put down the phone.

The New York friends who had accompanied Thomas let me know the next day that New York City's power company, Con Edison, suffered a ten-minute power outage over a third of New York City at exactly the time Thomas was speaking to Mr. Washburn, confirmed by the newspaper reports on the exact time of the outage. There had been no coverage of Thomas' UN visit.

Florida: Hazel, the Great Spirit and dolphins

A few weeks later, two back-to-back international women's conferences in Florida's Miami brought me to that sea-flanked state in which my parents had spent the last part of their lives before I'd gone off to Greece. I'd been asked to lead a panel at the Global Assembly of Women and the Environment, and afterwards visited my friend Hazel Henderson, who was living in St. Augustine, up the Atlantic coast.

Hazel, a Norwegian-English dynamo, had launched the clean-air movement while working for the government in Washington DC and was writing books to promote new ways of looking at and practicing economics for the benefit of all. While I was with her, she offered me the first 'residency' in her new Institute for Future Studies in St. Augustine, so I packed up once again in Tucson and quickly found myself walking the long sandy beach with Hazel as we shared our ideas for a more life-centered and better world.

That winter in Florida I also met and began writing a book with Ed McGaa, a Lakota Indian who had been in Vietnam as a fighter pilot while my elder brother was becoming a Lt. Colonel there in the US Marines. Ed and I co-led some sweat lodges as he was a firm believer in the need for gender balance in such ceremony, and in my bestowed Lakota name *Ina Kanghi* (Crow Mother) I could provide that.

To me, the sweat lodge is the most wonderful way of worship — to sit with my bare butt on sacred bare earth with others, mingling our sweat with Earth's, felt like such an honest and humbling way to express our human reality as part of all Nature. To play drums and sing around glowing, and then hissing, steaming, stones created the perfect misty atmosphere for the deep prayers of gratitude I loved. I could still not say the word 'God' but 'Great Spirit' gave me no problem at all.

The various prayers I was then using to open my brief personal evening meditations evolved into a longer morning prayer based on the Lakota medicine wheel of four directions plus sky and ground, and consisted of lists of things for which I was grateful. Life was good and gratitude came easily. The Great Spirit or Divine Oneness — names I tried out for whatever higher power might be at play in my own life — seemed to know what I needed far better than I did on my own.

Living in Florida, I also got to spend time with another girlfriend. Known as Captain Victoria, she grew up in Key West in boats — in her own words as a Navy brat — and developed her own business of taking people out to see dolphins. She also headed a reef-saving group of environmentalists and delighted in dancing in spike heels on weekend 'Duval Crawls,' as bar hopping is known in Key West, where gumbo is cooked to the sound of New Orleans jazz.

Vicky knew most every wild dolphin in the turquoise seas of her ecosystem and they flocked around her little boat as soon as she tapped out her identity code for them to pick up. She loved playing music for them and had discovered that Polish polkas were their favorite dance music.

Thus, my first year back in the US passed quickly and was almost complete when Darrell Posey gave me my first opportunity to go to South America. I had actually turned down an earlier invitation to the UN 'Rio '92 Earth Summit because some of my Native American friends objected to how indigenous people were treated in the planning process.

This trip to Santiago de Chile as an 'expert advisor' to the UN Working Group on Indigenous People seemed well worth doing as I could advocate for their interests here. While preparing to come to Chile, as it happened, I dreamed the message that I would "meet my Amazon guide in Rio," so I took that as another spirit call and revived the invitation to go there directly from Chile. Rio was then a free stop on the way back from this paid trip to Chile and the timing was perfect.

Andes adventure

It's 1992 and I've been back in the US for a whole year as I'm off to Chile on my first visit to South America. My fisherman still writes occasional letters but seems to be adjusted to my absence. I am going to write this new adventure in the present tense, dear reader, hoping that will bring you right along with me.

Together with around thirty indigenous people from all over the world, along with the UN's head of indigenous affairs, I have been traveling by bus for sixteen hours from Santiago to high in the Cordillera mountains across from Argentina. A Mapuche Indian delegate to the conference has invited us to attend a ceremony of her people in Quinquen, the last natural Mapuche village in a high valley surrounded by snowy peaks.

Our bus stops where the paved road runs out, and we are transferred to jeeps, bouncing in them along dirt tracks, several times straight through snowmelt rivers that send water up to our windshields and into our laps. My jeep gets stuck in one of them and we huddle together to keep warm, rubbing our hands with teeth chattering, holding our breath as an oxcart driver who has most fortunately come the same way slowly drags us out.

At last, we arrive at our destination where a small band of Mapuche Indians still living high in this remote part of the Chilean Andes greets us with their sacred araucaria tree ceremony. There is no village in sight as we pull up in a barren field where people are gathered around a small ceremonial tree. Their cheeks are painted an intense blue that shines like gemstone in their icy landscape under a low sun as they perform a sacred ostrich dance.

The blue chalk[35] decorating their faces is sacred to them, collected in these native lands, and rubs off onto us as each villager embraces each visitor with great joy. Visitors are very rare here and such an international group of indigenous people brings our hosts great joy.

The most memorable discussion held at the indigenous conference these past days was a long fight over whether we were addressing problems concerning indigenous people or peoples. People are individuals, no matter how many of a kind, but 'peoples' are entire ethnic/cultural/political entities that have, in a few cases, successfully demanded status as nations with their own passports. The United Nations finds that very difficult because such indigenous nations exist within their member nations, many of which resist such demands as illegitimate.

After the remote mountain Mapuche recount their tragic history under European domination, the indigenous people in our group — Australian Aboriginal, New Zealand Maori, Scandinavian Saami, African Watusi, Native Americas — return the Mapuche hospitality with their own greetings and dances. We then feast on the large pine nuts of the araucaria trees that provide almost their entire diet, mostly ground to paste with water and cooked like tortillas on hot stones.

As a rare treat for rare visitors on this special occasion, they have also roasted wild goats on iron spikes over open fires. To brew wild herb tea, they have a few tin kettles and cups — the only other artifacts from the outside world we see. The children play happily at breaking the ice of puddles big as small lakes while we adults blow much frozen breath on each other in our eager talk, using Mapuche interpreters from Santiago.

Our UN meeting was held in a large, nature proof UN building, as I call those without windows, burning thousands of lightbulbs day and night, recycling stale air that was artificially overheated and overcooled in turn. Yet the Bio Bio River, at whose headwaters we are now celebrating with the Mapuche, is scheduled to suffer strangulation by six dams in the coming few years, so that Chileans can have even more electricity.

A young woman who lived for years with the Mapuche calculated that more electricity could be made available by eliminating waste in the present system than by all the new dams put together. Yet those with vested interests in the lucrative business of building dams have no interest in rational arguments against strangling rivers and flooding land to pile waste on more waste.

Having returned to the US from Greece just a year before this trip, I continue to be determined to act on the conclusions I had reached in my book — that we humans will have to learn very quickly to organize ourselves by the principles of living systems within the larger living system of our planet or we might end up an extinct species. It is so obvious that native cultures knew and still know far more about this than do our now pervasive industrial cultures.

Rio: Kari-Oca and Indigenous rights

Sweltering in the heat after coming to Rio directly from the icy Andes, I am at the pre-conference gathering of Indigenous Peoples, happy to have opportunity to use the Mapuche greeting, *"Mari mari"* several times. Just before I flew here from Chile, a Mapuche woman with the Spanish name Maria Pinta gave me the beautiful silver Mapuche breast ornament from her own dress, asking me to tell other indigenous people gathered in Rio that the Mapuche were alive and well. The Pinochet dictatorship had apparently announced their extinction!

The first person who comes up to me in the specially built for this occasion Kari-Oca village greets me in English with a smile, saying, "I'm Mapuche." He has recognized the ornament. A few Mapuche had fled the dictatorship to Europe — he to London — but kept in contact and formed a Mapuche League.

The invitation to Rio has come from Hanne Strong, wife of Canadian gas and oil executive Maurice Strong who was Secretary General of UNCED, and thus heading the whole Earth Summit event. Hanne, whom I'd visited at her home in Colorado, where she hosted frequent gatherings of Indian chiefs, medicine men, Tibetan lamas, New Age gurus, alien abductees and permaculture practitioners, had assembled an international team of religious and indigenous leaders. She called them 'Wisdom Keepers' and intending them to hold the spiritual energy for this global political Earth Summit in Rio. She had invited me to represent Earth Spirituality.

Accepting her invitation affords me the opportunity to work on other programs, including Campaign for the Earth, the Earth Parliament, and working with indigenous peoples during this week-long pre-Summit Global Gathering in the Kari-Oca village they had built in Amazon Indian style in a beautiful valley near Rio Centro, where UNCED's array of the world's political leaders would meet to make agreements on environmental policy issues, some distance from the Global Forum in Rio itself.

The World Indigenous Summit is putting together a declaration to be presented at the UNCED conference, and Hanne's Wisdom Keepers are intended as a kind of spiritual bridge connecting all three of these events: the political UNCED conference, the NGO Global Forum of some 20,000 representatives of UN-sanctioned Non-Governmental Organizations (NGOs), which had built a large tent city in the *Parque do Flamengo* that ran all along one of Rio's major beaches, and the Kari-Oca Indigenous Summit.

The main part of the newly constructed Kari-Oca village is its three large longhouses completely covered in thatch, with earthen floors in traditional style. Two house eighty people each, the third is for ceremonies, meetings, and celebrations. All are cool by day and warm by night — a tribute to the knowledge of passive heating and cooling so common in vernacular architecture around the world, and so lacking in what the white man has built as his civilization has progressed.

The group I'm here with includes Chief Leon Shenandoah and Onondaga Faithkeeper Oren Lyons, who had both been at the Philadelphia Harmonic Convergence; Barbara Pyle, vice president of Ted Turner's CNN and working hard to get him to 'go green'; and Darrell Posey who has gotten to Rio though he could not make it to Santiago.

After seeing Kari-Oca village and greeting people we know, Barbara Pyle and I have a cool drink with a few young journalists and filmmakers, including a very handsome Kadjiwel Amazon Indian named Maksuara who acts in a daily Brazilian soap opera called *Amazonia* and aspires to using theater as a way for his people to teach the white world their culture.

Offered a leading role in the Hollywood film *At Play in the Fields of the Lord*, he turned it down when told he would have to cut his hip-length hair for it. Maksuara tells us the beautiful creation story of his people, and Barbara puts him on camera to speak of the many things his people have to teach our world.

In the dusky atmosphere of the longhouse, where light and air comes from the opening all around it where the thatch ends two or three feet off the ground, Davi Yanomami, who traveled to North America to plead for saving his people's Amazon forest, inhales the bone dust of his ancestors to contact the Creator, sweat pouring from his body during his strenuous sacred trance dance.

Eliane Potiguara, the Amazon woman with whom I will very soon be co chairing a Day of Indigenous Women, stands by Davi and goes into deep trance with him. Maksuara comments afterwards that Davi has continued his own story of creation; that nothing is accidental as all is woven together in a single design.

Hanne Strong's first event, still a few days before the Earth Summit formally begins, is the Sacred Earth Gathering of our Wisdom Keepers group, now in a spectacularly set mountain monastery overlooking the sea far below. We meet just as the World Conference of Indigenous Peoples is finalizing its Declaration[36] in Kari Oca, and as soon as it is done, Oren Lyons, the Onondaga chief — or Faithkeeper — whom I'd first met as we studied art at Syracuse University, brings it to our gathering.

We are sitting in a large upstairs monastery room, along a double horseshoe curve of adjoining tables with the speaker at the opening. As Oren speaks about the process of writing the Declaration, a spider appears on my table right in front of me. I think of the webs we are weaving and as I am in the back row, take it carefully to the open window to free it as I drink in the beauty of an orange flowering tree in the garden below the window and above a magnificent vista of forest all the way down to the ocean.

The moment I turn back to the room, Oren begins reading the actual Declaration. With his first word, I feel a sudden gust of cool air at my back and hear a loud downpour of rain behind me. I turn back to the window in surprise. Indeed, it is pouring rain where it was bone dry the moment before!

The rain stops just as sharply as Oren reads the last word of the Declaration. Leon Shenandoah, Oren's elder chief, tells me afterwards that the spider was a good omen. Without it, I realize, I might well not have noticed the precise timing of the rain's sudden beginning and abrupt ending. I know now that things are happening at levels my dominant culture white people cannot even fathom. The relationship of indigenous peoples with their sacred Earth is clearly still strong, and that feels very good.

The Declaration is good, too. There is no more asking the white man for concessions, but just a simple affirmation of indigenous rights. This fills my heart with passionate approval, for I have thought it fruitless for indigenous peoples to play by the white man's rules. None of us can afford to play by those rules anymore, I muse, for by them our world has been ravaged to a very dangerous degree.

Savages and politicians in Rio

Sarah James, enduring the heat of Brazil, is beating her huge caribou-skin drum to punctuate her words as she tells us about her Gwich'in Indian culture in the northernmost inhabited village of Alaska. I first met her at a WISN meeting in Oregon last year; this time she has made the trip much farther south to Rio for the Earth Summit. She describes her people's lives before contact with the white man — their sacred relationship with the caribou, their endless gratitude and care for these animal relations who give them everything they could want: food, bone and skin houses, boats, snowshoes, utensils, tools, clothing, drums, flutes.

She sings her welcoming skin hut dance song, then speaks of how rich their lives had been — rich with family and community, warm homes and clothing, plentiful food, much time for ceremony, music, dance, storytelling and laughter, much reason for celebration and thanksgiving for their bounty. But when the white man came upon them, he only saw people living in 40-degree-below-zero weather with only caribou to provide for their meager subsistence. "He called us poor savages" Sarah cries out, as she beats her caribou skin drum louder and smiles broadly, shouting out "Well, then let's *keep* Alaska *savage!*"

Sarah is making a clear statement of preference for her traditional life of simplicity over the modern world that brought her people real poverty along with the terrible dependencies of debt, alcoholism, and the glue-sniffing that has destroyed her own son's brain. She clearly makes the point that wealth is a matter of perception and priorities.

Northwestern indigenous cultures south of Sarah's northern Alaska, making and trading more complex material things, developed 'potlatch' and other giveaway ceremonies to divest themselves of excess possessions, as well as to practice generosity. My personal potlatch — back in Boston, in preparation for moving to Greece — has led to a more permanent transformation in my own life on a material level, living since then with less income and less 'stuff.' All in all, this has increased my happiness and excitement about life. Little money, no house or car, has led to fewer expenses, less negativity, more free time and flexibility, endless fascinating adventures.

Sarah's talk, for me, is the highlight of this Day of Indigenous Women's Voices I planned with Amazon Indian Eleane Potiguara at Kari-Oca. We are holding it in an inner-city people's park to avoid the stiff entry fees to the Global Forum on Flamengo Beach, the huge tent city where the 20,000 NGO representatives are holding their exhibitions and events in a beach park.

Our people's park dance floor has no walls, is just covered by a huge roof on poles, its stage at one end, and its loud if tinny sound system has been donated for our use, as have the food and lodgings in a former army barracks nearby, for all the indigenous people from around the world whenever they come into the city from Kari-Oca.

After Sarah's talk, we eat lunch at small tin tables set up in the graveled area around the dance floor. I'm facing a broadly smiling Senator Al Gore, the only politician to have come to us from the UNCED venue. He's sitting with me as his host, because I'm the event's co-organizer, and I could not be more thrilled, having just read his newly published book *Earth in the Balance*. He strikes me as friendly, intelligent, open and honest, as well as so knowledgeable about ecological issues that I come away with new hope for politics in Washington. And, indeed, it will not be long before his appointment as Clinton's Vice President!

Sapaim

Not very many highly trained medicine men have survived in the indigenous struggle for saving the Amazon forest, but Xingu *pajay* Sapaim is one of them. We meet during the Sacred Earth Gathering at the monastery on the hillside, when both of us gravitate outdoors at every opportunity. We have no spoken language in common, yet with the occasional aid of an interpreter, and with a handful of Spanish/ Portuguese words and much sign language when we are alone, we empathize and negotiate considerable communication in the span of three days.

As a healer who works through plants, Sapaim's knowledge comes directly from plant spirit teachings, not from another *pajay* (medicine man). That makes him the *"pajay of pajays"* in his own words. A small dark skinned man with wide cheekbones, intense black eyes, and hair in bowl cut bangs, he exudes the gentle but vital spirit of the forest. It is obvious he is more at ease in the forest than amidst the people and artifacts of our so called 'civilized' world.

All I can offer him as a gift is a smudge stick of white sage I gathered on my Greek Island, kept for a year in the US and brought with me. It is my last and I ask if he can use it or would like to take it to his people. Sapaim breaks into a happy grin as he accepts it and says he will tell me about it after sleeping and dreaming with it. Next morning, he speaks excitedly, so I run for an interpreter. My plant and his plant, he tells me, have been talking all night. They have both come very far to meet each other and are ecstatic at being together. They have much to say and their lively conversation is not yet finished. Sapaim and I hug each other in our people happiness at bringing the plant beings together. I ask whether the plants of the rainforest talk about the ongoing destruction. "Constantly," he replies. "They talk a lot about survival strategies." "Will they survive the devastation?" I ask. "Yes," he says gravely, feeling their pain.

We walk up a forest path I discovered, to a pool where butterflies flit in colors and patterns I have never seen before, where tiny monkeys occasionally scamper through the branches high overhead, sitting up suddenly to cock their heads and listen to the various bird calls and other sounds. A strong wind arises and trees rub each other with creaking sounds while the ground is pelted by a barrage of falling leaves, small branches and clumps of epiphyte plant matter.

I ponder this intense activity of the forest in maintaining itself through rapid recycling. It does not pursue 'progress' but works hard to stay the same, just as do the native people who have learned from it, who do not understand our passion for 'progress' — our destructiveness, our blindness to the ways they know to be good from their many centuries, if not millennia, of passed-on experience. Before we leave the little forest pool, I take from my pocket a handful of small uncut gems I was given in my hotel's lobby on arrival by a Brazilian jewelry factory representative drumming up tours. I show them to Sapaim before I fling them into the pool. He understands my action, that I am symbolically returning something to the Amazon that belongs there, and smiles.

Learning that Sapaim is a healer, people in our group come to him for help. But it is difficult for him to heal without his remedies. He has apparently left his home hurriedly, without even the herbal cigars he smokes in his healing rituals. Still, he manages a kind of psychic surgery to cure Chief Leon Shenandoah of a residual pneumonia.

As Leon describes it, he removed congested material from his lungs through his chest, and also healed severe stiffness, still there from when he'd fallen off a horse. I saw a lot of Leon in the following two weeks and can vouch for his lasting chipper mood and regained agility, even late into the nights of our long working days.

I introduce Sapaim to Dr. Vandana Shiva from India, a physicist by training, I've long admired for her profound understanding and scientific analysis of the disasters of hi tech agriculture, and for her passionate opposition to genetic engineering, to the colonization and patenting of seed held sacred by those who nurtured it for thousands of years. I ask Sapaim if he could give her the power to protect plants and he does a special ceremony for her toward that end.

On the last day of this meeting, as I sit in front of the monastery with Sapaim, a lady appears with a camera crew and whisks him off to film an interview. Suddenly, there is a flurry of people and attention focused on Sapaim, crowding around him excitedly. "He's a pa*jay*, a medicine man." "He's an incredible healer!" "He healed Chief Shenandoah!" "Can he cure my shoulder ... my tumor ... my back?" In the midst of this excitement, the lady rapidly explains through her interpreter that he will be taken to speak at a very special gathering here in Rio with the Dalai Lama and other dignitaries. She will then take him to New York; he must arrange everything to leave very soon. What did he need? How soon could he go?

The pushy intensity of this New York film producer's 'discovery' of a new medicine man, this dramatic imposition on his life, makes me want to protect him. I try to move closer, to speak to the lady. She brushes me off rudely. "This is none of your business; please move out of the way. I'm in charge here. Bring the cameraman ..." I try again: "I've just spent three days with this man; he needs to get back to his people; you don't understand ..."

As I am physically pushed aside, tears well up in my eyes. These people do *not* understand and haven't even rudimentary manners. But how can I explain what they don't understand? It isn't something to be said in a few words, in this curt North American way they operate. It is everything I have absorbed of Sapaim through my skin and other senses by spending quiet time alone with him, by attuning myself to his world, his energy.

There is so little I could even try to say — that his people need and want him at home in the Xingu territory, that what he could say before her cameras would be a few limited phrases in Portuguese that could never convey who he is. But who would listen?

A new medicine man in New York could build reputations. I try to stop my ears against the voices I hear in their Manhattan accents: "Oi've got this terrific new psychic healah!" "Wait till you heah about *my* Xing*u* pa*jay*!!" Inside I was screaming *"Rape!"* — the rape of yet another culture in our unwitting, bulldozing way.

Shortly after that, I find myself on Sugarloaf Mountain overlooking Rio. I've been invited to participate in an impromptu arts festival in honor of *Omame*, the Yanomami Creator God — also, I understand, a kind of Patron of the Arts. They want me to speak about Gaia, but I decide a speech is out of place, that I will sing instead — an Australian whale song about a mother and son who free a beached whale. It has been on my mind to do this, and when I was told that another participant was bringing a huge inflatable parachute cloth whale, I took that as confirmation that singing the whale song was indeed the right thing to do.

After we circle the whale, singing the *"Oo-wa-ee yea-ohs"* of the chorus together, I lead people into the whale through its tail opening and tell them a whale story inside. The story is from my favorite of Lyall Watson's books, *Gifts of Unknown Things*. It is of a whale found beached by Tia, a young girl dancer who keeps alive the natural religion of her Indonesian Island. The priest of the newer Muslim religion has forbidden the people to help her free the whale and return it to the sea because it is the month of Ramadan when touching animals is forbidden. Unable to free the whale by herself, she stays with it, pouring water over it from a coconut shell, stroking and singing to it until it dies. After that, she disappears. When she comes back to her village, she has the power to heal by laying on hands to close wounds and even brings a dead man back to life.

That whale story and song make me think of Sapaim, who would be alone like a whale out of water in New York. As soon as the session is over on that domed Sugarloaf rock, I find a great rubber tree with which to share my profound grief. I have never spoken to a tree in anything but recognition and greeting before. Through my tears I whisper to this tree in Greek — the language I've spoken for so many of my recent years and in which I still speak to animals and plants for some reason — telling it the whole story and pleading with it to tell my news to all the trees it can reach, to broadcast the news through the whole Amazon forest, to ask the forest to protect Sapaim any way it can.

The giant rubber tree is rooted well below the level of rock on which I stand, so I can touch its glossy overstory leaves. As I speak to it, one branch moves toward me and strokes me again and again. As with Sapaim when we were in the forest together, communication shifts to a different level, a silent connection in which we are joined in a field of mutual understanding. It is a long, deep interchange — not communication, but *communion*.

I see Sapaim only once more in Rio after the TV crew incident. He comes up to me in another setting, at an Indigenous Earth Parliament in downtown Rio. He is in very beautiful face paint wearing a crown of gorgeous red and yellow parrot feathers; I do not recognize him until I look closely into his eyes. We hold each other briefly and part soon after. I do not know that we are destined to meet one more time.

From Kayapo to concert

One night in Rio, I go to the formal opening of a museum exhibit on the Kayapo Indians. The living Kayapo are present. I know them by now as they, like myself, are spending most of their time at the Indigenous Earth Parliament near the dance floor where I met Al Gore and where no NGO conference badges are needed, where Indians are fed and housed for nothing, where the poor people of Rio can come, where anyone can speak at the microphone as people sharing pains and joys, projects, experiences, news, music, and dance.

The Kayapo are at this museum opening in full feather, sitting on a mat of banana leaves spread on the floor in the center of a huge hall at the end of the exhibit on their culture. The exhibit itself is beautifully done, with much of my ethnobiologist friend and colleague Dr. Darrell Posey's work in evidence. But the exhibit of live Kayapo, with the guests gawking and milling around them feels wrong. I leave before the celebratory drinks are served.

My mind has run to *People* magazine, which decided not to print an intended cover article interviewing Chief Paulinho Payakan because he did not come to his interview in feathers. I thought of this and of the reporters who followed us to the Mapuche ceremony in the Chilean Andes and were so disappointed when the Australian Aboriginal and the Maori danced in western clothes, asking if they couldn't find some feathers to don for the cameras. Occasionally the Amazon Indians spoof the reporters. Not about to do sacred dances on camera, they invented something they called the "press shuffle" that was as authentic as the Banana Clan the Hopi invented to initiate white folks they called "wannabe Indians," their word for white man being *bahana*. I saw people proudly wear their banana badges, oblivious to the lack of bananas in Hopi culture.

When will the focus change from exotic visuals to the vital teachings such peoples have for us? Whenever I speak with indigenous elders, they remind me how strange it is from their perspective that people want a "new world order." What, they ask, is wrong with their *old-world* order? The laws of nature, they have told me again and again, were given by the Creator long ago and will never change. When will the white man learn to live by them, honoring all Nature and doing no harm?

The Laws of Nature known by indigenous people are consistent with the principles I discovered in my independent scientific study of nature such as interdependence, give and take, balance and harmony, along with the sacredness of all life.

In my scientist mode, I have come to call them 'principles' or observed regularities, as my colleague Rupert Sheldrake calls them, because we agree that the word 'law' connotes a lawgiver and thus seems inappropriate to a science that has rejected God as Creator. I have no problem seeing them as the Great Spirit's laws in indigenous settings where there is no separation between 'religion' and 'science,' just a seamless way of life.

Euro American scientists derived their 'laws of nature' from laboratory experiments, such as the entropy law derived from the study of steam engines. By this law of entropy, scientists declared that living systems evolved their own order only at the expense of their environments, literally, by *degrading* their environments.

Like Teddy Goldsmith, I see only abnormal, unhealthy living systems — living systems out of balance — displaying such entropy, while healthy living systems contribute health to their environments, as well as to themselves by recycling whatever they do not consume. Would we not, then, do better to obey the Laws of Nature as indigenous peoples understood them — as those laws of balance, of harmony, of the necessity of giving as much as you take?

By isolating natural phenomena inside laboratories, all the deep connections among them in nature are eliminated. The study of nature can only reach the profoundest truths, as my indigenous friends know, by going *into* nature to study it.

With Sapaim, with Maksuara, with my whale song and the rubber tree on Sugarloaf, I begin to sense that my work is not only about bringing together the wisdom of indigenous peoples and the best of modern technology, but of moving into a deeper understanding of the plants, the rocks, the elder whales in the sea, the creatures of the forest and even the stars in their profound and sacred communion with one another.

A Guarana tree story

Maksuara, on another occasion, tells me the *Sataré Maué* people's story of the Guarana Tree, from whose berries the Guarana drink originating with them was made long before it became the national beverage of Brazil. The Maué, he tells me, also eat the dried guarana berries to gain clarity of mind, regularity of heartbeat, and general strength.

In the story of the tree, as he tells it, a pregnant woman prays for a son who will make his people strong to keep their forest healthy. When the time comes for her to deliver, however, she is alone in the forest with no one to help her and dies in childbirth. Without her milk to nourish him, the boy child also dies. But as he lies on the earth, the first guarana tree grows from his eyes. That is why the berries look like pairs of eyes. And as the guarana tree has always made the people strong enough to keep their forest healthy, the mother's wish is fulfilled.

In the evening of the day Maksuara tells me that story, I meet a young man named Morgan from Mexico City. He sits next to me at dinner, in a typical Brazilian restaurant that reminds me of a Greek *taverna*, and he seems to me a kind of bodhisattva. Almost losing his life in an automobile accident, he has been left with scars around his beautiful face and one of his soft dark eyes is blind.

Yet, in his urban neighborhood of open sewers, disease, unemployment, homelessness, and utter despair, he has organized youth group activities, including finding materials for them to build homes for the homeless as a 'Neighborhood of Hope.'

I tell Morgan the story of the Guarana Tree I just learned and recall Maksuara's words at Kari Oca on how Davi Yanomami had continued Maksuara's story of creation; how things are woven together. The story he gave me this very day seems continued by, woven into, Morgan's life and work. While I will never see Morgan again, I will remain deeply inspired by who is.

During this actual Earth Summit, our Wisdom Keepers group has moved to a lovely ranch cut into the forest close to where the politicians are meeting well outside Rio. We keep vigil in pairs around a fire day and night in rotating shifts, passing the time in conversation, silences, drumming, and song. On my night vigil turns, we drum prayers into the sleeping heads of the politicians, hoping to influence them toward positive decisions and commitments.

On the drives shuttling from the Earth Parliament or Flamengo Park to our ranch, I keep noticing a region rife with a nasty cesspool-like odor we pass through, but no one can identify it. Soon enough, however, I find out exactly what it is, when invited to give a talk to some rural people who turn out to live on the shore of what was literally a big cesspool just behind the pretty trees flanking the highway.

Only on the way there is it explained to me that developers have put up large apartment blocks nearby and are piping all their sewage into the small lake to which I am being taken to speak to people living on its shore, too poor to move somewhere else. To make things worse, I am shown the charred remains of a small house that belonged to a couple who dared protest the situation and were murdered for it, their bodies bound, stuffed into plastic bags, and thrown into the lake. And I am expected to give the survivors who still live there some kind of hope!

Never in all my life have I faced such devasting tragedy head on. I have beaten my head against the wall over napalmed children during the Vietnam war, yet I never faced their families up close and personal. What can I possibly say to these people?

As it happens, the first thing they do is take me out in a rowboat to show me their lake, which only makes their situation more graphic. I have to witness the floating sewage in a boat the gunnels of which are barely above the sludge, fish clearly killed by murky, toxic water floating belly up, white herons blackened by the sludge roosting in mangroves, the roots of which are trying desperately to vacuum up the hopeless, stinking mess.

All I can think of is the Guarana Tree story — the story of hope out of hopelessness, of life out of death. As my audience piles into broken folding chairs on a crumbling concrete patio outside a tiny general store and furnished otherwise only by the omnipresence on a Coca Cola machine, I tell that story humbly, as I have just heard it myself. Then I vow to ask university students and government people to look into their situation and try to build an advocacy group to work with them on a cleanup program — perhaps in the name of a possible eco-tourism project they could evolve with such help and benefit from economically.

I follow up on this promise as soon as I am back in Rio, exciting some students and politically connected people, praying hard that I am inspiring real follow up to my impassioned pleas.

Concert under the moon

Meanwhile, the idea of a big concert on the beach to celebrate the last night of the 20,000-strong Global Forum participants surfaces repeatedly in conversations with various NGO groups in which I am involved when not working with my Wisdom Keepers. There is SO much to do! Many proposals are made for artists, funding, staging and so on, but nothing seems to work; every plan somehow falling through. It seems to me there are just too many egos in contest with each other.

Suddenly, I think of a Texas lawyer I've met who seems to me the kind of person who can make something happen quickly. A few of us believe there is enough talent for several concerts on the scene already;

what we need is a stage set, a platform, a sound system, lighting, and a beautiful big mural as an onstage backdrop. Someone suggests the perfect street artist, a young man in a Los Angeles ghetto who would be perfect to paint that backdrop, so I talk the lawyer into flying him to Rio immediately. It only takes a few phone calls and gets done!

I am sure everything else will somehow come together around him once this part is done — and it does! People are excited and cooperate, the musicians come together, we keep the young artist company on the beach a whole night as he paints, the stage goes up, and the moon gets full.

As we stand on the improvised stage under that full moon on Flamengo Beach, the crowd gathered by the thousands, and the music beginning, I watch clusters of people form dance rings and other visible patterns. I flash on the great theater of Epidaurus in Greece more than ten years earlier, the night it seemed to me a huge cell nucleus with streaming people-protoplasm ebbing and flowing around it.

As I hold that image, our stage becomes for me the nucleus of another such cell, with people clumping and circling in clusters like cell organelles, the rest streaming about them. Some begin handing their small children up onto the stage to take pictures of them at this historic event and I see these, their offspring, as symbolic of contributing new DNA to this cell in formation, this cell representing a new, cooperative world of humanity!

CHAPTER 8

Living in the Flow

Sufi summer

Adnan Sarhan[37], a Sufi master from Baghdad who opened the formal Earth Summit with a drumming meditation, is one of our Wisdom Keepers. On this evening, we sit surrounding him on a large Persian carpet in an elegant basement room at the ranch, where he is drumming just for us.

When he has us swaying in a rapt trance, he gets us on our feet, his drum leading us in a belly dance session for beginners. We are all blindfolded so we cannot compare ourselves with others, told to focus purely on feeling the rhythm of his drumming, responding by letting it move our bodies as it will. Adnan has assured us there are no right or wrong movements; no judgment from anyone.

Drawn to Adnan's loving simplicity, I want to accept his invitation to come spend six weeks at his summer workshop in his camp in New Mexico but have to beg off as I have neither the airfare nor the tuition. He just smiles and insists, "You weel be there; eet ees paradise and you weel come out like high school gurrl."

When I get home to Florida, I find my first frequent flyer ticket in the mail and smile to myself. Am I indeed meant to go to Sufi camp? I call Adnan explaining that I still have no money; he simply asks when to meet my flight in Albuquerque. So, off I go on the free ticket.

Sitting among some sixty people on a large wooden floor with Adnan, in plain white t-shirt and khakis, on a low dais at one end, leading us in chanting simple verses from the Koran, I laugh inwardly, glad my children cannot see me and roll their eyes at what I'm doing *now*.

From my perspective, Sufi camp with Adnan takes me the next step in my spiritual development, learning through 'right-brain' activities such as chanting, exercising, drumming, whirling, and dancing to get out of my intellectual left brain and live simply in the moment. I lose weight on healthy organic food, get limber with exercise and occasional garden work, learn a bit of belly dancing, sleep sometimes under the stars, pray under the open sky in the morning, and come out feeling as youthful as Adnan promised I would.

Adnan has trained the best belly dancers in America and always has a flock of lovely girls around him eager for a lesson. He is not tall but solidly built and certainly does not move like them, yet, hooking his arm into one of theirs, he seems to transmit the dance directly. His star pupil, Dunya, who studied dance at Julliard, is here with us and marvels as she tells us how she had not believed a dance form could be learned without the usual kind of instruction.

Periodically, Adnan puts all sixty of us to sleep instantly by saying, "Time to sleep!" as he snaps his fingers and we fall back on our mats, then wakes us again ten minutes later with a clap and a "Time to wake up!" I love his completely unpretentious ways, but knowing how very perceptive he is, tease him about looking at my aura before I've combed it in the morning. It is clear he can see all our auras and he clearly tailors his sessions to our moods.

I finish the book with Eagle Man Ed, who comes to visit so we can work together, and get other work done, as Adnan said I would when I'd tried to use work as an excuse for not coming. He gives me the gift of seeing first-hand how when you live fully focused in the present instead of on your plans and efforts for the future, things flow to you easily from the future. Full awareness from moment to moment seems indeed to put me in the cosmic flow where things happen without pushing.

This simple but functional summer camp was donated to Adnan by Josh Reynolds of the tobacco company, who eventually supported anti-smoking efforts. Adnan, who always treats me as a colleague, tells me one day that the majority of people coming to his camp are addicted to one thing or another when they arrive and usually leave free of their addictions without his ever having mentioned them. In fact, he forbids nothing, even setting up an outdoor kitchen in the woods for people to cook meat if they wish to. Smoking and perfume are not allowed where we live and work, but nothing is said about elsewhere.

This same summer, *Mountain Light Magazine* publishes a dialogue between Fritjof Capra and myself, and after Sufi camp, I make my first appearance on New Dimensions Public Radio, distributed to three hundred National Public Radio stations. Yet, aside from a few paid talks,

I live on Audrey's kindness in Tucson and Hazel's six-week residency in Florida until I find my own place nearby. A few air tickets, gifts and 'freebies' come my way as I stay connected with spirit, believing in the bounty of the universe and remaining consciously in its service.

I pray to receive and to give whatever is in my own highest good and that of all life everywhere. I am aware that this means welcoming *whatever* happens in the confidence that it *is* in my own highest good, whether it is a fall on my face or a hot fudge sundae! Nothing helps meet tests better than the assumption that they will lead to learning and spiritual development.

Newly slim at the end of my Sufi Summer, I make a new commitment to continue exercising with a personally assembled and pleasant ten-minute ritual made of Japanese, Chinese, and Tibetan exercises, to keep trusting my intuition and following my inner guidance.

The latter really puts me to the test! At the beginning of the summer, I had planned to move to Key West in the fall, to accept Captain Victoria's irresistible offer to live with her, be near dolphins, and raise money for a whale research institute on whose boat I hoped to sail eventually. I had felt that whales would come into my life sooner or later, but no sooner do I get to Key West, directly from Sufi camp, than my inner guidance changes everything!

First, I am told to do a Quincentennial Columbus Day '92 meditation by full moon with friends on Bear Mountain in New York State's Hudson Valley, where I was born, and the means to travel there appear quickly as confirmation. While there, I visit a dying friend just upriver from that mountain, but, while at her house, I get yet another and very strong inner message to move, of all places, to Washington, DC!

Unable to imagine the nation's capital as a place to spend more than brief visitor time, I protest vehemently, telling the inner voice I cannot do that without a home or job there. In a matter of days — out of the blue — I am offered a free apartment in DC for six weeks. Shocked by *this* confirmation, I decide I had better go.

Washington, DC: The way up is down

So, I'm headed for the nation's capital on the strength of a very nice, if temporary, apartment, with only my summer Sufi camp wardrobe and a battered old tent in my luggage. I cannot even afford to go back south to St. Augustine to root for somewhat better clothing among the meager possessions I've left packed up in Hazel's garage, still waiting to be shipped down to Key West. Jumping to the conclusion I'm being sent to Washington to work in some professional ecological or political capacity, I intend to look for such a job.

Stopping off to visit a Philadelphia friend I'd last seen in Moscow, she outfits me with lovely Washington-appropriate clothing she'd outgrown, down to a lovely hand-tailored tweed suit with matching leather boots and bag. So, yet another need is magically met.

Things would seem totally magical except for my troubling failure to find a job in DC. Nothing works, however flexible I try to be in my pursuit of employment. I live from hand to mouth as frugally as anyone could, stretching the small fees or donations I glean from talks given here and there, mostly in people's homes.

Within weeks after moving to DC, I'm in New York City for the special UN General Assembly session on Dec. 10, 1992 — the long-scheduled session that will give voice to indigenous people, including Thomas Banyacya. In my work with him before this, I was only able to facilitate that very short visit to the UN for him, described in Chapter 7.

His Hopi elders had told him as a young man to "knock four times at the Great House of Mica" in order to tell the Hopi Prophecy there, and the visit I had facilitated completed that mission, even though he had only, as he now says in the General Assembly, "delivered a letter and the sacred prayer feather I had been given to John Washburn in the Secretary General's office in October, 1991."

This time, for the General Assembly meeting, he and Oren Lyons are the officially invited indigenous representatives from the US, along with quite a few other indigenous people from other parts of the world. When I was told that Thomas had actually been chosen at the last minute as one of the two, I called him immediately, expecting him to be all excited.

Instead, he said, sounding gruff and sullen, "I'm not gonna go. They closed that door too many times and I'm done. That's it; I'm not going." I was crestfallen. "No Thomas. You cannot do that now. This is the real thing, *the General Assembly*, Thomas, and they will give you time to talk there. *Please*, get up and pack your bags and go to New York."

On December 10, I am standing in the UN lobby, wearing a red sweater when Thomas walks in, wearing his red jacket. He looks at me in surprise and says, "I didn't think I'd see you here." I put my arms around him and say, "*I* didn't think I'd see *you* here."

Before the proceedings began, I also met my Brazilian Xingu friend Sapaim walking along a hall in the UN building — an even more wonderful surprise! The film crew lady had not succeeded in bringing him North; he had gone home to his people and came to New York only for this event, in entirely other and very good hands.

Sapaim happily told me, through an interpreter, that he was in NY just for a few days and had been given medicines to take back to his people — medicines for diseases brought in by white men and for which his native plants were unprepared. It seemed the trees I'd asked for help, the trees so integral a part of his world, *have* been able to protect him!

Oren Lyons opens the day's events, with the US delegation to the UN conspicuously absent and disgracefully poor overall attendance for what should be an important event. Thomas is to be the closing speaker, with all the other indigenous speakers in between. It is well into evening when he finally takes the podium and delivers his message.

When the session closes, we are told a huge storm is suddenly raging outside. The next day, we find that it is the biggest storm in a decade and actually blew the weather equipment off the UN building roof the night before. I might have written off as coincidences both this and the power outage during his earlier visit, if I were not piling up so many experiences in which indigenous people's deep connections with nature and its weather produce unmistakable effects.

Very soon after the UN event, I'm back in Washington, my six weeks in the apartment are up and I have no place to live. I ask my daughter to fly me to California for Christmas with my grandchildren, not telling her of my situation, of not knowing where I will live after that, or on what. I return to Washington as the new year begins in the conviction that something will break for me. After all, I have no spirit calls to go elsewhere, so I must go on trust.

Hard as it may be for you to believe, Dear Reader, within a few hours after stepping off the plane, still trying to decide from whom to beg couch space, I hold in my hand a letter containing an overdue check worth a few weeks' groceries, and a key to another beautiful apartment turned over to me by a relatively new acquaintance who knew of my situation and tells me she has no current need for it.

My New York City girlfriend Nancy, whom I see as my cosmic little sister because we share the same birthday, has founded an organization of flight attendant volunteers she calls 'Airline Ambassadors' who are offering their services at President Clinton's first inauguration — *on* our birthday.

Nancy stays with me and as the others volunteer to serve at the various balls; Nancy and I volunteer to serve at the Homeless Ball. There, what is left of my insecurity at my own homelessness gives way to amusement as I realize that if it comes to being a bag lady, I might be in a position to write a manual on living in the streets!

After all, I know how to find terrific bargains in thrift shops — my London Fog spring coat and my beautiful cherry red wool winter coat together cost a total of ten dollars — and I have learned that one can attend foreign embassy receptions loaded with food by greeting the ambassador with "How good to see you again, Dr. X!" *He* proves to be the one embarrassed at not remembering. I even reason one could pick up a cheap hotplate and plug it into the sidewalk outlets for Christmas lights to cook pigeons in the park if things got desperate enough.

When a street person asks me for a handout, I laugh and turn my empty wallet inside out for him, offering him the newspaper I just picked up in the metro I'd ridden with my last dollar. True as it is, I doubt he believes I really have no more money.

The whole point of this exercise seems to be to know deep inside that I have *whatever* resources it takes to survive, and to survive in style, as well as in good spirits. Only when I really believe that, really stop flinching when down to my last cent, do these spiritual tests of faith stop happening.

In the meantime, I have seen two sets of friends lose their houses and all their possessions to fire, so I *know* that *anyone* can be stripped of material things in a flash. And, as another friend, Carolyn Myss, told me, "Anyone asking for spiritual growth can be sure they will be tested one way or another. You can't invite the angels into your house saying you'll serve them and then complain about the tasks they give you."

One of the most wonderful things happens when I finally go to rent my own apartment. I have suddenly been paid $2,500 for a single lecture, my biggest fee to date, and I know exactly where I am meant to live — in a building at 1500 Mass Ave I've walked by and felt was where I belonged. I go there and apply for a lease before the paycheck even arrives. What an applicant I am — a woman with no job, no work history for fifteen years, no previous rental agreement, no credit cards, nothing!

When I call a few days later, I am told I'd been refused. I ask what their shortest lease is — three months — and as the studio apartment rent is $500 a month, I offer to pay the entire rent in advance. I'm told huffily over the phone they did not do business that way; that the decision could not be changed.

I am so sure I am meant to live in that very building that I do not hang up. Neither does the man at the other end. We hold the silence until suddenly he says, "Wait, wait, some new information has just come in ... you can have a six-month lease." I do not ask where that new information came from; I simply go to sign the lease.

It is a big, bright, sunny studio apartment just four blocks from the White House — my first real home since my return to the US two years ago. I am thrilled. I have come to love Washington, DC for its magnificent beauty, its cultural diversity, and the endlessly fascinating free things to do here.

Surely nowhere else in the world can one get as rich a free education. Volunteering or speaking at as many conferences as possible, I am getting crash courses in subjects ranging from international development to conscious birthing.

Attending public meetings of the President Clinton's Council on Sustainable Development, I even get the opportunity to speak briefly at one of them. And, while I never get any of the jobs I apply for, I give talks at the Environmental Protection Agency (EPA), at the World Bank, and at the Washington Evolutionary Systems Society's Interdisciplinary Conference on Evolutionary Systems at Georgetown University, among other interesting venues, including the UN.

In retrospect, after my Washington sojourn, I could see it was all about lessons in trust — faith that the Cosmos would provide if I continued to set my mind correctly 'in the moment' as Adnan had taught, and if I remained in gratitude for what I *did* have.

Whenever I was aware, I gave thanks for my health and for not having missed a meal or been forced to sleep in a park. It was not easy to avoid those twinges of guilt arising when someone seemed to be shaking their head at me for not getting a proper 'PhD job,' living without a home, without insurance, without the 'normal' accoutrements of a professional life.

Sometimes I still create such guilt myself, asking whether it was not my *obligation* to be staying more visible, publishing more books, giving more speeches, teaching more seminars, *promoting* myself. Only the hard-won strength of my inner guidance could still this voice.

Catching myself flinching when my minimal financial resources are exhausted yet again, I religiously shake off anxiety, embarrassment and guilt at my 'failure' to live as a professional working person, reminding myself I have a kind of scholarship to a school of spirit, a school that has taught me that faith — true and grateful belief — does get rewarded.

I am aware that the whole world is in transition; that each of us, at such a time, must march to his or her own drummer, even while cognizant of playing a role within the larger communal scheme of things. I *know* that my life has to be lived on more than this physical level alone; that I cannot limit myself to it, *whatever* others think of me.

To go to Greece, I had stripped myself of most things I owned; in Greece I was stripped of my entire professional image and linguistic prowess as the wife of a fisherman, unable to speak at even the daily intercourse level of my peasant neighbors. In Washington I was functioning again in my full intellectual capacities but almost devoid of life's basic resources in the modern world.

From prayer vigil to prayer chapel

A Washington highlight project I get involved in is the organization of a Native Prayer Vigil for Earth — a kind of Indian encampment between the Washington Monument and the White House. We have called together elders and others from different Indian nations or cultures to set up teepees on the Green for a 24-hour continual prayer, pipe ceremony, and other ceremonies of offerings to Earth.

Among the elders are: Thomas Banyacya representing the Hopi, Arvol Looking Horse and Harry Byrd the Lakota people, Grace Smith Yellowhammer and Roberta Blackgoat the Diné (Navajo). I host Roberta, an octogenarian grandma, in my studio apartment. She is fighting to keep her land from miners like so many other indigenous Americans.

Roberta tells me how thugs were sent to poison her doggies and break the legs of her sheepies, all to get her to leave her ancestral lands so they could be exploited by mining companies. After the Vigil, she wants to see the new Holocaust Museum and I insist on pushing her through it in a wheelchair as I know it will elicit a lot of emotion in her. I also ask the staff there about the possibility of an American Holocaust exhibit and am told to apply as there is a room for temporary guest exhibits.

I write a letter to President and Mrs. Clinton to explain what the drumming in the night outside their windows was all about — that Indian elders were praying for their wellbeing and for world peace all through the night. I receive a canned reply about all the US government is doing for Indians. We decide to make the Prayer Vigil an annual event.[38]

I soon manifest several further trips to South America. On one, funded by a small research grant, I go into the Amazon with Maksuara, whom I'd met in Rio. In one of my most memorable moments in the rainforest, I ask him to teach me to talk with the plants and animals. He looks at me hard and says, "Shut up and listen, Elisabet. They have been in conversation as long as this forest has been here. Your job is not to initiate a conversation, but to hear the one ongoing!"

In Washington, an endless stream of interesting meetings, volunteer projects and soiree dialogues in people's homes keep me busy. Among the wonderful people I meet is Candace Pert, the neurobiologist who discovered opiate receptors in cells and showed the effect of our minds on our health.[39]

A wonderful new friend, C. Jesseramsing, is the second most senior diplomat in DC as the ambassador from Mauritius, who is also the ambassador to Cuba, Mauritius being too small to send diplomats to single countries. He takes me to those embassy receptions loaded with fine food, while himself always carrying a pocketful of cloves, the chewing of which, he insists, prevents colds and other diseases.

Thus, I weave myself into Washington DC's cosmopolitan life, even seeing Al Gore again at a private campaign reception, now as Clinton's Vice President.

In Context magazine[40] publishes an article of mine, as do several European publications, and I am interviewed by Jeffrey Mishlove for his *Thinking Allowed* TV series and by Michael Thoms for his New Dimensions Radio shows. In the same year, on another trip to California, I get filmed by the Foundation for Global Community in Palo Alto, CA, for a video production.[41]

In Washington, it never occurs to me to visit the National Cathedral until an old friend calls to say she is coming to DC and would love to have me accompany her on a tour she'd signed up for to see it. I go with her and am awed by the imposing architecture, not even knowing it was built so like the old European cathedrals had been. Stone on stone, its enormous pillars rise through the main floor from their vast bases in the basement, where they are surrounded by a series of chapels.

As we walk into one of them, I'm so struck by the gloriously beautiful mosaic of a full-figured, dark-haired Jesus against a glowing background with a huge rising sun in a dazzling aquamarine sky, that I have a sudden urge to kneel before it. It is a strange and powerful feeling, yet I instinctively resist it, having never kneeled before a Christ figure, even in church as a protestant child. I take note there are butterflies all over the needlepoint covering on the kneeling bench in front of this great mosaic and my mind runs to the excuse that I cannot kneel on butterflies.

Still, the feeling persists and, seeing a space on the bench where there are no butterflies, I drop to my knees and grab the brass rail hard. Anger, of all things, is welling up inside me, a kind of despairing anger ... almost as if *I* had been the one betrayed. "Why, *why*," I blurt out, looking up into the haloed face, "have you let so many terrible things be done in your name?" I feel as though I am sobbing in some deep interior place, though outwardly silent and trying not to show what I am feeling in case anyone else is there behind me.

The *last* thing I expect is an answer to my anguished question. Yet it comes, as loud and clear inside my head as my guiding voice has been when giving me orders to move: "How would that make you feel if you were my mother?" it asks back. And tears come, as I instantly feel what I am meant to understand and make my peace with Him.

From that moment, I am able to say the word 'God' again.

A matter of metaphor

Most impressive of all my invitations to speak is one to give a Colloquium address at the Santa Fe Institute. It came about from my reading the new book *Complexity* by M. Mitchell Waldrop in the wee hours one morning and jumping from my bed to write a letter to the Institute. The book is a compendium of stories about the founding scientists of the Santa Fe Institute, and something truly exciting to me popped out as I read the book: a sentence to the effect that the task of science was finding the right, or most appropriate, metaphors.

This is a very big deal to me, because I have been so concerned about science using mechanical metaphors almost exclusively in describing life when they are, in my opinion, sorely inadequate given the essential differences between organism and mechanism.

I had, in fact, long considered choice in metaphors to be critically important to science, often speaking about how nothing new in science can be described in anything *but* terms we already understand — that is, in metaphors — and how these metaphors color our understanding of particular scientific findings, but I had never before seen such acknowledgment from within the ranks of mainstream science.

In Freud's day the brain/mind was described in the metaphor of a plumbing system of pipes and valves that could get jammed. The telephone brought us the new brain/mind metaphor of the neurological switchboard of communications connections; the computer was next, then holographic devices, and most recently, parallel processors.

Clearly the evolution of metaphors scientists employ in describing the brain has followed our technological trajectory. Yet all these metaphors are mechanical, so, to my way of thinking, science fails to portray — to understand — the real essence of brains, indeed of all the living entities characterized by the intelligent self-organization that is totally lacking in the manmade machinery from which science draws its metaphors.

Yet, whenever I argue with other scientists that it really matters what kinds of metaphors we use, I am met with blank stares or the flat-out counter argument that it does *not* matter what metaphors are used. So, what I read in *Complexity* truly excites me.

Just at this time, in a 'list serve' dialogue — a new communications tool the early Internet makes possible — I meet Eshel ben Jacob, a physicist in Tel Aviv who turned to biology and is studying the communications and behavior of bacterial colonies. He is discovering amazingly intelligent communications and abilities that he cannot account for in mechanical terms, even those used in the growing field of Artificial Intelligence. In other words, he cannot find acceptable scientific metaphors adequate to describing what he has been finding.

For example, when he moves bacterial colonies from milk sugar substrates that nourish and grow them to cellulose substrates they cannot live on, they are clearly stressed but do not die off as expected. Rather, the whole colony composed of billions of bacteria 'reinvents' itself faster than information can be chemically broadcast from one to the other across such immense numbers. Every individual is suddenly and simultaneously putting new genes into play to build new metabolic systems enabling them all to digest cellulose.

This is very important work as antibiotics are failing because bacteria build immunity to them in similarly surprising ways. No one could have suspected how fast they can change their physiology as the speed defies explanation by Darwinian adaptation, according to which change can only happen one generation at a time. Such dramatic metabolic reorganization would take many generations.

Eshel had run into a dilemma. He was seeing very complex, clearly intelligent, coherent communal responses to environmental stress that changed the physiology of billions of individuals simultaneously — as if the individual bacteria were all cells in a single organism.

It was a phenomenon for which mechanical metaphors were utterly inadequate. Imagine a billion automated factories running on oil suddenly having their fuel supply switched to a substance that can run only completely different machinery, yet somehow retooling themselves overnight to continue their operations smoothly, with no intelligent engineers involved.

Eshel knew he was witnessing reliably replicable instances of individual *and* group intelligence, putting immensely creative solutions into rapid play. Scientists did not believe bacteria — or the cells of *any* living creatures, for that matter — capable of anything like it. He asked me for ideas on how to explain his findings to his colleagues, having heard me give arguments for why Earth itself should be seen as alive and intelligent.

Now, the Santa Fe Institute is apparently willing to listen to my ideas, despite being a glaringly masculine enterprise. When I tell my economist friend Hazel Henderson that I'd written to them angling for a talk invitation, she calls it a boy's treehouse in which girls don't get to play.

So, I am utterly amazed and thrilled at actually getting the invitation … and am now scared silly at the same time. Not since my first speech as an independent scientist at the university in Catania, while still in Greece, have I written out a talk, but knowing how controversial my talk about a living Earth will be there, and how critical an audience I'll be facing, I have to think through my arguments and choose my words — and my particular metaphors — very carefully. The importance of choosing metaphors is my entry point of agreement to a subject they will likely find controversial.

Long ago, as a graduate student, I had taught myself an important lesson. One of my professors and a few male fellow students had occasionally reduced me to tears during scientific arguments when I felt personally attacked. I hated when that happened and felt they were taking advantage of my feminine capacity for easy tears. So, I worked hard to convince myself that there was absolutely no reason to take logical arguments personally; my job was just to make sure my arguments *were* logical and not some flawed feminine opinion.

It was a wonderful breakthrough. If I lost an argument, I realized, it was because I had not argued well enough in terms of logic or because my opponent was less logical or because he had the better case. I never had a problem with being *proven* wrong as I was always happy to adopt better scientific answers than I had. I *wanted* to evolve my ideas, and academic argument was one way of doing so.

Finally, I'm at the Santa Fe Institute and there is only one woman in my audience; none among my hosts. She does not engage in the post-talk dialogue. I practice my 'Tai Chi tactic,' taking the energy thrown at me and deflecting it gently back to the men by asking *them* questions and getting them arguing with each other instead of with me. None of them come out in clearly voiced agreement with my talk, but they seem to have no good arguments against what I actually said in carefully defining life and then going through the ways in which Earth merits being called a living planet.

It is the woman in my audience who walks me back to my car, and she lets me know she really appreciated my talk but did not dare say so publicly. I tell her I suspect that within a few years the ideas I have presented *will* be adopted by at least some of the men there, but that they will likely be citing, when they do, scientists other than myself, probably even other than Jim Lovelock, to back up a claim that the living Earth is nothing new, but rather something long known.

Sure enough, an obscure chemist from decades earlier, whose name I have forgotten myself, will actually be pulled out in this manner at the Institute just a very few years ahead. Neither Lovelock nor Margulis, whom I had of course cited, will be mentioned by them.

J. Allen Boone

My discovery of a small book called *Kinship with All Life*, by J. Allen Boone, starts the delicious adventure of reading all four of Boone's books, despite considerable difficulty in finding old copies of the three others, all out of print. I quickly count Boone as one of my greatest mentors, though sadly he left this life before we could meet.

I began this book quoting him on how we are each responsible for making life worth living, and the human world in which we find ourselves worth living in. Boone, an early film producer and global journalist was known as the St. Francis of Hollywood for his great love of animals, and his acknowledged mentor was the very first Hollywood dog star, Strongheart.

Strongheart came to Hollywood in the 1920s as a highly trained German Shepherd police dog whose training was gently undone by Larry

Trimble, a most unusual 'trainer' who unconditioned him to restore his natural intelligence, and that led to his becoming a fabulous screen actor.

Boone's interaction with Strongheart came during six weeks in which this amazing actor dog was entrusted to him while Trimble was away. So awed by the amazing dog, Boone decided to spend his days and nights according to the dog's rhythm and inclinations, following his leadership as a humble student.

During their perambulations in the mountains overlooking the Pacific, Boone learned from Strongheart the art of what I have come to call communion — the direct transmission of ideas and information — to distinguish it from communication by languages.

As Boone reports in describing their eventual hours a day of deep conversation, "Neither of us was expressing himself as an original thinker or an independent source. On the contrary, we were being *communicated through* by the mind of the universe."[42] He also noted that the flow was always interrupted if he elevated in the least his end of the "mental bridge" between himself and Strongheart — any time he lapsed into the notion of superiority of man over dog.

As a *Washington Post* correspondent, Boone roamed the world with fascinating people such as actor Douglas Fairbanks, Sr. and his equally famous wife Mary Pickford, beloved stars of early cinema. The three of them were in exotic 1920s Shanghai, pondering where to go next: "… an expedition into the Gobi Desert to capture some long-haired tigers, a hunting expedition into Indo-China, a flying trip into remote parts of Russia, a visit to Tibet, or a wild but alluring scheme for prowling around with a bandit band in the back country of China."

So, Boone asked a renowned explorer of jungles for his opinion on the most exciting new frontiers for the best adventures. To his surprise, the man answered:

> *My personal preference is for sitting in a rocking chair, and exploring the undiscovered regions in my own mind... We explorers have conquered practically all the geographical frontiers, but not the mental ones. We know almost nothing about the oceans and continents still lying undiscovered in the hinterlands of our own minds. That is the real challenge of the future. Geographical exploration is comparatively simple. Mental exploration is more difficult. It takes more initiative, more daring and more courage, but the returns in accomplishment and satisfaction are much greater.*[43]

On reflection, after his initial shock at this answer, Boone realized that the world's greatest teachers had come to this same conclusion:

> ... that though one explore every spot on Earth, fly as high in the stratosphere as machinery and oxygen will lift him, or burrow deeper underground than anyone has ever been before, in the end he can arrive at but one conclusion. This! That the greatest wonder to be found anywhere is one's own self ... his mind ... his consciousness ... his subjective state of being ... his thinking areas ... his world of awareness ... that which makes him so uniquely what he is.

As Boone reported it, this explorer recognized that:

> ... we would all have to become mental explorers sooner or later, because of the way the scientists were causing the material universe to disappear before our very eyes ... insisting with ever-increasing proof ... that the universe of mechanized matter is not external to us at all, but inside us — that is, inside each individual mind — and that it is made of the same substance as mental ideas.

How was it possible that the explorer Boone met in Shanghai in the 1920s so clearly recognized this critical finding of quantum physicists who had turned to ancient Vedic science to understand their findings? And how fascinating that Boone immediately adopted it.

Apparently, this concept was spreading across the world mouth to ear in this way a century ago, even before astronomer Sir James Jeans published his statement that "the universe looks more and more like a great thought than a great machine" in his 1930 book *The Mysterious Universe*.

CHAPTER 9

The Call of the Andes

Peru calling

One morning, I wake suddenly, having heard a very clear voice in my ear, saying "Go to the June solstice festival in Peru with Mazatl!" No visual images, just that voice. It's 1994 and I'm still in Washington DC, not having seen my Mayan/Aztec friend Mazatl since the Findhorn conference in the late '80s and have no idea where he is.

I get up and call a mutual friend in California to ask if she knows where he is, and whether he might be going to Peru for solstice. She says, "Yes, he is; so am I. Are you coming with us?" I reply that I'd love to, having 'dreamed' I should go, but have no money to do so. She laughs and says, "You'll be coming; six of us had the dream, including Mazatl himself, who actually cancelled an opportunity to do a concert with Peter Gabriel to take us!"

Shortly after we speak, a check big enough for the trip shows up in my mail — money I'd actually forgotten I was owed. Without hesitation, I book my ticket to Peru. But before it is time to go, I have another trip, already arranged, to speak at the annual International Transpersonal Association meeting, this year in Killarney, Ireland.

While there, I am taken on a boat ride to see the famous Dingle Bay dolphin between conference sessions. After that lovely experience, a man who heard my talk comes to me and invites me to teach biology seminars the following summer aboard an ocean-going, whale-watching sailboat!

I make him repeat what he said, not believing my ears. It seems my Key West dream is to come true after all. I had continued to hold the desire to be with the whales but had let go my efforts to do so. Once again, I am shown this essence of what we call magic: the paradoxical focus of desire or intent while at the same time letting go of the outcome.

It isn't easy to desire and let go of the desire simultaneously, but it seems to work sooner or later. The boat, which belongs to his marine biology research institute, is in California and we will be sailing along that coast. I will be paid to teach aboard: what heaven!

The trip to Peru, filling in part of the time till the whale trip, is thrilling. The altitude is heady; Cusco is colorful with crowds of indigenous people, many of whom have trekked from afar to gather for the June solstice festival — winter there, with crisp bright sunny days.

They come by the thousands to the sacred site of Sacsayhuaman with its immense ancient stone walls and great open field between them. From Cusco, we go on to awesome Machu Picchu, then travel farther to the splendor of Lake Titicaca and pre-Inkan Tihuanaco in Bolivia, each breathtaking and deeply spiritual in its own way as we do our ceremonies in each place.

While walking a street in Cusco one day shortly before we leave, my inner voice speaks up once again, telling me to come back there by fall for at least six months. I am reluctant, to say the least. Alone? In the rainy season? Knowing almost no one and not speaking Spanish? With what resources?

I fight the message for twenty-four hours, then succumb and announce my plan to do so to the roommate I've been paired with, John Denver's ex-wife Cassandra, who calls him regularly to check in on their little girl, Jesse Belle. She thinks it's great and the following day I tell my whole group.

Need I say the money shows up? Back in Washington, a small grant I'd applied for so long ago that I'd given up on appears in the mail. It permits me to work on the grant project for the rest of the summer and then I can continue the work in Peru, where the money will last six more months if I live very frugally, and so I will be back in time for the whale-watching trip in California next summer.

On one of Tony the astrologer's tour groups to Greece, I'd met Nancy Gottlieb, who lives in Santa Barbara. We'd really hit it off, stayed in touch, and she's been urging me to come live there. As the whale-watching trip is to be mostly in the Channel Islands just off Santa Barbara, this seems a wonderful idea. Especially as my daughter Johara and her partner Deb — both medical doctors now — have really settled in California with their three children, by now all in school.

My first grandchild Nick was joined by Maya and Phoumara, adopted in Cambodia. They live in Oakland, right next to Berkeley where my son Philip, who has stayed in Greece, was born. If I lived in Santa Barbara, they would be in far easier reach. So, before returning to Peru,

I again reduce and ship my possessions off to be stored in the basement of Nancy's gigantic pink Santa Barbara landmark Victorian house while I'm in Peru.

Cusco

Contrary to my expectations of feeling lost in language and without friends, I make myself at home from the moment I arrive back in Cusco, now noticing how much its streets resemble those of Greek islands, with red-tiled roofs, whitewashed walls, stone stairways — like Hydra, except the donkeys have been transformed into llamas.

The city as a new home, rather than just a tourist attraction, is lovely with its astonishing Inca stone walls topped by Spanish architecture, its squares with flowers and fountains, the Quechua craftspeople vending their wares.

I quickly find a small one-room casita I turn into kitchen, bedroom, office and living room in one; the toilet and shower outside are shared with two other tenants in a small complex. Across a garden I have a view over the undulating tile-roofed city with the mountains in the distance beyond.

The fresh market I can walk to easily supplies everything I could possibly want to eat, and I am there daily as I have no refrigerator. This is life at its simplest and I enjoy the challenges, as I did in Greece. There are spectacular arrays of temperate and tropical fruits in endless variety and vegetables both familiar and new in the huge market. Line-ups of women with blenders give me amazing choice in what to ask for in smoothie combinations. I soon settle on a favorite of beets, apples, carrots, and ginger.

My breakfasts in the little casita are delicious thick shakes I make by hand in a glass jar by adding water to big spoonfuls of my dry mix: high protein powdered *kaniwa* or *kiwicha* grains, sugar, cocoa, and powdered milk. Suppers are more elaborate stews and stir-fry's, cooked in a big pot or frying pan on my single-burner electric hotplate.

Only a few weeks after my October 1994 arrival, in the first week of November, a full solar eclipse will be visible from the high Peruvian desert near Arequipa. Too good to miss, I endure the long bumpy bus ride through the mountains to join people from all over the world who have come so much farther to dance ecstatically to the music of Andean flutes and churangos in the sand under that spectacular sky show over the desert.

The full darkness with stars luminous at midday and the diamond ring corona are awesome, and with Venus brightly visible just before totality it is no wonder the media dubs this awesome event the Love Eclipse.

Back in Cusco, I settle in and begin working hard at learning Spanish, reading library books on Inca history with a dictionary and setting out to make friends with local people instead of tourists. I soon have magical encounters and many of my evenings are spent listening to live Andean music and dancing, making friends with native musicians. I also make friends with a very young professor of 'informatics' at the university who gives me one of the ten e-mail addresses they have been granted, few other professors knowing what to do with them.

One of my native friends is a tour guide in the exquisite ruins of Machu Picchu, and lets me stay or sneak in after hours, even letting me spend the night there, sleeping on a bed of straw in a cave, llamas snuffling about in the dark. By moonlight, the stones sparkle their crystalline content and the stars are exquisitely bright and more numerous than I've ever seen.

It is so special to be able to step over ropes and enter sacred places forbidden by day, doing my own ceremonies, then lying on the stones of temples on my back to find the dark spaces in the Milky Way, which the ancient Peruvians saw as shapes equal in importance to those of star pictures.

Intending at first to write a book bridging the western physicists' new understanding of 'hyperspace' with Andean cosmology, I soon realize how presumptuous it was to think I could understand either side of that cross-cultural task in a few months. I also feel ever more strongly that I am there to get *out* of my intellectual head and into my heart to make further spiritual progress.

I turn to studying my dreams using a handbook brought with me, having long intended to use it and seeing my Peru time as a good opportunity to do so. In talking to new friends about my experience with it, I soon find myself succumbing to requests to teach others to do so, in the Spanish still so new to me. More opportunity for practice!

My greatest insight from that experience is that the native people in my class tend to know the meanings of their dream symbols because dream sharing is part of their cultural heritage, while those of Spanish and other Euro-American descent have to work at discovering the meaning of their individual dream symbols, each of them having to construct their own symbol 'dictionary' through analysis as in the guidebook I had brought. It is a fascinating revelation of how our contemporary culture of putting the individual ahead of community, even of losing community, impacts us at the deepest levels.

My greatest opportunity for service in Cusco becomes helping native friends who are struggling in various ways to keep their Andean culture alive. Back in Washington DC, I had attended a lecture at the World Bank on Inca agriculture that credited it with the finest and most extensive experimentation and development in the history of the world.

Over half the food eaten in the modern world, I heard there, was derived from its crops, including the staples of maize/corn, amaranth grains, such as quinoa, and potatoes, plus the other nightshade family crops of tomatoes, eggplants, and peppers that eventually found their way to the Mediterranean and around the whole world.

Now, although a few restorations have proven the ancient farming methods still superior today, chemicals banned as too toxic in the North are being pushed onto local farmers in Peru and all South America through endless radio advertising. My new indigenous friends and I together start a coalition we call Casa Andina-Amazonica, working to reinstate methods of growing traditional foods, preserving traditional instruments and music, recording stories told by elders, and collecting ancient weavings.

Journey to Hapu

Some native men from a remote mountain community called Hapu have trekked on foot to Cusco in their rough handwoven brown ponchos, barelegged and wearing the ubiquitous Andean rubber tire sandals on their feet.

They look so remarkably like the Kogi natives in Alan Ereira's film that I feel I am indeed meeting real Kogi. Making supper for these visitors one evening, I'm astounded at the amounts they eat until someone warns me that they will not stop as long as I put more food on their plates.

Their remote village, Hapu, it turns out, has never even been visited by an anthropologist, or any outsider, for that matter, other than a schoolteacher who comes there by horse each summer and stays through the winter. The men so want us to come visit them for the annual festival they will shortly be hosting for many mountain communities gathering in their location that we — Juan and Kike, two native friends, Diana, an adventurous young English woman and I — agree to do it.

We start out just days later, finding ourselves squashed among other riders and a load of goods in one of the forty-ton Volvo trucks that ferry food and fuel between Cusco and the Amazon on a single-track road across the mountains, going one direction Mondays, Wednesdays, and Fridays, in the other on Tuesdays, Thursdays, and Saturdays. Hour after hour, we ride through barren mountain heights above the tree line, then wind our way along the edges of ever more precipitous cliffs.

I have to shut my eyes, or look away, to reduce my fear, until at last we reach the highest point on the road and get off. In a crude building the driver pointed out, we four sleep on a cold concrete floor, huddled together under a large but light down quilt I've brought in a stuff-bag. Setting out in the morning on foot, we trek upward until a Hapu village man meets us as planned to guide the rest of our climb — a very difficult and lengthy one over a 16,300-foot, snow-covered pass to his village.

At nearly sixty, and at this altitude, I'm finding this physically the most difficult thing I've ever done; the bone-chilling cold of the icy heights is exacerbated by the bone-aching effects of making this effort in the exhaustingly thin air.

My head aches fiercely despite chewing coca leaves we brought with us and herbs our guide picks along our way, assuring us they will help. Each step seems to become an achievement. Yet every time we have looked up to what seems the final height, reaching it reveals yet another upward climb, despite our guide's repeated smiling assurance that from now on it is all *"pampita, no mas"* to assure us this was little more than flat terrain.

Months after this, a California friend driving me back to the airport for my return to Peru after the whale-watching trip, schedules a stop at an I-Max theater to see the very realistic 3-D film of St. Exupery's Andean mail plane crash in the Andes.[44] As we watch the downed pilot clamber about in the snowy heights for days before his rescue, my friend turns anxiously to me asking whether I am okay. Unaware of my own gasping, heaving, empathic breathing, I stop and laugh, whispering "Been there; done that!"

Anyway, we do eventually reach the high point of the pass, from which we head into hours of wading through snowmelt rivulets everywhere amidst patches of snow on the sunstruck downward side to the Hapu community. I kick myself for being in very leaky hiking boots, rather than the waterproof ones Diana wears. Whenever we sight a house in the distance, thinking we are arriving, it turns out to be just a single-family farm, one of many scattered sparsely across the steep landscape.

Just before sunset, we reach the valley floor, where two rushing little rivers meet, green growth is lush, half a dozen stone houses seep smoke through grass roofs that rises to meet the low clouds. People in colorful handwoven clothing mill about, decorating llamas and feeding them corn-beer *chicha* from bottles. The celebration has already begun. Peasant farmers have come from all over the surrounding mountains and next morning, more and more arrive from farther and farther away.

The festival lasts three days and three nights; the pattern of events becoming gradually evident. As many people as possible cram into a stone house through its very low door following an elder village governor — a *varayoc* — inside for music, dance, song, eating, and drinking around an altar of three crosses decked in silvery sacred *phunia* plant, representing the three *apus*, mountain gods, that guard this community. Thus, ancient traditions are preserved within the official Catholicism forced on the Andean peoples by the Spanish.

The leaders then blow conch shells called *pututus* one at a time in a pattern of *ptuuuuu-tu-tu-tu-tu*, answered by the same rhythm from another conch, going round and round. Other men play high-pitched reed flutes as they dance, while the women stand in a ring around them, singing an endless series of verses that praise the flowers, plants, animals, mountains of their world, and speak of the circumstances of their lives.

Their melody is based on a four-tone chord, such that each note harmonizes with all others and the song can be entered like a canon by the various women at various times. While very formal and repetitive, there is much creativity as individuals add their own verses in their own timing.

Suddenly, the exodus from this house begins and all follow the leader in trooping to another house for another round of the same, then on to the next and so on throughout the nights and days. The black, trampled earth between the houses becomes an ever deeper richer muck as rains come frequently and chicha beer flows through the men's bodies and into the mud, women generally squatting a little bit further from the common path. The hours and days and nights of repetition keeps people going in a trancelike state.

Juan and Kike, who had brought Diana and me with them, explain that festival songs in other places are usually about love and other personal feelings; that this veneration of nature in song is a far more ancient ritual. We are very grateful to be assigned the schoolhouse floor for sleeping when our festival endurance flags.

It takes me a long time after this amazing journey to see the festival rather as I had seen the play in the great theater at Epidaurus in Greece, and the concert on the beach in Rio, as symbolic of bacteria forming nucleated cells in primeval times. The Hapu festival houses are the nucleus, a center where DNA is gathered and traded symbolically in the sharing of song, ceremony, dance 'in-formation,' people streaming like protoplasm, joining many communities into one larger cooperative entity. Could this be how in ancient human times the first real villages were born as trade centers, then slowly growing larger into towns and cities?

Because of my e-mail address, I am able to share my written account of the trip,[45] photos included, with my Native American friends in Washington DC, who had introduced me to the Internet. How I appreciate this happy marriage of indigenous culture and our modern technology — symbolic of what a better world for all humanity can look like when we integrate the best of our human past with the best of the present. I even begin to wonder whether the Internet will play some kind of role for all humanity that will weave it into a new kind of enormous body or global cell.[46]

In Cusco, my best friend, not of native descent, is Cusco's official Minister of Culture, in charge of historic sites. I tease Pepe about the large ornately gold-framed paintings in his office, of Spanish Conquistadors in helmets, armor from which lacy, rather silly looking, tutu-like ballerina skirts project and metal shoes with long skinny toe points. Why not decorate your walls instead, I ask Pepe, with the gorgeous weavings, the pottery, the musical instruments of the real Peruvian culture?

When the Hapu men next visit Cusco, I take them to Pepe and his wife Gloria's home, where I am often invited to lunch, to show them the Kogi film I brought with me. On the soft couches, the Hapu men can barely stay awake, but occasionally raise an eyelid and comment that these are their brothers, their language clearly not strange to them.

Puma and the spirits of the Andes

Walking across the main square in Cusco to the market, I keep running into a young teenage boy selling woven belts, unlike the other boys who sell postcards and cigarettes. He is a bright-eyed, bouncy, and outgoing boy — in profile the perfect Incan culture poster, with his intricately-patterned knitted *chulyo* hat above a gently convex nose in a warm smooth honey-brown face. He has learned English remarkably well from tourists, and asks, whenever he sees me, "Are you looking for me? Taking this as a sales come-on, I laughingly blow hm off, but there is something unusual and intriguing about him.

A very psychic friend, Tanai, visits from the US for three weeks and, as we sit in a coffee shop together, I see the boy across the narrow street through the glass door. I call her attention to him, and suddenly he bursts through the door grinning from ear to ear and I invite him to have a hot chocolate. Tanai is so blown away by Puma's immense aura, she later asks me, "What is he? Something like the Deepak Chopra of the South?"

His name is Fredy Quispe Singona, and after Tania leaves, introduces me to his very reluctant eighty-five-year-old teacher and grandfather, Don Maximo Singona Puma, a medicine-priest in the ancient tradition. Don Maximo, in a worn brown suit and speaking his native *Runasimi* language, is extremely shy at first, but with his grandson translating, we get acquainted, and he invites me to participate in a ceremony he conducts for his own people, not for tourists.

As I get to know them better, I learn that Don Maximo has helped his grandson understand the deep and complex dreams he'd already had between the ages of three and six — some of himself as an adult in other lives — and then, at six, already a shepherd, Fredy was struck by ball lightning while swimming in a river, out alone with his animals. He recovered and as soon as he got home told his grandfather, who said this marked him in his culture as the one to be taught formally. And so, by twelve, Fredy knew how to heal with plants, set broken bones, and deliver a baby under supervision.

His grandfather made him stand for hours in thunderstorms, at freezing temperatures, teaching him to move souls from darkness to light. He had to learn the long ceremonies of paying tribute to Earth — *Pacha Mama* — as well as to the mountain *Apu* deities. As I get to know all this, and as Fredy has begun calling me 'Mom' even though his own mother is younger than my daughter, I urge him to call himself 'Puma' after his grandfather, rather than Fredy, which seems too undignified for what he is becoming.

In light of what I have myself been taught by my indigenous WISN colleagues, I also urge him to call himself a medicine priest, and never a 'shaman' as that title is a Siberian designation that does not belong to the Americas, much as it has been adopted by Cusco's midnight cowboys to seduce women tourists. I do not want Puma ever to be confused with them, or with 'instant Indians' — white people who have had a few lessons from native teachers, or taken a few workshops, and then call themselves shamans. A genuine medicine priest must earn that credential through long apprenticeship to an elder in his or her own culture, as Puma is doing.

Puma is 14, in a regular public high school in Cusco, known for his sunny disposition and helpfulness, even helping his teacher with her English, all the while keeping his training as a medicine priest to himself. He is obviously unusually intelligent; I recognize his eidetic imagery ability — he can tell me the page and location of anything in his schoolbooks he has seen there — and he has an uncanny mapping ability, decidedly useful for a boy who has tended wandering sheep from the time he was very small and has had to find his way home. His phenomenal knack for picking up languages makes it easy for me to communicate with him on the deepest subjects.

The Andes are a place of very strong energies, both positive and negative; it seems that no one can go there from outside without being transformed somehow. Some say it is a place to quickly clean up karma, and it does seem that opportunities to learn lessons are thrown thick and fast at people who stay longer than transient tourists. One new friend actually dies there; another tries to commit suicide in front of my eyes. Others get sick and run home, yet some welcome these challenges. I find myself among the latter, thriving on the thin, clear air, feeling energized by it. Cusco is around 11,000 ft in altitude; Machu Picchu only 8,000 — a long gradual downhill train ride away.

I stay consciously open to learning from experiences of all kinds. Tanai, after three weeks here, commented as she left that the real Peru made the newly published *The Celestine Prophecy* book — about people facing spiritual tests in the Andes, but written by someone who seems not to have actually been there — look like kindergarten!

While I am having a marvelous time, I'm eventually severely tested myself, passing out when strangled and robbed one night as I'm foolishly walking home alone through an alley, very late at night after an evening of music and dance. A stranger finds me still lying on my back on the stone slabs paving the alley, just coming to and wondering foggily why I can see the stars overhead from my bed. He gets me to my feet and walks me home, assuming I am drunk and had passed out. I am too foggy to put together what has actually happened yet, but a few months later I meet him again in a shop and he apologizes, as he himself has been similarly assaulted just a few weeks after finding me. Pairs of such robbers, he has learned, are known to come from Lima; finding someone alone, they come up silently from behind to attack.

The morning after the assault, I seek out a friend of a friend whom I know to have a massage table and ask him to clear me of the dark energies I feel within my body. As he works on me, I recall something Don Maximo said to me. Knowing that I was developing a special relationship with the Apu Ausungate, whose mountain I can see from where I live and have been drawn to, he did a special ceremony for me, naming me *Kuntur Ruy*ac — White Condor — and warned me that two dark guardians would be sent by this mountain's spirit lord *apu* to test me.

Suddenly it makes sense. My mind clears as I remember the two men that came upon me from behind in the dark, one sweeping my feet off the ground as the other put his hands around my throat. Now, on the table, I know I have a clear choice, to suffer or not to suffer by forgiving my assailants, knowing they have given me the opportunity to pass a spiritual test. Despite a sore voice box that will last for some time, along with severe bruises, I leave the session feeling otherwise back to normal. To my surprise, in the coming days, I find that other people do not find my positive attitude appropriate, wanting me instead to suffer from the attack.

Interesting that the only valuable piece of jewelry on me when the thieves struck was a string of ancient, museum quality, Peruvian coral beads on which hung a hand-worked sacred stone *chacana* cross given me in ceremony — a symbolic map of the Inca lands reflecting the stars of the Southern Cross. Inexplicably, the thieves had not taken it although they had pulled off another necklace that was actually of far less value and stripped me of watch and rings.

Taking Puma north

In May of 1995, my six-month 'Cusco call' technically more than completed, I have the opportunity to bring Puma, now fifteen, to Washington to speak at an international conference titled *When Cosmic Cultures Meet*. I convinced the organizers, who had invited me as a speaker, to invite him as well, and to pay his travel on top of the speaker's fee. The intention of the conference is not to prove the existence of aliens, but to dialogue on appropriate ways to interact with them in the event of encounters with them. Puma's culture accepts aliens as part of their reality, since it is apparently not uncommon for people in his culture to have actual encounters. I, myself, have come to feel that the rural Andes mountains are indeed a great place for spaceship landings, since any aliens making it there are apparently assured friendly reception by humans.

Puma blows everyone away with his talk. He goes up to the podium and begins by building community around himself, pointing out that his uncle has knit his hat, an aunt has woven his poncho, his grandfather has taught him much of what he will say, so all of them are part of his own presence. Then he looks down at me from the stage and says, "Come up here and sit with me in case I don't know a word, Mom." His most memorable point is made by asking the audience, "Why is it that in school we are taught the history of humanity as a history of war, and never as a history of love?" It seems to stun them. Puma has learned both, one in school, the other from his grandfather.

At the end of the conference, Puma and I are invited to the White House for a special after-hours evening visit by a conference participant who is in charge of one of the Situation Room computers that monitor the world for situations that might require waking the president. Although I lived just four blocks from the White House for years, I have never been inside it and am as fascinated as Puma.

I am especially struck by the peaceful Wedgewood blue and gold beauty of the Oval Office. On leaving it, I ask the night shift guard at the door, who looks Native American to me, whether past presidents ever come to visit it again. "Yes, Ma'am," he says quietly, maintaining his erect stance and barely moving his lips. "Oh," I continue, "which of them comes back most often?" With quiet dignity, he replies simply, "Abraham, Ma'am." As he does, I am being called away to move on and can only smile and thank him quickly. It is certainly not an answer I anticipated, but one I will never forget.

After the conference, it becomes possible to take Puma traveling to meet some of my Native American friends in Arizona, and in Mt. Shasta, California, where he jumps into an icy river to swim as he would in Peru. Everything we need and everything we could possibly desire materializes for this wonderful month-long trip from Peru to Washington and then across the United States.

Everyone who meets Puma feels his heart touched. He has become a very special responsibility for me — a spiritual son, one who had adopted *me*. The Andes are increasingly seen by Native Americans as a leading spiritual center for the whole Earth; even Tibetan lamas are coming there to do ceremonies, saying the energy is shifting from the masculine

Himalayas to the feminine Andes. Traveling across the US with Puma, people everywhere, hearing where we've come from, often declare, "Oh, I've always wanted to go there!" or "I must go there soon; it is such a deep call in my life!"

One day, I ask Puma how his *Runakuna* culture — called *Quechua* by the conquistadors — understand the concept of 'reality.' He explains quite easily that reality is simply everyone's experience. Runakuna cultural laws — basically, "don't lie, don't cheat, don't steal, work hard" — are all about integrity in community. As Puma explains, it is as if people say to each other: "Tell me your reality truly; do not distort it to manipulate me and I will accept it as your reality without having to make it mine." People can also make up stories from their imagination, as long as they say so.

This definition of reality has me surprised but pleased. Looking up dictionary definitions of reality, they all include the word 'real' — rendering them fairly useless as definitions, but eventually I find one Webster's Dictionary online in which the fourth definition for reality is "non-derivative experience," which makes me almost whoop and holler with joy. *Non-derivative* means first-hand! *My* experience, *your* experience, *all our experience* as reality!

Puma's Runakuna culture and Jane Roberts' 'Seth' and this lone dictionary are all agreed on what reality is, yet my culture has ignored this as religions and science alike imposed their 'realities' on us, each of them claiming to have the real reality! I cannot do anything about religious realities, but, as a scientist, I can lobby against the imposition of a single reality on all humans, without denying the great value of scientific theory and research in any culture. This becomes an issue I become deeply involved with for the rest of my life: the validity of different views of the same universe in which we all live.

In a culture such as Puma's, everyone's experience includes plenty of things they can agree on from which to build a common cultural reality, but the different ways individuals experience the world are acknowledged and validated. Strong community is natural in a close culture where people know each other personally; humans evolved as social creatures. Some ancient cultures lasted thousands of years in close cooperation, with no need for police or jails or extensive personal possessions, and, as paleoanthropologists have noted about these 'refined subsistence' cultures, they had shorter work hours and more leisure for cultural activities than do modern societies.[47]

Central to Puma's *Runakuna* culture is the concept of *ayni*, inadequately translated as 'reciprocity.' It means community in the fullest sense of deeply reciprocal relations among its members, all sharing work and play, all contributing unquestioningly and happily to each other's wellbeing, in stark contrast to our Darwinian concepts of competitive self-interest as human nature. Such socially mature wisdom and practice is passed through generations as the very core of all its knowledge. As Nicolas Aguilar Sayritupac, an Aymara Indian from the Lake Titicaca region, wrote:

> *The human being of the West has abandoned being human and has turned himself into an individual: man, woman, child, elder, separate. Community, the ayllu — the essential unity of humanity has died in them. The existence of Western people and society has been destroyed by their egoism. On the contrary, we Indians have things well in our heads, our feelings in order, determined to do what we can; it is for this reason that we do not go away much from our home and family, for this reason that we have kept ourselves away from the equivocal ideas of the men who find themselves in the place where the Sun hides itself.*[48]

The concept of reality as whatever people experience is not the same as the 'cultural relativity' taken up in the Boomer generation, where the beliefs and practices of every culture are considered equally valid. Puma's culture imposes common human values on all its members as the foundation on which the accepted diversity of realities is based. Thus, no one can claim, for example, that in his reality he should lie or steal or shirk all work or harm another. In this same sense, I would argue for 'cultural relativity' *only* if all cultures agree on basic human values to underlie that cultural diversity. The time and culture-tested Golden Rule would be a good start. The universal practice of kindness to each other advocated by the Dalia Lama is even simpler.

I am very much in favor of diversity in languages, beliefs, and other cultural matters as long as common values unite us as a global family of distinct cultures. I also believe it would serve our global family well to teach all children any agreed upon global language along with their native language. Unfortunately, we have found that languages cannot be artificially constructed because they are natural, living extensions of human thought. Esperanto was a brave attempt at a universal language, but no one dreamed in it or used it to write good poetry.

What it demonstrated is the livingness of languages that evolved naturally and the impossibility of constructing new ones. The construction of Esperanto can be compared with the construction of artificial cells by biologists, which has not worked either. The choice of a global language as one of our existing natural languages is thus a serious matter. English has so far won out because of colonialism and two world wars — not the best of credentials — and may need reconsideration when, if ever, we truly form our Global Family.

At the end of our trip, Puma and I spend some time with my daughters in the Bay Area of California and I thoroughly enjoy watching him rolling around on the floor in delight with my grandchildren. He joins them in an Aikido class they are taking, and the teacher says to me afterwards, "Boy, what I could do with that kid in six months! It takes me longer than that just to get kids here into their bodies."

I put Puma onto his flight back to Peru, knowing we'll see each other again in the Fall after the whale trips and picture him doing Aikido rolls on the sidewalks around the town square in Cusco in the meantime. I have not completed enough of what I started with the Casa Andina-Amazonica for it to fly on its own. Santa Barbara, where my boxes already wait for me, will have to stay unopened somewhat longer, though I will be onshore enough during the whale-watch summer to get acquainted with life there.

Santa Barbara whale summer

My whale trip adventure begins by sailing with the captain and crew of the sleek ocean-going *Dariabar* from Sausalito, just north of San Francisco, where she is moored, down to Santa Barbara. I get my sea legs easily, being used to boats from all the years in Greece. As we sail down the coast, observation seats on both sides of the main mast provide turns at phenomenal views and gasping moments when she leans so hard the seats almost graze the waves and you have to hang tight to stay in them.

Emerging suddenly and dramatically from a solid grey fog bank into the sun on the third day out, we pass through nature's dramatic curtain dividing northern and southern California. On the fourth day, we arrive in Santa Barbara, where I stay a few nights with Nancy as we pick up paying guests and settle them in before heading out among the Channel Islands. My work is easy as no one wants formal classes, so teaching turns into dialogue on subjects I love, such as our human relationship to the rest of nature.

Our most spectacular sightings are of two unexpected blue whales that follow us for several days. We hear them snuffling around us at night and by day see their snouts almost touching our stern. Quite a few acrobatic long-finned humpback whales and a huge school of dancing dolphins fulfill everyone's hopes; I could hardly have asked for more. Occasional opportunities to wander on the islands themselves, with their craggy rocks and grassy fields where foxes play, make them so much more real than when I had looked out at them from shore.

Between trips, I stay in Nancy's spacious "Pink Lady" Victorian house, which gets repainted this summer with the help of many volunteers. In unpacking my boxes, I decide I still own too many things, so I hold a sidewalk sale at which Bruce Bigenho, a Korean American musician who lives across the street, buys a number of my books and we become instant friends through our obviously common interests. It is Bruce who takes me, on the way to the airport for my flight back to Peru, to that 3-D IMax film about St. Exupery's crossing the Andes at which I gasp in empathy with the downed pilot.[49]

Back in Cusco, I find a small house to share with another woman and get back into the swing of daily life. Soon, my old friend Audrey arrives, bringing two girlfriends with her from Tucson to trek the newly rediscovered short branch of the Inca Trail. Puma is our guide and manages to collect all our heaviest gear onto his amazingly strong back. Along the way through deep gorges and past plunging crystal waterfalls, Puma spots a family of three Andean spectacled bears — *ukumari* in his Runasimi language. While we observe them, an official ranger happens by and is astounded, saying he has never seen even one in eleven years of patrolling the area.

The Casa Andina-Amazonica struggles along with no funds. My efforts at raising them while in California by appealing to American companies who had profited from Andean and Amazonian products, such as cat's-claw medicine, natural green and brown cotton plants, quinoa, and other high protein grains put into 'astronaut food' and sold in the now proliferating health food shops, failed but for one $300 donation from Arrowhead Mills. Nevertheless, we stage a picnic at Cusco's ancient Sacsayhuaman site, mount an evening performance in a cultural center and participate as a group in other public events as we continue building the collections of instruments, weavings, and stories.

Puma's grandfather comes to understand my personal crusade against the toxic farm chemicals touted to Andean farmers on radio from morning to night while — or perhaps because — they have been banned in the US as too dangerous to human health. Local farmers cannot, or do not, read the instructions on the bags and spread them with dangerous abandon, assuming 'the more the better!' At first, Don Maximo's neighbors indeed grow bigger potatoes using this regimen, but it turned out that this did not last. I hear updates over the ensuing years on their crop failures while grandfather's crops remain a stable island of good harvest.

Puma's education continues, as it will for another nine years after I leave, until his grandfather, by then well into his 90s, 'graduates' him and allows him to marry at 24 years of age — making his training 21 years long from the time of his three-year-old childhood dream processing. He is allowed from time to time to come to the US and later other countries as I introduce him into organizations such as YES! (Youth for Environmental Sanity) and INAYA (Indigenous and Non-indigenous Youth Alliance)[50] wherein the cultural practices of indigenous peoples are revered as essential models for co-creating a better world for all. This inspires him to teach his own peers in the Andes to take pride in their heritage, practice their traditional music, dance, crafts and ethics, rather than only wanting to escape unthinkingly into the modern world.

When I return to Santa Barbara to stay, I find my own snug little studio apartment just a short walk from Nancy's and in easy walking distance of the entire downtown area. Beautiful as Cusco is, Santa Barbara's own Spanish heritage in whitewashed, red tile roofed architecture and ubiquitous florescence makes for a gorgeous setting that also includes the undeniable comfort of those modern conveniences I've learned to do without yet welcome back into my life.

Santa Barbara is a haven for artists and musicians, enormous resourcefulness manifesting in a seemingly endless string of festivals around the year with spectacular costumes, amazing float parades, and a strong community heartbeat. I quickly make many friends as groups easily come to life through potluck dinners and dialogues or salons in people's homes similar to what I'd been part of in Washington DC. I can stay in touch with my DC friends and others all over the US and even abroad, as e-mail is by now more widely available. Indeed, I sign up with a local server just a few blocks from my home, getting the beautifully simple address: elisabet@rain.org.

Having gotten Puma on email as well, we never lose touch and I bring him to the US at every opportunity I can arrange for him as a speaker or workshop leader. Whenever he comes, we make a special trip to Santa

Barbara's relatively posh and amply stocked thrift shops where he first buys one or two of the biggest suitcases they have and then stuffs it with shoes and clothing carefully chosen for his mother, sisters, cousins, aunts, uncles, and friends.

CHAPTER 10

Weaving My Reality

Moon over Brazil

Another spectacular full moon in Brazil reminds me of that over Flamengo Beach at the Earth Summit — this one hanging like a huge lantern over a fragrant flowery garden in Sao Paulo, where I sit next to Edgar Mitchell, the moon-walking astronaut, pinching myself to make sure it's all real. Ed and I are in the largest white wicker armchairs, just opposite that spectacular moon in a circle of progressive business leaders with whom we've just had dinner in this gorgeous private home. They are all waiting eagerly for what Ed and I are going to say to them before dessert is served to cap off the evening.

Ed and I don't know what we're going to say — only that we've both been asked to share something at this celebration following the first *Imaginaria* conference on Brazil's possible future, to which both of us were brought as speakers. It took place in an old factory, converted by these business leaders into a huge, architecturally exciting community center, theater, and subsidized restaurant for poor people. This afternoon, at the final celebration of the conference, we were also in a circle — a huge one with hundreds of people, including some of Sao Paulo's poorest, all holding hands and singing. I was myself holding the hand of a poor woman whose face was flooded in tears of joy, expressing her amazement at participating in such an event — all of us with the highest hopes for Brazil's enormous potential for role-modeling a better world for all people.

Ed and I briefly converse, as the last guests take their seats in the garden circle; neither of us having a plan for what to say. I'm suddenly reminded of meeting the larger-than-life Human Potential movement founder, Jean Houston, when I was visiting in New York while still living in Greece. She asked me what I would most love to do in life, and I replied, without reflection, "Dialogue with the finest minds on the planet." So, I look at Ed and ask, "Why don't we just have an impromptu dialogue?" He readily agrees and we both sigh with happy relief that we can now have fun instead of performing.

The energy we build is terrific as we feed on everyone's palpable enthusiasm and enjoy weaving in and out of each other's ideas. Our voices flow and merge in a conversation like an interlude in time and space — we two, the others, the great flowering bushes and vines and the moon weaving a wild and wonderful instance of Life itself. It is a peak experience I know I will never forget. Looking back on it later, I have no recollection of any specifics of what we said, just knowing we talked about our mutual interests in cosmology, physics, and biology and how they weave our world together. Those present with us were clearly delighted as they kept bringing it up as a most magical evening during my subsequent visits to Brazil.

There turns out to be another fascinating encounter with Ed in Brazil a few years later, still during my Santa Barbara years, at another *Imaginaria* conference, this one held in the capital Brasilia — like New York, a city with its state's name — hosted by its governor. After Ed speaks, showing slides of his moonwalk, a little old Amazonian lady comes up to him in great excitement to tell him how much she loved seeing his pictures of the moon. With the help of my interpreter, I watch her exclaim, "It looks *exactly* as it did when *I* went there many years ago, and I knew back then that we would all be here for *this* meeting. I am so very happy to meet you now!"

I flash on stories indigenous people elsewhere have told me of journeys to the center of Earth and other places impossible from the perspective of our usual reality, and ask myself, *"Why not?"* In the universe, according to Jane Roberts' channeled Seth, we all create our realities individually and together, within our consciousness, and so such things are possible. I have, after all, still not encountered any universe I find more intellectually, scientifically, *and* spiritually appealing than Seth's.

A day or two after Ed's talk, the governor of Brasilia sends a small military helicopter to take me out into the countryside where he has asked to meet me in order to show off some ecological projects he initiated. Seeing Ed in the hotel hallway on my way to the helicopter, a phone call to my room had announced it was parked outside waiting for me, I asked if he'd like to come along for company. He accepts, and as we settle in behind the two pilots and take off, he asks a few questions about the 'copter that made the pilots ask if he has ever flown one himself. When Ed answers affirmatively, they ask what other craft he's flown and when he includes spacecraft, including a moon lander, on his list they are blown away and decide to give us an extra tour.

We hover above Brasilia, a modern city in the midst of Brazil's rainforest, treated to breathtakingly close views of its cathedrals and other massive architecture from above, then cruise toward a lake where our pilots have seen anacondas sunbathe along the shore and decide that would be of interest to a biologist, as it would indeed have been, had we found any. When we don't, I ask jokingly whether we could fly to Varzhinia to see the aliens found there according to a newspaper report I read.

"You know about the Varzhinia ETs?" one of them asks in surprise, then adding, "My brother was called out there when they caught them running across a field. He told me the US sent their military people there right away; they caught one of them and took him away to a base in Florida."

Unfortunately, Varzhinia is too far off our course, and the ETs are no longer there anyway. For my part, I love finding people who corroborate such stories, and I'm happy just to add one more ET encounter story to my growing collection of them.

The projects we are shown by the governor are admirable and very much what's needed around the world — farmers processing and packaging food right on their farms to make their local economies more sustainable — and yet it is the helicopter ride itself that stays with me as most amazing.

More reality-shifting stories

Having heard quite a few ET stories, in the Andes and elsewhere, I find myself at Hanna Strong's house in Colorado, meeting a woman who told me her story of an encounter she'd had while a high school student in Miami. I wrote it down, and will call her Michelle to protect her identity, as she'd requested if I passed it on:

> *One of her classmates was an oriental–looking girl who seemed to have no friends, and asked Michelle if she'd walk home with her one afternoon, as she might be going away soon and wanted to show her something. The girl took her through a large home and across a garden to a small cottage, where she said she lived by herself.*

> *Inside, she pulled some papers from one of several filing cabinets and showed Michelle they were reports of meetings between high-level US government officials and aliens. She then said that she was actually one of the aliens, who had taken on human form to live among us undetected. Then she demonstrated her 'real' voice, which Michelle said sounded like a dolphin through quadrophonic speakers.*
>
> *She went on to relate how the girl explained that her people were here from Venus to try to stop us from our nuclear explosions because they were tearing up the dimension in which her people normally live — different from our dimension and therefore invisible to us, and apparently one in which Venus is not forbiddingly hot and toxic to its inhabitants. The girl also said that the people in the big house were not her parents, just pretended to be to cover for her. She would be leaving soon and wanted someone to know her kind were benign, here to help humans stop doing damage beyond even that of which they were aware.*
>
> *The following day the girl was not in school, nor was she the next two, so Michelle went back to the big house. The kindly silver-haired man who opened the door, apparently more the age of a grandfather than a father, simply confirmed that, yes, she had had to leave. Michelle did not question him or go back after that. The alien girl had given her a way to contact her should she ever be in serious danger, and as she never had been when she told me this experience, she had not tried.*

As I have adopted Seth and Puma's definition of reality as everyone's experience, I collect these stories as other people's experiences. As in Puma's culture, I do not have to make them my own reality in order to respect them as someone else's. In such an inclusive larger reality, there is no need to sort reports religiously into the bins of fact and fiction that our education system so drills into us, and I *like* living in that version of reality. More and more I am seeing how we construct our realities from the stories we make of our experiences — not just the way I am doing consciously now, but ubiquitously, in all cultures, with or without awareness that we are doing so, individually, as well as collectively.

To my surprise, my Native American WISN friend, Paula Underwood in California, became another such informant. She taught leadership workshops, derived from her father's cultural teachings, as a business consultant and, during Willis Harman's presidency there, Paula worked at IONS, the Institute of Noetic Sciences that Ed Mitchell had founded. Paula told me rather matter-of-factly one day, years after we became friends, that her ova had occasionally been harvested by aliens, as her mother's had been. When I asked why she had never told me that before, she replied, "Oh, people make too much of such things and just get distracted from what I have to teach." She clearly knew 'her' aliens to be benign beings to whom she had willingly given her contributions to breeding hybrid beings.[51] After her donations, she never attempted to see what became of them; simply respected them as far more intelligent and benign than we are and so trusted them.

Tanai Starr, whom I'd met in Asheville, North Carolina, and who had visited me in Cusco, also had a fascinating story, which I also wrote out for my collection when I heard it from her in Asheville:

> *As a child in a southern Baptist community, she'd been visited by three angels who became regular playmates, until as a teenager, she found their presence conflicting with her social life as friends made fun of her, and so she asked her angels to leave. Before they bowed out graciously, they told her to go on to college and to study physics. She did so, became a chemical engineer, and then found a good job with an engineering company. Part of its mission was designing weapons systems, and she became dismayed when her own boss got involved with such a project, knowing it was almost certain she would be asked to participate in it, which she really did not want to do. Remembering the angels, she decided to try calling on them and, sure enough, they returned. Tanai no longer knew whether they were angels or aliens, only that they were interdimensional and benign, and she willingly performed deep meditations they assigned her to nullify the weapons systems while also teaching her a new kind of nuclear physics that included speeds faster than light, thus not limiting the properties of matter in the way of standard-model physics.*
>
> *One day, her boss walked into her office asking her to come to his. She panicked, thinking he somehow must know about her meditations and was about to fire her. He closed the door to his office behind him, looking very concerned, then proceeded to confide in her that he no longer felt good about the weapons system and wanted to drop it; would she think ill of him for doing so? Needless to say, she was greatly relieved at not being found out and happily empathized with him, encouraging him in making the good decision.*

I loved hearing such stories and was collecting enough of them to build a convincing picture of life beneath or behind the usual surface of things. Even Ed had told me that although he'd never seen an alien — much as newspapers and fringe media occasionally said he had — he did believe in them. When I asked why, he told me, "Because of the high-level meetings I get called to in Washington." He also told me he had been shown 'helicopters' taking off noiselessly, clearly based on technologies he'd never heard of and assumed had been copied from captured craft. With the Cold War ending, I could only hope both the USA and the USSR would open up about such things.

One evening in Santa Barbara, the six o'clock TV news reported that UFOs had been sighted flying over a West Coast US military base and an officer on the base testified on camera that their missiles had been deactivated during that overflight. I called all my friends and told them to watch the next newscast at nine o'clock and then tuned in myself. The piece had been pulled; there was no mention of it. Obviously, it was not part of the reality the owners of TV news — or whoever could dictate their content — wanted to project.

A few years later, I became friends with the retired chief missile designer of a large aerospace company who told me of watching a craft spiral around a test missile as he watched its trajectory crossing the Pacific on radar, knowing we had no craft that could do that. I also met a commercial pilot in my travels who had reported being closely followed by an alien craft on a flight along the US West Coast for over 20 minutes and had reported it. He said he would never report such an experience again as he'd been held in an underground facility for endless repetitive questioning over a period of weeks.

Revisioning biology

Willis (Bill) Harman, with whom I'd exchanged those meters-long faxes on deep scientific/philosophical questions while in Greece, was still president of California-based IONS and got back in touch with me when I moved to Santa Barbara. He asked whether I'd consider writing a book with him on the subjects we'd batted about back then. Specifically, he wanted the book to answer the question: How would biology, and society in turn, change if consciousness were considered primary in the universe, rather than as a late emergent property? I agreed enthusiastically and suggested that we write the book itself as a dialogue, so that we need not agree on all points and readers would know which of us believed what. He liked the idea and also my proposed title for it: Biology Revisioned.

While writing my first book in Greece, I had also been in dialogue with Jim Lovelock, especially when he actually visited me on my island, and repeatedly urged me not to appear "New-Agey" lest I lose my scientific credibility. My book had hardly mentioned consciousness as I deliberately wrote it to stay within the bounds of what I call 'western science' despite its globalization. I felt it was radical enough to flout convention by arguing that Earth was a living planet and by claiming that Darwinian theory covered only the youthful, competitive phase of a natural maturation cycle, ignoring the mature cooperative phase following it.

I presented nature as holistic, with everything interdependent, suggesting that we not limit ourselves by seeing individual creatures against background environments, but as whole ecosystems — as what I had called "rabbits in rhabitats." This holistic view, with its maturation cycle, showed how simultaneous self-interest at *all* levels of holarchy, from cells to multi-celled creatures to species in ecosystems, led not only to tensions, but to negotiations and mutually beneficial cooperative arrangements in the mature phase. This had made sense to me of the types into which ecologists had sorted ecosystems, from Type I in which species are highly competitive and expansionist to Type III in which they are stable and cooperative, although the process of maturation from one to the other was not recognized by them.

By the time I wrote *EarthDance* in the late '80s, I had been convinced by Erich Jantsch's arguments for a self-organizing living universe[52], but when I tried to introduce that concept to Jim Lovelock as a logical extension of his living Earth concept, he begged off, saying Earth was as large a domain as he cared to consider. Nevertheless, I did tell my story of a living Earth within the context of a living universe, carefully eschewing the concept of consciousness despite my personal adherence to the conscious 'Sethian' and Vedic universes, in order to push the boundaries while remaining acceptable as a scientist.

I was thrilled when MIT Press offered to publish EarthDance after I'd taken the rights back from Simon & Schuster[53] because of serious contract issues, so I happily signed the new contract. A year later, MIT Press broke the contract, saying that half their reviewers had considered it leading edge science, but the other half questioned it as insufficiently scientific. The sticking points were both the living planet concept and my insistence that indigenous peoples had demonstrated the practices of systematic science. I had used the OED definition of science to convince MIT's editor it was a valid designation, but the review committee overruled us, and I resorted to the rapidly growing world of self-publishing to get it back into print in an expanded version of the original *Gaia* as Simon & Schuster had named it.

Thus, it was Bill Harman's request that brought me out of the closet on the issue of consciousness. My views were clearly going to be controversial no matter how hard I worked to give my terms operational definitions and to defend my arguments logically. Academic scientists could defend their fortress; I had no more need to scale its walls to get in and was content to stand on my views.

Aware that Bill Harman is also a Jane Roberts fan, with all her Seth books on the bookshelf in his Bay Area IONS office, I am thrilled to find new Seth books, published while I was in Greece, seeking them out in Santa Barbara's delectable Earthling bookstore. With its dark green walls, elegant crystal chandeliers and central fireplace surrounded by comfortable reading chairs, the Earthling pioneered the bookstore café and free evening events, from films to poetry readings. Little did I know these practices would soon be copied by encroaching 'big box' Borders and Barnes & Noble bookstores as they drive out our beloved Earthling.

In working with Bill over the years, I had asked myself how science itself might have evolved had a single scientist made a plausible alternative choice — if Galileo, for example, had fashioned the new lenses of his day into a microscope rather than a telescope. Instead of looking out at the heavens he understood as vast God-created mechanism, he might then have looked down into a drop of pondwater, an utterly mysterious and squiggly world of inarguably living creatures that defied explanation as machinery. Might biology in that case, have become the leading science rather than having to fit life into the mold of mechanistic physics? Would this have led in the opposite direction, to extrapolating life to our planet and all the cosmos? *Was* western science seriously biased by 'accidents' of history?

The toughest questions scientists had faced, I felt, were how life comes from non-life, consciousness from non-consciousness, and intelligence from non-intelligence. These big questions had led to complex and convoluted theories neither Bill Harman, nor I, nor other paradigm-shifting scientists, had found convincing. That was why Bill and I had engaged in such long dialogues on the paradigm shift — on how it was leading to different fundamental assumptions about our universe at the very foundations of science. Now I was ready to take this big step into the question of consciousness with him as my ally and make the results of our dialogue public as a book.

Views on consciousness

To see consciousness as primary in the universe meant adopting that belief as a fundamental scientific assumption — a replacement for the existing belief in the foundational concept of things the other way around: that matter was primary and consciousness a late emergent product of its biological evolution. Consciousness as the primary source of all the material/energetic universe we know *is* a fundamental assumption in ancient Indian Vedic, Chinese Taoist, *and* Japanese Kotodama philosophies and sciences. Western science had differed radically from this view to the point of being antithetical to it, yet a number of western scientists, especially physicists creating or inspired by quantum theory, along with at least one prominent biologist had looked back to the ancient East because their research results could not be fit into the worldview mold they had been taught.

In 1931 astronomer James Jeans had published his view that *(my underline)*:

> *Today there is a wide measure of agreement, which on the physical side of science approaches almost to unanimity, that the stream of knowledge is heading towards a non-mechanical reality;* <u>*the universe begins to look more like a great thought than like a great machine*</u>*. Mind no longer appears as an accidental intruder into the realm of matter; we are beginning to suspect that we ought rather to hail it as a creator and governor of the realm of matter ...*

This view may not have been as widely held as Jeans wrote; in any case, it was quashed by limiting quantum theory to mathematical quantum 'mechanics' and instructing physics students to 'suck up' the weirdness of the implications and focus simply on the undeniable usefulness of the mathematical formulas.

Harvard's Nobel Laureate biologist, George Wald, in his essay, 'Life and Mind in the Universe,' spelled his view out this way:

> *Consciousness is not part of that universe of space and time, of observable and measurable quantities, that is amenable to*

> *scientific investigation. For a scientist, it would be a relief to dismiss it as unreal or irrelevant. I have heard distinguished scientists do both.... Unfortunately for such attitudes, consciousness is not just an epiphenomenon, a strange concomitant of our neural activity that we project onto physical reality. On the contrary, all that we know, including all our science, is in our consciousness. It is part, not of the superstructure, but of the foundations. No consciousness, no science. Perhaps, indeed, no consciousness, no reality.*

Clearly Wald understood that consciousness belonged in science not as a late emergent phenomenon, but as its most fundamental concept. In this essay, Wald went further, expressing:

> *The thought that mind, rather than being a late development in the evolution of organisms, had existed always: that this is a life breeding universe because the constant presence of mind made it so.*

Within a few weeks after coming to this idea, he wrote that he had discovered he was *"in excellent company,"* citing physicists with similar ideas, to wit:

Erwin Schrödinger: *"The world is a construct of our sensations, perceptions, memories. It is convenient to regard it as existing objectively on its own. But it certainly does not become manifest by its mere existence."*

Sir Arthur Eddington: *"The stuff of the world is mind stuff ... The mind stuff is not spread in space and time.... Recognizing that the physical world is entirely abstract and without 'actuality' apart from its linkage to consciousness, we restore consciousness to the fundamental position."*

Carl Von Weizsacker: *"A new and, I feel, intelligible interpretation of quantum theory ... Identity Hypothesis: Consciousness and matter are different aspects of the same reality."*

Wolfgang Pauli: "To us ... the only acceptable point of view appears to be the one that recognizes bothsides of reality — the quantitative and the qualitative, the physical and the psychical — as compatible with each other, and can embrace them simultaneously .... It would be most satisfactory of all if physis and psyche (i.e., matter and mind) could be seen as complementary aspects of the same reality."

Some of them put consciousness on a fundamental par with matter; the others went all the way to derive matter from the ultimate foundation of consciousness. Perhaps my favorite George Wald insight is:

> *If I say, with Eddington, 'the stuff of the world is mind stuff,' that has a metaphysical ring. But if I say that ultimate reality is*

expressed in the solutions of the equations of quantum mechanics, quantum electrodynamics, and quantum field theory — that sounds like good, modern physics. Yet what are those equations, indeed what is mathematics, but mind stuff?

George Wald greatly honored me by writing to tell me how much he had appreciated my *Gaia* book, as published by Simon & Schuster in 1989 while I still lived in Greece, even though I had not outed myself in it as a believer in consciousness as primary.

On the whole, scientists left the explanation of consciousness to philosophy — the name designated by the Greeks *as* natural science, although western scientists declared philosophy to be *independent* of science. Such exercises in dividing the world into separate compartments was clearly now crumbling. I thought a lot about the fact that mental conceptualization was as fundamental to science as mathematics was its tool of choice. Our minds have no boundaries; all our experiences occur within consciousness. There is no way to escape it, to look at it 'objectively' from the outside.

The 'axioms' of science are concepts of the universe that scientists formed in their minds; beliefs that constitute the paradigm — the worldview — on which the enterprise of science was built. All scientific theories are necessarily built on that conceptual foundation, as my philosophy of science professor, J.R. Kantor had taught way back in the 1950s, when his discipline was still taught to new scientists.

Writing *Biology Revisioned*

Bill Harman's big question to me, already back in Greece, was whether we were 'paradigm shifters' developing a broader context for science, in which the old would remain embedded, or whether we were developing an entirely new science? If our fundamental concept of a conscious universe was diametrically opposed to the paradigm of western science, I responded, how *could* the latter be logically embedded within it?

Now, both in California, if in different locations, we eagerly took on our task and continued to have wonderful conversations, mostly by email, that we turned into our book. Both of us liked Arthur Koestler's concept of holons in holarchies as the nested entities of the universe from subatomic particles to multi-celled creatures to the cosmos itself. Bill argued that *"If there is consciousness anywhere in the holarchy — in the scientist holon for instance — then it is characteristic of the whole."*[54] But this elegantly simple statement did not convince me as truly logical until I could work through more complex reasoning.

From Walter Pankow's work (see Ch. 3) I had understood the logical 'openness' of living systems evidenced by their self-transcendence, their self-referencing — their ability to 'know' themselves. He had summed this up so simply, but with such deep meaning, in the words *"It takes a living system to know a living system."* 'Knowing' implies awareness, and awareness is a common definition of consciousness.[55] So I recognized Pankow's insight as being very much akin, if not identical to, Bill's simple statement that consciousness found anywhere implies consciousness everywhere: "everywhere' defined as living. So it all comes down to All That Is being alive.

Consciousness cannot, after all, be contained in time or space. If we conceive the universe itself as alive, everything evolving naturally within it is alive and therefore self-transcendent, consciously knowing itself and thus knowing the whole at the fundamental level of cosmic consciousness. This is not an easy concept in our western world, where science gained the authority to tell us our most fundamental creation story. But science is a fallible and evolving 'authority,' subject to its own internal revolutions. Yet it has great responsibility, as it has the prestige of telling 'the' story at every stage of its life.

If the living universe story is true, then my cells are conscious, intelligent beings in the great community of my body, and every mushroom and mongoose knows its place in its living community. Looking at all nature from this foundational conceptualization changes everything. As I wrote in our book:

> *The new biology would show us that mature ecosystems do not evolve toward the sole survival of the most aggressive and clever, as they sometimes do in early stages of self-organization or when invaded by very aggressive 'outsider' species. Rather, they evolve toward intelligent and cooperative mutual support communities in which every species has a valid and valued role. In such a community, the bottom line is not profits, but output useful to other species in a virtually 100% recycling economy.*[56]

Writing *Biology Revisioned* was a great step in integrating the basis of my spirituality — the conscious cosmos — with my science, and I followed the writing of it with several essays on formally modeling science upon the concept of universal consciousness.[57]

Almost immediately after we finished co-writing the book, Bill was struck down by a brain tumor. Despite his admiration for the Sethian worldview and knowing every alternative healer in California and many elsewhere, he bowed to family pressures to undergo surgery with chemo and radiation treatments afterwards. Because I had met a number of people in Brazil — one a businessman with the same kind of brain tumor — who had been healed by Rubens Faria, an extraordinary 'psychic surgeon,' I urged Bill to go see him after the surgery but before the chemo.

Faria claimed to be the third person in sequence to be taken over by the spirit of a self-proclaimed 'Dr. Fritz,' a surgeon who had lived in Germany during the Second World War. I had first run into this phenomenon years ago in reading a book by the first of the 'Dr. Fritz' healers, Zé Arigó, described in a book called *Surgeon with a Rusty Knife*. My Brazilian friends, all professional people, swore by this third Dr. Fritz, by trade an engineer with no knowledge of medicine.

Bill agreed to go and, to prepare him for the trip, I arranged for a Sao Paolo friend with a cell phone to go to Rubens Faria's clinic and put him, while in trance as Dr. Fritz, on the phone with Bill in his home in Palo Alto. I was there, on an extension, listening to their conversation, in which I heard 'Dr. Fritz' say, *"I cannot restore dead brain cells; I can only contain tumors safely, but I must see you in person. However, I do not want to come between patients and their doctors, so you will have to make your own decisions about whatever your doctor tells you to do."*

After the conversation I ran to where Bill was, eager to help arrange the trip to Brazil, only to hear him say, *"He told me to do whatever my doctor tells me to do."* I was stunned but could not convince him otherwise. He and his wife Charlene took a short trip to Europe and then he began chemo and radiation. Months later, he was declining rapidly and suddenly decided he wanted to go to Brazil after all.

When I contacted my friend there again, sending him a photo of Bill to show Rubens, the response came back that there had now been too much damage for a successful healing. Bill wanted to go anyway, and I worked with him to get his IONS board president Paul Temple and his wife Diane to fly Bill and Charlene first class — Bill by now on a stretcher — to Sao Paulo.

Paul had an intractable knee problem no doctor had been able to solve and came back showing off a hairline scar around his beautifully healed knee that had been cut open with Dr. Fritz' usual dirty scalpel. When I asked why he let himself be cut that way — Faria often explained it was not necessary to the healing but seemed to increase people's faith in the results — he told me he simply wanted the experience after watching others go through it and could now testify that although the cut had been deep, there had been no pain and very little bleeding. Tragically, Bill passed away shortly after they returned. As Rubens had said, he could not undo the extensive damage. His loss came as a terrible blow.

Our book was with the publisher by then, but not yet in print. Rereading the last chapter of our manuscript, I suddenly saw Bill's brief telling of his life story and his philosophical conclusions about the meaning of life in that chapter as his own exquisite epitaph. And in a flash, I also got the real meaning of something he had told me when I agreed to write the book with him: that the book was the last of six tasks he had been given in a meditation. I had felt happy to be such a big part of that last task, but, as most of us have series of tasks on our agenda at any given time, it had never for a moment occurred to me that those six tasks were given to him as the *last* six tasks needed to complete his life!

Willis Harman was a true renaissance man, a pioneering holistic thinker, and a lovely personality, greatly missed. In what I dubbed his own 'epitaph' in our book he had written:

> *It's fun to realize that at some deep level of ourselves we choose to age and die, and to watch the process with as much fascination as a new father might delight in watching the birth of his child. It becomes more obvious each day that I am merely a part of the whole, that the deepest pleasure in life is serving that whole, and that subtle and manifold are the ways we can discover to that end.*
>
> *Out of that experience, which I have taken the liberty of sharing quite intimately, I am brought to several conclusions. One is that real learning does not come solely through assimilating knowledge; it involves coming to hold one's conceptual framework sufficiently lightly to allow in experiences that don't fit well with existing frameworks. More and more people are coming to this attitude regarding the prevailing science, despite its impressive successes.*
>
> *Another conclusion is that if our belief systems fundamentally change, through whatever process or experiences, our perceptions and everything else about our lives will change. That will be true individually and collectively. Which is to say, the consequences of adopting such a holistic concept of biology as we have been talking about are hard to anticipate, but they will be profound!*[58]

Seth at the Salk

While we were writing our book, Bill announced he was going to Tucson, where I'd stayed with my friend Audrey on re-entry to the US, to attend a consciousness conference at the University of Arizona, where she is still teaching. Seeing an opportunity to visit her while doing valid book research, I asked if I should go, too, but Bill only laughed, "Oh no, it will be very boring — all scientists trying really hard to squeeze consciousness out of the brain." We used such language between us as we'd come to believe that consciousness creates brains, rather than the other way around. That is, after all, what our book argues. But he felt he needed to go to that conference in order to stay abreast of this growing field. I asked whether I could, in that case, go to another conference on our IONS book project budget, and when he heard I wanted to go to a Seth conference in Oregon, he readily approved.

And so, I set out in eager anticipation and, indeed, it is everything I could have wished for — a happy group of people gathering to share their Sethian worldviews, food, and fun, more like a three-day party than a conference and named *The Magical Reality* after one of Jane Roberts' Seth books.

The participants are ordinary middle-class Americans — a postman, a few teachers, a librarian, secretaries, an electrician, and so on, along with a handful of science professors and researchers, all of whom have read and adopted the Sethian worldview — including the belief that we create our own realities — all of us thus free of victimization and blaming forces outside ourselves for anything. That makes this a happy lot; they have no gripes about their lives and seem not to suffer when ordinary adversity strikes them. I'm amazed at how they take everything in stride as another adventure from which to learn, looking into why they've created or attracted whatever happens in their lives. I have never encountered a group like it before and love being with them at my first ever Seth conference!

On the tables, around which we sit as speakers talk, are modeling clay, colored markers, glitter, scissors, glue, paper, pipe cleaners and other things to delight chronic doodlers — people like myself, often labeled as having ADD (attention deficit disorder) despite all of us having great interest in everything said. One of our exercises begins in mid-afternoon, when we are all presented with milk, cookies, and sleeping caps, the snack followed by instructions to go to our rooms, lie down, imagine us all on the beach together, doze off into a nap with that image, and come back to report our dreams. It is a group dream-creation exercise, and it works, with a remarkable overlap of specifics in the dreams reported after our naps.

The conference was initiated by the founders of SethNet International, Stan Ulkowski and his wife Lynda Dahl, who had met in the context of IT companies for which they worked. Both had become very avid readers of Jane Roberts' books, and they had attracted Norman Friedman, a successful engineer and also a 'Sethie' who had just published a book called *Bridging Science and Spirit: Common Elements in David Bohm's Physics, the Perennial Philosophy and Seth*.

Norm has brought his delightful wife Leah, as these four were already friends. Andy Hauck, a very playful self-esteem coach and small-plane pilot, who actually attended live Seth sessions in Jane Roberts' home, is another member of this 'inner circle,' as is medical biologist Bruce Lipton, who is developing the new field of epigenetics that shows how our conscious experiences actually affect our genes.

I've met Bruce before, through my friend Molly Hart, an animal communicator friend and fellow Sethie who urged me to come to this conference. Molly is friends with all of this core group, and was also friends with Jonas Salk, who built the renowned Salk Institute in San Diego after discovering the polio vaccine named after him. Unfortunately, Jonas passed on last year, but Molly, who lives in San Diego and had gotten to know others at the Salk Institute, has brought a leading Salk research scientist, Walter Eckhardt, and his wife Karen to the conference. Walter was acting head of the Salk Institute during the search for a new chief, and he is completely new to this world of Seth.

Jonas Salk himself had actually looked me up while I still lived in Greece. When he'd announced his name on my telephone, which rarely rang in my remote location, I had stuttered, "Er, uh, the ... *the* Jonas Salk?" Assuring me he was, he explained that he had come to Athens for a medical conference and was calling to see if we could meet because a Greek philosopher friend who lived in Paris had given him my *EarthDance* book[59] and he had so liked it. Was it possible for me to come to Athens and spend a day with him and his wife Francoise Gilot? She, I soon discovered, had formerly been married to Picasso and was Paloma Picasso's mother.

Of course, I had jumped at the chance as it was quite wonderful to have another famous scientist's recognition of my work. He was very interested in the evolution of humanity as a whole and had proposed that we were following an "S curve" trajectory of increasingly rapid growth economics through a current inflection point that would, if all went well, lead to a leveling off into sustainable economies. Thus, he liked my closely parallel concept of an evolutionary maturation curve in which we were heading from a highly competitive youthful growth phase to a mature cooperative phase. He wanted to assemble small teams around the world to promote such ideas and suggested I begin one in Greece, also urging me to visit him at the Salk whenever I was back in the US to talk further, giving me his private number to call at any time.

While I was not able to take Jonas up on his offer to visit him at the Salk Institute before he died, Molly now quickly draws Walter, Karen, and me into this Seth Conference core circle of scientists where we all find each other so compatible that Walter invites us to continue our conversation in a weekend at the Institute not long after the conference.

By the time we meet at the Salk Institute in San Diego, Walter has also invited a few other people he was sure would be interested, including Jonas' son Peter, also a Salk research scientist, as well as a practiced TM meditator, and his artist wife, Ellen. After spending a weekend together that Fall, we feel so like a 'soul family' that we agree to meet regularly two or three times a year from then on.

My own magical reality

Before we even meet at the Salk, I have a truly fascinating confirmation of "The Magical Reality" right after I return home to Santa Barbara from the conference. The weather had gotten very hot and I was kicking myself for not having bought a perfect white window fan I'd seen in a small outlet shop on State Street just the week before. The largest front section of this deep shoe-box shaped store is devoted to clothing, with a small household appliances section at the back, where I had looked at the fan. Eager to buy it now, I am seriously disappointed to see it is gone. Back at the front, the woman at the cash register assures me that all the fans have been bought because of the heat wave except for the blue floor model I had indeed just seen and also remembered being there on my previous visit. Clearly, no one else wants it any more than I do now.

Unable to take 'no' for an answer, I go back again to take another last look for it, recalling exactly how this fan I so wanted had looked: white plastic, a side panel adjustable to the width of a window, the price tag, and a sign on it saying "FOUR SPEEDS; ONLY THREE WORK; NO REFUND. I am happy now to settle for three but my fan is simply no longer there, and there are too few items all told for it to be hidden from sight.

Noticing a door ajar at the back corner, I push it open, see a man at the back of a storage area, and call out to him: "Do you have any more of those white window fans like the one I saw here last week?" Like the lady at the front, he tells me the heat wave has cleaned out all their fans except the blue one.

Still refusing to accept my fan's absence, I stand stubbornly staring at the spot where it had been, and then, just as I finally let go my futile persistence in order to leave, it is suddenly *there*. No fade-in materialization; just suddenly there exactly as it had been last week. Eyes wide, I step over to touch it. Solid. And with the tag about the missing speed still on it!

I pick it up and carry it through the shop to the cash register where the lady blanches as she asks, "Where did you *get* that?" I reply simply, "Back there; may I pay for it?" What else can I say? I have done nothing intentional to materialize it — it seems somehow to have come into being through my fierce stubbornness. What can she do but ring it up?

Back home, I am surprised to find all four speeds functioning perfectly despite the disclaimer. Naturally, I wonder a lot about the fan's appearance in thin air. Suddenly, I recall a book on magic I'd read in the '70s that spoke of holding strong and clear intentions at the same time as letting go the outcomes — something I knew to be far easier said than done! I'd had several minor experiences of such 'magic' — finding a ring Audrey had lost, making an odd change in an electronic component — but had explained those outcomes away to myself as coincidences.

In this case, however, I was *not* trying to materialize anything; rather, it seems my stubbornness produced the 'magical reality' as I visualized the fan so clearly and strongly in an emotion of stubborn refusal to accept its absence. This must have built up the same kind of field as would actual intention by conscious practitioners. If I had built up this field strongly enough, it might have overlapped with the moment of my letting go to produce the simultaneity of intention and letting go — exactly what that old book described as magic. This, at least, provides me with an explanation that might one day be measurable and accepted in science.

Whatever the case, it is fun to have come from a conference called "The Magical Reality," and then be presented with overwhelming evidence that physical reality *is* more than science can encompass — at least with its present assumptions.

CHAPTER 11

Strands in the Tapestry

A walk through time ... and space

After finishing the book with Bill, I begin to feel that life in Santa Barbara is almost *too* good — that I am spending too much time just enjoying it and not getting enough done. The old Puritan ethic I thought I'd shucked forever in Greece is coming back to nag at me. I begin feeling tall northern pine trees calling me — appearing in my mind as symbols of uprightness that might counter creeping sloth, and it isn't long before I actually find myself among exactly such trees on an island off Seattle, but first a lengthy stop along the way.

I actually left Santa Barbara to spend a few months with my daughters and grandchildren in the Bay Area, where I had been interviewed during a previous visit, while living in Washington DC, by the video crew from the Foundation for Global Community in Palo Alto. The video — about emerging new worldview stories — had been released as *The Unfolding Story* and had gotten repeated airings on PBS ever since. Staying this close to that crew, I am able to participate in their local events, and begin giving occasional lectures and workshops in their spacious Palo Alto headquarters, even bringing Puma up from Peru for a very special one.

Emilia Rathbun, who had founded FGC with her late husband Harry under its original name, Beyond War, quickly becomes a good friend, as does their son Richard, who headed the film crew, and others in their foundation. I love visiting the stately, loving Emilia, now in her eighties, in her delightful home behind a small front-yard jungle. Her inside walls are painted in the gorgeous reds, purples, and oranges of Mexico, where she was raised. Her artistic hand is everywhere on hand-painted furniture and in a profusion of flowers, both real and artificial. She keeps endlessly busy teaching workshops, gardening, and rearranging all her décor with every change of season. I wish I had known her earlier, when she and Harry and Bill Harman and their friends, including Aldous Huxley and other prominent intellectuals, frequently gathered for what must have been fabulously rich dialogues.

Emilia claims, quite adamantly, not to believe in reincarnation. Once, having lunch with her, I cannot resist telling her I was quite sure we'd been together in a past life. While denying such a possibility, she seems interested enough as I describe having been kept in a kind of convent for girls being trained to give their lives in sacrificial ritual in ancient Mexico and having sneaked out occasionally for a tryst with a lover despite the watchful eye of the matron in charge of us. Emilia smiles and looks me in the eye across the lunch table, saying quietly, "You know I was always a little lax with the rules."

It is the Foundation for Global Community that soon brings me my next writing venture. One of their members, Sid Liebes, whose career was built at Hewlett-Packard, had been granted permission by his employers to develop an exhibit on biological evolution. Sid had worked with a fleet of biologists, notably Lynn Margulis whom I met when she came with Jim Lovelock to the Gaia Conferences Teddy Goldsmith had staged in England a decade earlier.

A Walk Through Time tells the story of Earth's 3.8-billion-year evolution of life in a series of colorful and informative poster placards, designed to be mounted and stretched out along a mile-long walk where every step people take represents millions of years. This makes it startlingly clear that three quarters of evolution was solely about bacteria and nucleated single cell creatures, both of which still play their indispensable roles today.

With Lynn's vital participation in the design, all this purely microbial life is depicted in great detail never before seen by most people, showing multi-celled creatures evolving only at the start of the last quarter of the trajectory, and we humans a mere and very new blip on the evolutionary screen in the last step of the entire mile. What had been written off as 'primeval sludge' is now demonstrated to be an exceedingly complex world in which the most important steps in evolution had already been taken by the time most teachers begin the story!

Wylie & Sons, a leading New York publisher, is offering FGG, which hosts the exhibit, a contract for a coffee table book on the exhibit and wants the manuscript fast in order to present it in time for Christmas shoppers this year. They say they will make it their top promotion for the season, and I am recruited to write it as quickly as possible. The Prologue is to be written simultaneously by cosmologist Brian Swimme; the Introduction and Epilogue by Sid Liebes.

Just at this time, David and Fran Korten in New York City, board members of a magazine called *YES!* that evolved from its predecessor *In Context*, for which I had written, have bought a new house on Bainbridge Island off the coast of Seattle, where *YES!* has its offices. As I need a quiet writing retreat location and they need someone to keep the house warm for the winter as they cannot move into it till spring, our needs mesh perfectly ... and those tall pines beckoning to me become my reality.

Arriving on Bainbridge, I have just six weeks in which to write the entire manuscript, Wiley having told me exactly how many words they want, since the book with all its color illustrations — the Walk's placards — has already been laid out. I had literally prayed to get my life more organized and now I must work out the daily quota of words to fulfill if I want even just Sundays off to breathe in the cool scented air of those trees. Surrounding me everywhere, I reckon they are there to insure against any sloth on my part!

Brian sends me his draft for the Prologue, which begins: "Imagine a comet looking back at its tail ..." Wiley's editors are aghast. They are a reputable, academically respected publisher and comets do *not* look at their tails! Nor are we to mention a word such as *consciousness*.

Alone among my upright pines in a snowy winter landscape, I am thrown back into my old academic box, having to drop all the context of *Biology Revisioned* as I draw on my cross-cultural skills to see what I *can* get away with. I scrap the first version of my first chapter and start over with lines such as these, which happily pass muster:

> *... Today the cosmic evolution of Earth as a planet is a commonplace, for we can actually see it from space, along with other planets, cosmic clouds and distant galaxies. The natural evolution of Earth's creatures, from the earliest and tiniest bacteria to ourselves, is also real to us. We see it everywhere from museums full of fossils to computer animations on giant movie screens. It is our story.*

> *But our grandparents' grandparents, representing only a few human generations in the past, had a very different picture of origins. Before Darwin, people who thought about it at all believed Earth was only six thousand years old, measured in Biblical generations from Adam, however ancient that seemed at the time. Most people were shocked when scientists such as Mr. Darwin, late in the 19th century, told them it was vastly older, and that they were kin to apes and other animals that had evolved gradually, one kind from*

another. Imagine their reaction if he had told them they were even kin to germs — the name we still sometimes give bacteria.

The answer is that our present understanding is far from complete and not to be taken as dogma, for, like the planet itself, our story will continue to evolve. It is virtually impossible to know just how we will understand our evolution in another century.

Today we accept Earth's age as billions of years, and most of us can contemplate microbial ancestry without batting an eye. But wait — if the Cosmos evolves, if Earth and its creatures evolve, and if our human knowledge evolves with the most blinding speed of all, then how do we really know that we understand evolution now?

Feeling good about my diplomacy, I go on to present the four biggest steps in our current understanding as ...

- *an ecological systems view that is blurring distinctions between geology and biology as we began to consider Earth as a living planet, a matter still controversial; to be decided on the basis of how we define life,*
- *the revised 'tree of evolution' that now gives such great weight to the importance of our microbial ancestry,*
- *the new view of DNA as a complex self-organizing system responding to events both inside and outside its cells and creatures, and*
- *the creativity of life in response to crises.*

All this is accepted, and I also get away with using the word 'intelligence' where I would prefer the word 'consciousness.' Somehow, this, too, is acceptable, and calling all life intelligent leaves only a small step to 'conscious.'

No sooner is the book published as *A Walk Through Time: From Stardust to Us: The Evolution of Life on Earth*[60] than it gets a rave review from the prestigious *Harvard Educational Review*. Unfortunately, however, and for reasons we are never told, Wiley drops it from their priority Christmas marketing and gives it virtually no publicity. The world of publishing has gone the way of proverbial 'soap sellers' and has to preserve its narrowing margins as best it can, putting the weight of its publicity only behind one or two books per publisher in each season, depending on estimates of what will bring in the greatest revenues quickly before being dumped. Biological evolution is apparently not on the public radar enough to push it in a coffee table Christmas book.

As for me, the writing task was grueling on such a short deadline, and with severe constraints. I vow never again to pray for my life to be better organized!

Cross-cultural insights on religion

To my surprise, I am increasingly often called on to speak to religious organizations and church congregations, even giving Sunday sermons on occasion. I learn about the growing wave of churches professing 'servant leadership' and 'caring for creation,' including the rapid growth of independent 'New Thought' churches such as Glide Memorial in San Francisco and the Agape Church in Los Angeles, both drawing huge crowds, as well as the more established Religious Science and Unity churches that seem to be doing better across the US than most older protestant churches.

Episcopalian Bishop Spang in San Francisco founds a global venture called the United Religions Initiative (URI), and I make more new friends at one of their first conferences, among them the bishop of the National Cathedral in Washington, who loves the story of my encounter with the Jesus mosaic in the basement, and Bawa Jain, the lively young head of the American Jains. There are people from all continents at the conference, very excited about the new venture except for one seemingly glum young indigenous lady from southern Argentina. When I find myself at the same table with her in a conversation among eight people who are asked to name our religions, she folds her arms tightly across her chest and says, rather belligerently, "My people have no religion."

Everyone else at the table seems stunned, so I ask her what, then, brought her to the conference? She replies, "I want to see whether you people can make peace among yourselves, because more than a dozen religions are fighting over converting *my* people."

Remembering how I had seen the same missionary competition playing out in the Peruvian Andes, I recall a conversation with our guide from Hapu, the village I'd trekked so far to reach. He had three young children and in registering their births in the nearest real town had been talked into joining one of the missionizing Christian denominations on the grounds that he needed a religion to pass on to his children. He, too, had believed his people had no religion but, unlike the young lady at URI, had become convinced he needed one. I had carefully explained to him that he actually *did* already have a religion — that all the worshipful ceremonies his people performed, such as the one I'd participated in, making offerings to the deities of mountains, sea, and all else in nature, along with their practice of the ethical laws taught by these deities, *were* what the white man calls 'religion.' His eyes had widened and, according to our interpreter, he said, "No problem, I can still get me out."

So, I tell that story to the young woman and she seems much relieved. Over the next two days, I watch her brighten visibly and gradually engage in our activities with some enthusiasm. On the last day, she actually walks in our procession of religions, each with their own flag, in the chapel of Stanford University. There she is, carrying the Earth flag, her black eyes flashing with pride above her broad happy smile.

Cross-cultural communications have long been fun for me, especially when they can resolve conflicts. The seamless worldview I have been working to develop over the years is much more like those of indigenous peoples than like that prevailing in my own culture, wherein things are put in such rigid boxes or silos that conflicts are perceived where I see none. Why should science and religion be incompatible? Why should people think their economies have nothing to do with nature? How can publishers, not to mention scientists, be so rigorous in their designations of fact and fiction? Clearly these sharp divisions are what makes holistic thinking so difficult for 'my' people.

I reflect on my first indigenous name of *Kanghi Ina*, Crow Mother, meaning 'keeper of sacred law,' the second, *Kuntur Ruyac*, White Condor given me by Puma's grandfather in Peru, and the third, *Atlan Xalli*, Sands of the Seas, bestowed in Mexico by a Mexica (said Mesheeka) grandmother. The black and white birds of North and South made me think of my fascination with the ancient Taoist yin/yang symbol of inward and outward spiraling forces in balance — mirrored by the *Hunab Ku* galactic symbol of the Mayans — the most elegant symbols I know for how the universe works. 'Sands of the Seas' represents shifting boundaries to me; boundaries as connectors rather than separators, the most obvious natural boundaries on our planet. My indigenous names thus beautifully represent my Big Picture Reality in its perpetually energetic motion.

Chasing grand unified theories

Now the late '90s, I come back to California and settle in Burlingame, halfway between Palo Alto and San Francisco, almost next door to my cosmic little sister friend Nancy, who has moved there from Washington DC. By now, I've been involved with several groups of leading-edge scientists, mostly physicists exploring the nature of the material universe in terms of the primacy of consciousness. They chase after the fundamental geometries of matter and form, along with other aspects of how our world works, most of them dedicated to developing an integral science, if not 'the' Grand Unified Theory.

In one symposium of leading-edge PhD scientists in California, I find the courage to ask how many are familiar with, and influenced by the Seth books and, to my surprise, about 60% of them raised their hands. All of Jane Roberts' papers are archived at Yale University and are still much visited there by people from all over the world. I, myself, have spoken several times by now at annual regional Seth conferences. When the mechanistic worldview has been honored and laid to rest at last, I believe its successor will owe more than acknowledgment to the unparalleled Jane Roberts/Seth alliance.

Virtually all mainstream physicists have bought into the concept of an energy universe by this time, as Einstein convinced the world that matter is transformed energy. But discarnate Seth, whose worldview, I discover, is as known and intellectually appealing to most of the scientists I work with as it is to me, insists there is much more to this energy than mainstream science has yet uncovered. Seth says energy moves not only linearly as in light traveling through space, but also inward and outward in ways that I assume has something to do with the appearance and disappearance of subatomic particles — with their movement in and out of a source field, as most physicists accept, but which might have deeper implications, such as the nature of wormholes and other new interests of theoretical physicists we discuss.

One of the areas in which academic physics has gotten stuck is in considering atoms to be inanimate entities that remain indefinitely unchanged, except for those decaying radioactively. Why, indeed, should atoms be fundamental? My Greek island experience, with the sudden sand vortex smashing into me along with the vortices of the shells I'd picked up, had suggested vortices were the fundamental forms of self-organizing living entities — the fundamental geometry of the universe. Vortices at all scales from wheeling galaxies to subatomic particles; vortices ancients had depicted in their symbols, such as the Taoist yin/yang and the Mayan Hunab Ku.

The obvious vortices at our human scale of perception are always embedded in some medium on which they depend as source for the matter they form and as a sink for the matter released after flowing through them, such as whirlpools 'embedded' in surrounding water, and tornadoes in surrounding air. One of the poems I had written in Greece includes the line, "Try taking a whirlpool out of the river, or a whirling cloud from the sky." If seen as living entities, these geometric formations clearly depend on their surroundings for 'food and waste disposal' like all recognized living entities.

While still in Greece, I had read about and written to Hal Puthoff, a theoretical/experimental physicist in Austin, Texas, who was working on zero-point energy, to ask whether he thought atoms might be made of vortices feeding on that zero-point energy to keep themselves going for eons. He wrote back saying he thought that entirely plausible. So, I'm delighted to be invited now in California to a series of brainstorming meetings organized by Foster Gamble and called the Sequoia Seminars.

Foster is an independent researcher into the nature of the universe, and especially of atoms as bundles of vortices. His mentor is Arthur Young, an engineer and cosmologist who had designed the Bell helicopter, founded the Institute for the Study of Consciousness in 1972. Like Foster, I was intrigued by his theories from the time they were published while I was still in Greece. The first part of Young's cosmological theory of evolution concerns the *devolution* of consciousness into matter,[61] which tallies with Seth's descending speed of vibration from pure consciousness, through energy and into matter. Young followed this version of devolution with the *evolution* of material life as we know it, so meeting Foster, with such parallel ideas, is truly exciting.

To my great pleasure I am finding kindred spirits, wonderful thinkers and researchers including mathematicians and physicists of considerable renown, along with passionate and dedicated amateurs, all working on alternatives to mainstream cosmological physics.

Among the amateurs is Nassim Haramein, a brilliant young man Foster encountered living in a beat-up old trailer and, after hearing his theories, taken under wing by setting him up in a better place to live with computer and laboratory equipment. Nassim is working hard on a complete unification theory that many of us find more convincing than other candidates we explore.

Nassim's theory immediately reminds me of Itzhak Bentov's in *Stalking the Wild Pendulum* (see Chapter 4). Like the ancient Taoists, and like Ben Bentov, with his doughnut model of a simultaneous black/white whole, Nassim sees radiation (expansion) and gravitation (contraction) as the basic, equal and opposite, forces in the universe. Working with

Elizabeth Rauscher, the first woman to get a Berkeley PhD in physics, Nassim has learned the math he needed to work from Einstein's equations in order to show that these two forces can account for all four forces in the 'standard model' of academic physics. In doing so, he and Elizabeth built a very elegant new model in which the strong and weak nuclear forces are accounted for by gravitation at that size scale, and so there is no need to postulate any dark energy or dark matter in the universe because the equations balance without such factors.[62]

Biologist George Wald had actually written of the same conceptualization in his "Life and Mind in the Universe" essay cited earlier: (again, my underline)

> *Finally, we have a cosmic principle: To have such a universe as this requires an extraordinary balance between two great cosmic forces: that of dispersion (expansion), powered by the Big Bang, and that of aggregation, powered by gravitation. If the forces of expansion were dominant, that would yield an isotropically dispersed universe lacking local clusters, galaxies, or planetary systems; all the matter would be flying apart, and there would be no large solid bodies, hence no place for life. If, on the contrary, gravitation were dominant, the initial expansion produced by the Big Bang would have slowed up and come to an end, followed by a universal collapse .... There would be no time for life to arise, or it would be quickly destroyed. We live in a universe in which it has just lately been realized that those two forces are in exact balance ... "*[63]

Wald gives no source for that extraordinary last statement — that it had been realized that radiation and gravity were in perfect balance in our universe — as if this were now established knowledge. In my experience, only very few leading-edge researchers have come to this conclusion.

Nassim is finalizing just such a mathematically elegant toroidal model, with radiation spiraling out one side from its tiny hole and gravitation inward on the other side, like Bentov's earlier intuitive model *and* like the model published by Walter Russell, a remarkably little-known American genius with whose work Nassim is familiar. And at least in the Scottish Royal Society, it had been spoken of as the 'smoke-ring universe,' before Einstein's theory took over. I am ever more convinced it was known by the ancient Chinese and Mayans on opposite sides of the world, with their balanced black/white Yin-Yang and Hunab Ku symbols and that in our seminars we are formalizing all these brilliant insights with mathematical precision.

My introduction to Walter Russell's work comes through Japanese philosopher Yasuhiko Genku Kimura, a former Zen Buddhist priest living in California and president of the University of Science & Philosophy, which had been founded by Walter Russell in 1949. Yasuhiko has attracted his own group of leading-edge scientists working on unification theories with overlap, now including myself, from the Sequoia Seminar group.

Walter Russell, born and bred in Virginia, was a true Renaissance man excelling in the fields of architecture, painting, sculpture, business, philosophy, science, and anything else to which he put he put his mind and hands. As a scientist without academic training, he revised the chemical elements table in the 1920s to predict several new elements later discovered, and he then developed a unification theory rooted in the primal energy field he called Cosmic Light. As an artist, he was official portrait painter to Teddy Roosevelt and later sculptor to FDR. With no training in that mode, he sculpted the Mark Twain memorial — a commission requiring a single sculpture of more than twenty of Twain's characters, considered impossible by other sculptors. As a businessman and philosopher, he was a founder of the progressive Twilight Club, intended to keep capitalism ethical and including notables of his day such as Herbert Spencer, Andrew Carnegie, Ralph Waldo Emerson, Mark Twain, and Walt Whitman.

Russell's achievements were awesome[64] and he attributed them all to his direct line to God, established during a 1921 'cosmic epiphany,' which enabled him to achieve anything he could approach without any doubt whatsoever of his success.[65]

This concept of 100% belief, or zero doubt, becomes fascinating to me relative to Seth's insistence that we create our realities through our beliefs and focus. Ever since learning about Russell, I have looked for other examples — people who did the impossible by total belief that they could.

One of the few I found was Joseph Chilton Pearce, whom I knew for his books, such as *The Crack in the Cosmic Egg*, and learned when we met that he had done truly amazing things by proving the power of absolute belief to himself while a young man. As he described some to me, I asked why this was not in his books, and he told me he was warned by his own guidance to stay more consistent with the beliefs of our culture at large. Perhaps, I ponder now, recalling his stories, it was because, unlike Russell who discovered the power of belief as a mature man and used it to create beautiful and useful things of benefit to the world, he was too young in his discovery, showing off or using it selfishly. I'm sure he would have told me that himself had our conversation not been cut short.

Speaking of Seth, soon after my return from Greece, the Internet still in its earliest stages, I was in a 'list serve' dialogue group that included Howard Bloom in New York, and had sent the members some pages of Seth quotes, not telling them that they were channelled material. I was trying to get this group, mostly scientists, to look at Sethian cosmology without prejudice — to show them Seth's version of creation; how source consciousness is stepped down into electromagnetic energy and then into matter and more about multidimensional existence.

A chemistry graduate student at Harvard was the only one in the group who really responded, sending me the most wonderful note saying, "I spent several weeks one evening in that world and I loved it and find it self-consistent, but I came back knowing that none of my colleagues would follow me there." Such a poetic description of the power of herd mentality; the need, as with Joe Pearce, to *belong*, to stay in bounds despite the great appeal of going beyond them.

Still, by the time the Sequoia Seminars began, you could read about things only Seth had talked about earlier — even 'probable selves' in 'alternate universes' — in *The Scientific American*. Pure Seth language! And almost certainly because some credible research scientists were also Sethies! Now, over twenty of us in the group Yasuhiko put together are working on integral science models together and I finally get up the courage to ask: How many of you have read the Jane Roberts' Seth books and have been seriously influenced by them? Well over half of the group raises hands, and yet none of us had ever mentioned it.

Mark Comings, a Berkeley graduate physicist in that group, tells me, when we are alone, that he had actually been sent to a mental hospital by his parents for his 'delusional' ideas, and that he'd been hugely relieved when a friend brought him a Seth book that confirmed his views. Such stories increasingly make me believe Jane's Seth books really have had a huge impact on the paradigm shift in scientific worldviews.[66] Most of the leading-edge scientists I now meet on the conference circuit readily admit to knowing and appreciating them, as had Bill Harman.

Cosmic consciousness has been described by practiced meditators throughout the ages as an utter stillness pregnant with possibility, not unlike the ancient Greek concept of *chaos* as no-thing-ness with the potential for everything, later called by the Latin name *plenum*. The Sethian description of cosmic consciousness as the source energy that slows itself down to become electromagnetic energy and matter is also elegantly compatible with The Taoist model and had come to resonate with me as my truth on 'how things are.'[67]

Krista

We met while I still lived in Washington DC, but Krista and I only have a real opportunity to deepen a friendship when I move from Santa Barbara to Burlingame in the Bay Area in the late '90s, living not just next door to our mutual friends Nancy and her husband Dave, but also in walking distance from her.

Since returning from Greece, I have still not acquired a car, managing well without one in Tucson, Florida, Washington DC, Peru, Santa Barbara, and on Bainbridge Island. Being carless has indeed become a chosen way of reducing my energy consumption 'footprint' on our beleaguered Earth. So, Krista and I meet mornings for long walks to and in a large park of wonderful tree beings.

On the surface, Krista is an elegant, attractive woman, very successfully running her own pension fund investment company, which transforms large investments into retirement benefits for a great many people, while making companies in which she invests greener and more socially beneficial. She is far more successful by our culture's standards than I am and doing so much good at the same time. As a supporting member of the progressive business Social Venture Network, she draws me in to speak at their annual conference.

As a result, I become an official SVN 'fellow' and love meeting other amazing businesspeople interested in my concept of Living Economies, including Judy Wicks, who runs an actual living economy business in Philadelphia out of her White Dog Cafe and David Korten, an economist who has written a book called *When Corporations Rule the World*. Soon, eight of us are writing a collaborative paper on Living Economies, and eventually BALLE — Business Alliance for Local Living Economies — is born, primarily through Judy's initiative, as a way of spreading her practical expertise across the country in locally developed communities.

Krista is thrilled with these developments, yet my deeper fascination with her is focused on her inner self and how it relates to her outer world, which is obviously very different from my own, not the least because there seems so much less division between her inner and outer worlds than there is in my own experience.

It became quickly apparent to me that everything about the way she perceives herself and the world is far broader, deeper, richer than I've encountered in anyone else I've known personally, reminding me over and over of Seth's descriptions of how the universe works in us and through us as we co-create our world — at what Krista calls its 'leading edge.' She is for me living proof of everything that draws me back to my beloved Seth books so often; living proof that we humans can open doors to parallel and alternate worlds, to escape the foolish confines in which we imprison ourselves, cleanse and open 'the doors of our perceptions,' as Aldous Huxley put it, to all that is 'behind' the surfaces of our perceived world.

To know Krista is to know spirit having a conscious human experience and being fully aware of that. Her perceived world, as I understand it, is as an energy hologram with all the dimensions of all our senses and a great deal more — more than I can fathom, which accounts for my endless questions. Over years of knowing her, I never find anything dubbed 'psychic abilities' lacking in her, though she would simply say she has a different way of perceiving. Through her gradual sharing of her experiences on multi-dimensional levels, I learn more and more. At the time I was really getting to know her, she was spending a good part of her non-business-work time sitting with dying or coma patients to both learn from and help them endure, and then accompany them in their transition into beyond-death realities.

There had been and still are downsides to her extraordinary existence. As a small child, she had no way of knowing how she was different from other people, even in her own family, having to learn the hard way that other people do not read each other's minds and would not even want such transparency. By the age of six, she had to be taken on a trip by her nanny until her parents calmed down to prevent her from being shipped off to a private mental hospital. Animals have always been her refuge, especially horses, as she has always been able to commune with them, as well as by all other animals, domestic and wild, and be understood in ways few people can fathom.

Krista makes me more deeply aware of the world as sentient process — of everything in it intelligently interwoven. I understand such conceptualization from the analyses of human process languages as Whorf had taught me, from the physics of Bohm, from Taoism, from Seth, from J. Allen Boone's writings, from my own Sufi master for one summer, from the writings of masters throughout the ages, indeed from almost countless sides by now,[68] but here is an actual living friend whose entire direct experience of the world *is* of this endless flow. Sometimes I feel at a disadvantage, with my mind transparent to her while hers is opaque to me. Other times I am frustrated by the limits on what she can or will share about her abilities and experiences. But knowing her is invaluable in reinforcing and expanding my own worldview, and I cherish our psychic relationship, a closer one than I've ever had with anyone else.

I soon begin taking her to talks I give so she can tell me how people relate to me energetically, whether I truly hold their attention, whether heart chakras open as I speak, and to hear her tell what kinds of non-physical entities, including deceased people, gather in the room with us. I get her to go with me to the Dalai Lama's science dialogues in Dharamsala as I can invite a guest, and to a Seth Conference, where I actually get her to sit on stage with me in dialogue.

Grounding cosmic love

The Holocaust, exposed at the end of WWII while I was myself still a child, left me outraged, and the later agony of seeing children napalmed in Vietnam on TV made me beat my head against a wall, but my responses to these agonies was to dig deeper, to learn, to teach, to participate in demonstrations and campaigns, and then to organize them myself. I am inclined to want to fix things, not one to jump ship, and I desperately wanted to stop these terrible human horrors. In one of many poems a Bengali poet I had met in Canada wrote for me during the Vietnam War is this line: *"Somewhere the tears and the agony are stored into the chest of thunder"* — thus supporting me in transmuting the energy of painful rage into positive action.

I believe that any intelligent youngster, my son included, who sees our human condition at all clearly must at least contemplate checking out at some point in the painful process of growing into maturity with awareness of the human condition. But my way, as I said, has not been to jump ship in despair, and Krista's take on the world has given me a more spiritual perspective on working with individuals.

Another of my dearest friends became very worried about his own son's potentially suicidal thoughts, expressed in very dark poetry. He asked me to talk with his son, and so I contrived to run into the boy when I knew he was taking a walk on a beach where we were all on a retreat. Inviting him to sit with me on the rock where I was when he came by, I was able to connect with his pain — Germans call it *Weltschmerz*, world pain — but without intellectualizing, rather by just being in my heart with him. I got his attention when I said, as if musing to myself, "There's only one problem with checking out …"

"What's that?" he asked quickly, without denying what I implied was on his mind. So, I talked about Mitchell's archangel, and then about my image of ourselves as keyboards of vibrations from matter to energy to pure consciousness; about how when you kill your body you cannot come back to it to play in the low keys of matter and are thus stuck in the higher frequencies, like those angels, making much less rich music without those bass notes.

I told him that only from *within* your body can you reach all the way up the keyboard to your own soul, taking vacations, so to speak, from the human world. I had proven to myself that you can leave your body and come back to it, suggesting he might try that instead of a drastic solution. He was decidedly intrigued, and we developed our own friendship as he grew into a wonderful young man who became a nurse and works to save African tribes on the edge of extinction, as well as getting involved in other positive actions.

Krista sees rapidly growing numbers of truly special children incarnating now — kids who bring conscious knowledge of their spiritual origins to Earth, and who know their soul missions, though they need grounding through our human love to carry out their missions of helping humanity evolve. Without such grounding, they can get lost or retreat altogether from this life. She sees many of them as having little or no previous experience on our planet, so those of us with many incarnations — with all sorts of physical world experiences under our soul belts — are needed to help these relative newcomers to adjust.

She is adamant that the more we ourselves can ground cosmic love in all our cells, down to our toes, the more we can be of use to them. Cosmic love in turn, she holds, benefits from this humanizing of it, the extension of it into what I call the 'low keys of matter' on my keyboard. I find this reciprocity of humanity at the leading edge of evolution making its contribution to love at the level of Cosmic Consciousness utterly appealing as a story to live by.

Down to business

From speaking in Brazil about the future of the country, I am now speaking there more and more about the Biology of Business. I have been pulled in that direction because the sponsors and organizers of the *Imaginaria* conferences are all high-level businessmen, and because Krista has pushed me so strongly to work in the business world.

Working more specifically with progressive businesses on seeing themselves as living systems, I call my workshops "From Mechanism to Organism." These workshops and lectures are held in businesses considered progressive for their social conscience and programs, in Sao Paulo's leading business school, and at business conferences.

Invariably, the companies I work with, however progressive, have been designed from engineering diagrams of hierarchical boxes and flows, forcing their living people, from management to workers, into structures inimical to vibrant company life. So, we play with more flexible and more holarchic organizational possibilities, show them how their own body economies work in awesome cooperation and all the other political and economic lessons I draw from nature. Through this work, I continue to develop my list of the essential Features of Healthy Living Systems.[69]

One Sunday afternoon, I'm invited to a coffee party at the home of one of Brazil's top bankers. The immanent new millennium is much on people's minds, so when I have him to myself briefly, I ask, "Sir, what does the future of the world economy look like now from your perspective?" He responds, "I'm afraid we are all going over the cliff; it cannot last." Surprised by this candid assessment, I ask him whether his colleagues agree with him, and he replies, "To a man." Pressing further, I ask whether they do not talk with each other about how to avoid such disaster and he shakes his head, saying, "There is no way." Foolishly, I then asked him how that makes him feel as a grandfather, only to have him turn his back and walk away. Speaking with other business leaders, I get the impression that many business owners in Brazil dream of nothing more than selling their companies to multinationals so they can avoid disaster and retire to play golf in Miami.

This is however, not true of the ones I work with and learn from — those who have become personal friends, such as Rodrigo Loures, the very progressive founder/CEO of packaged food company Nutrimental and Tamas Makray, founder and ex-CEO of Promon, which built the largest hydroelectric power dam in the world in Brazil, with great concern for people and environment,[70] retiring after thirty years with the company but leaving it completely worker-owned. Another such friend is Max Feffer, the founder/CEO of Susana, one of the largest paper companies, deriving paper not from Amazonian trees but from eucalyptus plantations that usefully drain swamps.

Max's wife, Betty, also becomes a good friend I continue to visit even after Max passes away, after having funded a new Opera House for Sao Paulo and built a small city to be owned and run by his workers. These men are utterly dedicated to making Brazil a better economy and a better place to live and work. Still, as in other countries, such role models for a better future, even though at the top of their national economy, are still a small minority.

More opportunities to work this way come via invitations from New Zealand and Australia, where I get to work on transforming businesses and government departments by seeing them as living systems. I am fascinated by the tasks with which I am presented, such as one call to work with the National Tax Office of Australia on changing people's view of taxation to one of willingly sharing their incomes with their societies by letting them have some choice in how their taxes are spent.

For this challenge, I draw on a favorite essay called "Thinkers & Treasurers" by Barrows Dunham, a wonderful, but sadly little known, American philosopher. Dunham points out that all organizations from Boy Scouts to governments are funded by dues or taxes and work well only if these require no force to collect. Therefore, they also must include thinkers with the purpose of rationalizing why they should be paid. The best organizations are those, he says, in which the thinkers can tell the truth. The further implications, of course, are that such transparent governance, to avoid using force, will have to meet the wishes of its people. Australians, at this time, were to know the government's budget and have a say in where their taxes would go.

Increasingly, I am hired explicitly to get people who are advancing up the corporate or government ladder to "think out of the box," which becomes my favorite assignment, as it gives me more leeway for embedding them and their roles into the bigger picture of planetary and even cosmic life over billions of years. In the Netherlands, for example, I am asked to lead a workshop of this kind for all the people acceding to positions as heads of government departments including Education, Housing, Healthcare, Defense, Social Services, and so on. At Boeing headquarters in St Louis and for Siemens at Stanford University, the participants are men in their thirties, aspiring to move upward to becoming department heads in their companies.

The men in the Siemens group have just been given a new version of the classic Monopoly game called Super Capitalism. After my initial talk on how capitalism might evolve into something that resembles a stable mature ecosystem more than the highly competitive physical growth economies of youthful ecosystems, they ask whether I now expect them to throw those games away. "On the contrary," I respond, "I *want* you to play them now, but very consciously, thinking about how you want things to be in the future."

On the evening before my Boeing workshop, I watched Boeing's own channel on the TV in my hotel, which was part of their St. Louis headquarters complex. Seeing the documentary on the company's history, I caught the enthusiasm of the young founder-inventors who had been so eager to conquer the skies, and how this seemed to be a spirit of adventure that had persisted through the years in this company. It makes me a little more playful in the next day's workshop than I normally am, and that seems to help them "get out of the box." When the workshop is over and the men invite me to have a beer in the pub with them, the first question they ask me, now that they are, so to speak, out of school, is "Do you believe in UFOs?" It is all fun from there on, as that boyish enthusiasm for further adventure is unleashed.

Dharamsala

Through several invitations to speak at conferences organized by the huge 'New Thought' Agape Church in Los Angeles, I become friends with its minister Michael Beckwith, his musical director, and eventually wife Rickie Byers and Barbara Bernstein, who lives in Santa Barbara and is deeply involved in their jointly founded Association for Global New Thought. AGNT has connections with the Dalai Lama, which leads to his invitation to bring some 20 thought leaders in a variety of professions to meet and dialogue with His Holiness in Dharamsala, where he founded a Little Tibet community in the Himalayan foothills of northern India. As soon as I am invited to participate in this marvelous adventure, I know I want Krista to come along, to expand my own perceptions through hers.

In Dharamsala, we share a room in the special guest house where Richard Gere stays during his visits with the Dalai Lama. Big monkeys perch on the rails of tiny balconies outside our windows; blue Himalayan peacocks fly by trailing their long waving tailfeathers against a background of tall forest trees; near life-size Tibetan people look down on our beds from more balconies in murals painted on our room's walls.

Getting to Dharamsala entailed a long ordeal of airplanes followed by a long train ride, and then a sleepless overnight in a ramshackle bus with no springs below or in our seats, bouncing its way over gnarly, pitted mountain roads, yet we were all in high spirits throughout the endurance test. Once arrived, our spirits soared like the mountain peak that appears magically through the clouds to frame our meeting temple like an enormous triangular halo before disappearing again, reminding me of the Corcovado Jesus statue that appears now and then through clouds on its peak over Rio, seemingly hovering in the heavens and then disappearing again behind the mists.

Organizing American professionals in Dharamsala is like herding cats, though even harder given our well-established egos. Rather than behaving consistently with the dignity called for by the occasion, we let conflicts erupt when the Dalai Lama is not present. We argue about the carefully planned schedule, how and when to do or not do things, even occasionally descending into petulant competitive sallies on who deserves more access to His Holiness, whose physics theory is more important for the great man to hear in detail, and so on, much of it captured on film and making future audiences laugh at us in the movies that come out of this event.[71]

There is also dissent among our guests, as they are not allowed in all the meetings between the Dalai Lama and his invited group of professionals. They are welcomed into a number of our scheduled meetings with His Holiness, allowed to raise their own questions and make their own comments, and to all meals, entertainments, and visits, including our final personal encounters with His Holiness. Krista, being one of them, does us all an important service in persuading them that holding energy for the invitees is a very important role and teaches them how to play it while not actually with us. I believe they are thus able to prevent a serious breakdown in our more privileged invitees group, which obviously has a lot of inner work to do individually and together.

For me personally, it is very special to have at least a secondhand view of Krista's perceptions and insights on all the, to me, invisible strands of energetic interaction throughout this once-in-a-lifetime experience. And once back home, she continues to help me understand how few people are fully embodied and how important it is for all humanity to become so. I have been aware myself of this lack of embodiment, especially among intellectual men in the academic world, who sometimes seem to be all head dragging around their bodies like sacks of potatoes. Such perceptions, as I learn to trust them, are now growing more acute and less abstract.

Krista's experience of the world often reminds me of favorite books from the 1970s by Alan Watts, Lyall Watson, Aldous Huxley, Gurdjieff, and others besides Jane Roberts' Seth books. One of her own contemporary favorites is *Meetings with the Archangel* by Stephen Mitchell, whose wife Byron Katie is doing wonderful work on freeing ourselves from negativity and suffering.

In reading Mitchell's book myself, I am struck by the archangel explaining to the human that angels envy the things humans can do, that the angelic world is without 'push-back,' without sorrow to balance the endless joy. Angels, unable to feel the physical emotion of passion, he writes, have no ability to feel *com*passion. As the archangel explains, "Bliss can go only so far in understanding the *I Am*." In Krista's world, the angels are lined up for human bodies, and I see more why she is so adamant that full embodiment, in order to ground cosmic love down to our very toes, is critical to our human evolution. We *have* to learn to play what I keep seeing as a whole keyboard of matter, energy, and spirit vibrations.

More business world leader encounters

Among the truly progressive businessmen I become friends with elsewhere in the world as I learn from them is Takashi 'Tachi' Kiuchi who was CEO of Mitsubishi Electric in America up to his retirement. Tachi takes businesses along an eight-step path from accountability to shareholders to accountability to stakeholders. In his view, doing business to increase the wealth of shareholders is obsolete; the future lies with increasing the wellbeing of everybody affected by a business, every stakeholder. If you are in the food business, for example, the stakeholders are all those involved directly or indirectly in every aspect of production and distribution, from machinery, fertilizers, pesticides to delivery systems, every child eating the food, all their families, even the plants, animals, earthworms that nourish the soil that provides food for the cows, and so on — everybody and every creature affected by the business.

Thus, Tachi claims, if you want to do good business, create value for the poorest people on Earth. If you make the children healthy with good food, your stakeholder community will keep you in business. And the better you serve your stakeholders, the better your shareholders will do! Together with environmentalist Bill Shireman, Tachi visited, even by parachute, rainforests around the world to study the economics of nature, concluding in their book[72] that no problem faced by a business has not been faced and solved in a rainforest. This kind of thinking is of course highly compatible with my own growing work on living economies, and Tachi's arrangements for me to speak to business audiences in Japan are a great pleasure.

All this work in very different locations and venues give me ever more insights into global economics, as well as individual businesses. I see more and more parallels between biological evolution and the evolution of human society, as well as ways to integrate economics with my consciousness-based science and my views on evolution in particular. I write essays on "The Biology of Business," and on "The Biology of Globalization."

I use my early training in art to make beautiful PowerPoint slide shows to tell the big story of evolution — especially the positive heritage of species and ecosystems maturing from competition to cooperation — designing my shows to hold interest through gorgeous images of the natural world, animations from spinning Earth to flapping butterflies, relatively little text, attractive fonts, and elegant formatting. I am determined to demonstrate that slideshows can enhance lectures in the business world, as well as elsewhere rather than inflicting what had become known in business circles as "death by PowerPoint."

My "Biology of Globalization" essay is a direct response to something painful in my life. Teddy Goldsmith, who had become such a dear friend in spending time with him on various continents and occasions since the Cornwall Gaia Conferences, had begun an Anti-Globalization Campaign with San Francisco-based Jerry Mander and friends of mine including Vandana Shiva and Helena Norberg Hodge, both women teaching economics for a better world through their international experience.

I pleaded with them all that globalization was an evolutionary process far broader than global market economics, including the globalization of transportation, scientific cooperation, interchangeable currencies, Parliaments of World Religions, the development of the World Wide Web, altogether a necessary evolutionary step toward global cooperation for humanity that one could not be against, however much I agreed with them in deploring the exploitative human and ecosystem practices of most multinational corporations.

As Teddy could not accept my arguments, I am cut off from his friendship for years, much to my dismay. Fortunately, I eventually get the opportunity to convince him we are on the same team and the wonderful friendship is restored well before he passes on, with happy visits to him at his home in England and his manor in Italy.

All along, I keep meeting with wonderful businessmen and thrill to new tools for transformation in business. By the turn of the century, Karl-Henrick Robért in Sweden is making waves in the business world with his project *The Natural Step*, showing the way to sustainability by recycling all minerals, fossil fuels and manmade materials, ceasing the destruction of nature, increasing our resource efficiency, and promoting justice for all people.

Natural Capitalism by Amory and Hunter Lovins and Paul Hawken focuses on the same issues and shows how to redesign every business process to achieve these goals. Thus, I am drawn ever deeper into working within the business world, as Krista intended.

CHAPTER 12

Expanding Worldviews

(R)evolution in religion

On a late '80s trip to the US while still living in Greece, I had met Jean Houston — a founder of the Human Potential Movement that grew tremendously while I was off on my lengthy 'midlife retirement' in the Greek Islands. I thought of her during my dialogue with Ed Mitchell in Brazil, when I recalled her asking me what I'd most like to do in life and responded, "Dialogue with the finest minds on the planet!" Jean not only proved to *be* one of those astonishing minds, but also became a friend and introduced me to other world changers.

Soon after we met at her home just north of New York City, she took me to meet a Catholic priest named Thomas Berry, who lived near her on the banks of my familiar Hudson River Valley birth ecosystem. As she explained, he had followed in the footsteps of her own mentor, the great French philosopher Teilhard de Chardin,[73] whom she'd actually collided with while running in Central Park in Manhattan as a child and gotten to know as 'Mister Tayer.' Thomas, like Teilhard, had studied Sanskrit and Chinese to become a deep scholar of biological evolution and paleontology in Teilhard's Jesuit tradition.

Sitting by the river with Thomas on a glorious autumn day, squirrels cavorting around us in the thick fallen leaves, we are having a most engrossing conversation in which he suddenly says, "Jesus was a lousy ecologist." Shocked at this from a Catholic priest, I counter, "Well, he sure was good on gender equality," to which he comes back with, "That does not excuse him from being a lousy ecologist." Even more surprised, I try, "Well, I suppose there wasn't much green in the desert where he lived ..." and then I burst out laughing, "Oh my, what am I doing defending Jesus to a Catholic priest when I'm not even a Christian!?" We have a good laugh at that and Thomas explains that there just isn't enough in the Bible about concern and care for Creation on Jesus' part. Thomas does not believe we can tell the human story without telling Earth's story and building human love for it, as he does in his book *Dream of the Earth*, and I have to agree.

I meet him again while still in Greece, at the international peace conference that took me to Costa Rica, and because of these meetings with Thomas I'm invited to the very first conference I speak at upon my return to the US in June 1991. Held at a lovely Catholic retreat center on a lake in Canada, it is called *Three Women in Dialogue with Tom Berry*. Our host is a handsome priest with a shock of snow-white hair who wears shorts until the last day when he appears in a beautifully embroidered white surplice to do an outdoor mass under a big tree, complete with a communion ceremony using a handmade pottery chalice and a loaf of home-baked bread. He tells a short story about three divinity students in search of God, with one a woman who finds God swimming with dolphins.

Thomas then does a baptismal ceremony for a couple of new babies that have appeared in our midst, filling a tin sandbox pail, decorated with Disney characters, at the garden hose, then declaring *all* water as sacred and following with a Native American blessing that receives these new babies into their lives on Earth with love and gives them the responsibility of care for all life in turn. I smile to myself thinking I'd better get out of here before they make me a Catholic!

As I keep weaving spirituality with science and economics, I get calls to speak in New Thought churches, such as Unity and Religious Science, from Key West to Chicago to Hawai'i, as well as at annual conferences sponsored by the Agape Church in Los Angeles. In these communities, a spirit of love, joy, and openness is pervasive; music and ritual are amalgamated from various world religions; the focus is on building loving, inclusive community.

It is more surprising to receive invitations to speak from leaders in traditional religions. First, an order of Catholic nuns invites me to speak at a conference in their huge stately mansion on Long Island in New York, then an Episcopalian bishop brings me to his parish in North Carolina!

Upon my arrival at the Long Island mansion, I note a bumper sticker on one of the cars parked in its private lot, reading WE HAVE FAMILY IN IRAQ. The US has levied crippling sanctions on Iraq as it demoted Saddam Hussein from ally to evil dictator adversary, now drawing endless negative press — how curious for the nuns to have family there, I wonder. When I ask, they explain: US sanctions have affected their sisters tending to the poor and sick in Iraq by depriving them of needed medications, now more difficult and expensive to obtain from other sources. Saddam has never given them any trouble, as he values their social services. So American nuns flying to Baghdad have been carrying very significant cash to them as a mercy mission. I'm amazed at these feisty, gutsy gals living their spiritual mission.

In North Carolina, I'm warmly welcomed to the weekend event — a symposium of invited guests presenting their work to each other. On arrival, we are asked to fill out a 'get acquainted' form that includes questions about our favorite color, animal, and food. As it turns out, this is a ruse for surprising us on the last evening with a glorious banquet table laden with every person's favorite food in sharing quantity. Imagine the steak, lobster, crab, apple and cherry pies, along with more exotic delicacies laid out before us as every gastronomic dream is fulfilled. Never before or after have I experienced such a loving presentation of food.

Fascinating as these two memorable visits are, what endures as their highlight in my memory is — in both cases — very personal requests to help with redefining God for these new times. Few things in my life have moved me as deeply, and none make me feel greater humility than to do this. First a nun, and then this bishop, in turn making the same request of me. Taking it very seriously, I beg time to think it through carefully and then write the bishop a letter[74] explaining how I reversed the scientific story I was taught from seeing consciousness as the end product of evolution to seeing consciousness as the *source* of evolution — as what the Vedics called *All That Is*: the source of our entire universe. I see this Source as the aware intelligence, the Cosmic Consciousness that different human cultures personified as God under many names. My letter ended:

> *On a recent Sunday, I gave the sermon at three services in a Unity Church, for a minister friend who needed a break. I urged the three congregations to remind themselves occasionally to see themselves as the creative edge of God (a phrase I learned from a dear friend) — as God looking out through their eyes, acting through their hands, walking on their feet, and to observe how that changed things for them. After all, I can only describe the worldview/Godview that makes sense to me at this point in my lifetime of exploration. We have only our stories to go by, and each must necessarily be at least somewhat, if not radically, different — for God has become very complex, albeit eternal Unity!*

I pray that all the religions will recognize the importance of the uniqueness in each story within that unity of All That Is. I pray that scientists, who have been given the role of secular society priesthood, with the right to tell us "How things are" — will soon officially recognize that there is one alive, intelligent universe in which spirit and matter are not separable. I pray the indigenous people who never separated science from spirituality, and who have always honored the inner senses along with the outer ones, will be honored for that. It is time for the true communion which alone can save our species and all others, which alone can bring about the perfectly possible world we all dream of — a world expressing this understanding of ourselves as the creative edge of God!

Dissonance and resonance in Japan

Facing the massive bronze Buddha at Kamakura after a bullet train ride from Tokyo is an awesome experience. I'm walking around its lovely park setting with Elaine Valdov from the UN in New York, who is in Japan with me, our guide scurrying to keep up with our western pace. The gigantic Buddha is framed by a green mountain background, and when we get to it, I soon discover a door in the huge statue's stone wall base around one side. Seeing that it is ajar, I push it easily and find myself inside what I immediately sense to be a huge acoustic space of the kind that always lures me to try my voice out in it.

I've always loved the physical feeling of resonance in my body when a song or chant bounces back from the surfaces of such spaces. It is like singing through a mike, but better without the electronics; I'm vibrated from the inside and outside at once as everything becomes one — me, the sound, the form of the space. So, whenever I see and feel what appears to be a good acoustic space, I try it out — those wonderful Greek tholos tombs at Mycenae, an empty school hallway at night, the stairwell of the Capitol building in Washington DC, any chapels I find empty of people, the three or four geodesic domes I've had the privilege to visit, caves, the much smaller but just body-sized bells at the Vedanta temple in Santa Barbara. I've even stuck my head into large amethyst geodes occasionally found in rock shops for an 'Om' or two.

Standing now in the center of this great Buddha, a timidly sounded *Om* confirms the resonance effect and hooks me, so I try another, raising my voice a bit louder as I slow my way through its delicious vowels: *Aaoouuuummm....* Bathed in the rich vibrations now surrounding me,

I do not want to stop. I ask Elaine to chant with me and she does. The Gayatri mantra really rings this enormous bell, and I am entranced:

Aum bhur, bhuva svaha

Tat savitur varen yam

Bargo devasya dimahi

Diyo yona pracho dayat ...

Time stops as we chant until I suddenly notice a tiny but older and bent-over woman who has come in to stand beside our stunned guide. In the dimly lit space, I see she wears a grey uniform and holds a broom. Clearly, she belongs here as we do not. Embarrassed by this reality check, I approach her and ask my guide to convey my apology. But she is not angry with us; rather she is crying and smiling at the same time. My guide interprets: "I just want to thank you for what you have done. When you were chanting, the spirits of the people who built this Buddha came in. I have been cleaning this Buddha every day for many years, but I have never seen them before. I am very grateful."

We had done something 'from the inside out' — from our hearts, in simple, childlike joy, and I like to believe we thereby set up in this place a resonance that attracted these spirits connected with it. I hope we made the Buddha happy as well. I am humbled, once again reminded that my reality is but the surface of the deep cosmic ocean in which we all live, and that the least stranger I encounter may be far more present to its vast intelligence than I am.

Back in Tokyo from our quick trip to Kamakura, Elaine and I ready ourselves for this evening's big event, for which we have been brought to Japan by a Japanese businessman who had offered our dear friend Robert Mueller his intention to fund and co-found an international environmental organization modeled on the Club of Rome. Robert had been UN Assistant Secretary General when I met him, and was one of the first people to really appreciate my work, making a wonderful cover comment for my first published book, Gaia, and putting it into the UN bookstore. We've been dear friends ever since.

At the very last minute before coming to Japan — all air tickets in hand — Robert had received a phone call warning him there might be something 'off' about this businessman, Hogen Fukunaga, our Japanese host; that he should be careful with his reputation. As it proved impossible to reach and stop two other prominent colleagues of Robert's already flying to the meeting from Europe by the Asian route, Elaine and I had offered to go to Japan to check things out and head them off by passing on this warning as soon as they arrive.

And so, Elaine and I find ourselves in the enormous Tokyo Dome stadium, a chorus of 120 voices on stage belting out Beethoven's "Ode to Joy" as *he* — Hogen Fukunaga — appears in the limelight. He cuts a distinguished and imposing figure with his more than six-foot height, white hair, matching white western-style suit, shirt, tie, and even white shoes, a diamond tie clip sparkling on his chest. With the chorus behind him, children in white carry him flowers and his closest followers, also in white, kneel at his feet on stage beneath an enormous screen showing him in close-up; four other screens almost as large are spaced around the stadium.

It seems our wealthy environmentalist businessman is some kind of charismatic cult leader. I count five cameras on Hollywood- style dollies, tracks, and cherry pickers, keeping him on screen from all angles as he paces back and forth giving his lecture ... or is he haranguing his devotees? Periodically he begins chanting and then hyperventilating into the microphone for disconcertingly lengthy interludes during which our bones rattle with his breath through what must be the largest sound system in the world. The entire audience's chests are heaving with him as instructed, apparently going obediently into trance as they chant.

When it is my turn to climb reluctantly on stage and speak into a sea of klieg lights screening the audience from me, I have to limit myself to about three words at a time to let my voice bounce around the vast dome without talking over my words any more than is unavoidable. Needless to say, I make my talk as brief and innocuous as I can get away with, as does Elaine with hers. What a bizarre contrast to our earlier experience in the surrounding silence and perfect acoustics of the Kamakura Buddha.

I call Robert as soon as we are back in the hotel to explain why it is a good thing he did not come and that he ought to try to stop the sale of the book he wrote with Fukunaga as it is already advertised for sale on billboards pointed out to us in Tokyo streets.

Robert is not aware that it has already been published. Elaine and I are further shocked next day, as we are taken to a lavish temple Fukunaga has built to himself as a world savior, his imposing statue there in line with Christ Jesus and the Buddha, and a high tech 'heavenly' domed temple where devotees buy glittering faux-gold stakes to assure their place in heaven.

Before we leave, as gracefully as possible, I have a conversation with him on issues related to his proclaimed PhD in environmental science, and surmise it is a complete fake, granted by some questionable online 'university' to which a devotee most likely wrote and sent in whatever work might have been required.

Fukunaga was arrested within a few years after this encounter with him, eventually sentenced to twelve years in prison for his massive and predatory fraud, bilking people by the thousands for indoctrinations presented as cures for disease and for those special places in heaven. My adventure into his lair made me more aware of how easily people's beliefs can be manipulated — how we humans can deceive ourselves, as well as others.

Fukunaga is not the first or last charismatic cult leader to convince himself he is saving the world; his followers were adults who gave their money willingly, believing he was giving them something to live for that they did not find elsewhere. Charismatic leaders don't need to use coercion. So, where does responsibility lie — only with them? — or also with the followers who enable them?

We live in a world where taking advantage of opportunities is promoted as a positive way of life even if it often entails taking advantage of our fellow humans.[75] We are told it is human nature to get what you can however you can get it; we are conditioned socially to admire those that have climbed their way to the top of the heap, and we measure success in money and the glamorous lifestyles it buys. We keep the aspiration game going by telling ourselves that in a democracy *anyone* can be president, or head of a lucrative enterprise, or a highly paid pop star, or whatever else we desire to be, never considering how very few 'anyones' can actually make it to the top.

Japan has been plagued by cults but is hardly unique in giving rise to them. Fukunaga found his way to the top of his own mountain; then fell off it. He is just one more example of how the lust for power plays out when traditional power hierarchies are toppled and replaced by open competition. In the Darwinian king-of-the-hill game we call capitalist democracy, anyone may be able to reach the top, but to suggest that everyone can is certainly misleading.

Cultural creativity

In the year 2000, almost a decade since my return from what I have come to call my midlife retirement in Greece, Paul Ray and Sherry Anderson call it something else in their book *The Cultural Creatives: How 50 Million People are changing the World*. In the section written from their extensive interview with me, they call my Greek years "an ancient rite of passage with demarcated stages," which they delineate as my Separation, In Between, Return, and Integration, in the classic manner of cultural transformation stories, especially the many Hero's Journey tales, which Joseph Campbell brought to such wide attention.

At first embarrassed by seeing my Greek 'retirement' years dignified this way undeservedly, I eventually come to see its validity. Indeed, I had separated myself from my possessions, gone into a situation where I had neither recognized degrees nor even language, cooked from scratch and washed clothes by hand, reinvented myself, so to speak, 'from scratch.' I had pondered Nature and the human condition endlessly and taught myself to see the patterns of my world in evolution. When I returned, my best male friend, a long tenured professor at MIT, admonished me, albeit admiringly, "How dare you go off on a 13-year holiday on Greek islands and come back ahead of us who kept our noses to the academic grindstone?"

As Paul and Sherry quoted me:

> *The conclusion I'd reached was that we humans will have to learn very quickly to organize ourselves by the principles of living systems within the larger living system of our planet or go extinct.... A larger intelligent system surrounds us and works for us — call it by any name you choose — if we acknowledge and let it guide us, so I remain an open-minded seeker and a server at once. While I am not good at taking orders from humans, I accept the guidance of Spirit more than willingly, for life has never been better than under its auspices.*[76]

I *have* been able to make my 'big picture' view of living systems in evolution, along with my evolving spiritual beliefs, relevant to so many areas of human life that I get opportunities to speak in a very wide variety of venues around the US and by now on all seven continents — from global UN conferences to Parliament of World Religions, from MBA programs to corporate training programs, from conferences on business and consciousness to those on science and consciousness, from futurist organizations to government agencies, environmental groups, indigenous and community assemblies, yoga teacher training ashrams, the entertainment industry, religious leadership conventions, churches, university and community lecture series.

Even when I'm not called by bookings, my accumulated air miles get me to exotic places of my choice for personal research and writing retreats — one in Bali, one in Tuscany, another in Hawai'i and one locally in a deep redwood forest right near where I live in California.

Travels are a wonderful way to pursue my passion to understand 'How Everything Is' — people, planet, and cosmos. Being in service to the wellbeing of people and planet is, as always, the passionate desire driving me, so I must live life in ways that fulfill that desire and always stay open to new ideas and points of view. I'm aware that I devote far more energy to my global human family in my hopes for its evolution into mature cooperation, than I do to my own children and grandchildren — hoping they will one day understand and forgive me.

I've been privileged to glimpse some of the different ways life plays out in different languages and cultures with different belief systems. Gradually, I have come to see how much my life's path has anticipated what we must all now do, individually and as whole cultures — give up the idea that some single human authority, whether religious, secular, or scientific, can tell us the absolute truth about human nature, about the universe at large and our role in it.

Obviously, that is not a new idea. Anthropologist Franz Boas introduced the concept of 'cultural relativism' to the world early in the 20th century and my children's 'Boomer' generation has taken it up as a central view, but somewhat blindly from my perspective. Clearly, it was important to recognize the right of every culture to determine their own beliefs, values, and practices, but a recognition of and respect for cultural diversity did not free us from evaluating — in every culture including our own — what works toward the wellbeing of all and what does not.

Humanity is global now; all of us affecting each other, learning from each other, or imposing our values on each other. Values are primary; the very foundations of culture, and if we are to form a true human family, our best human values must be shared globally, across cultures, without homogenizing our precious diversity. We could all share values of peaceful cooperation, caring, mutual respect, and more.

Science set itself the goal of finding how things *really* are by looking outward into our material world, only to find that world dissolving into pure energy at its very foundations; every religion, its 'truths' coming through inner revelations, has found itself at odds with other religions in which the revelations differed. If the goal of discovering or determining a single Reality has not been reached, does it mean there *is* no ultimate Reality for us all to discover?

Our own multi-cultural society is often deeply divided by intolerance. The Dalai Lama has suggested that the only religion we truly need is Kindness — everyone treating everyone else with kindness, he suggests, would go a long way toward harmonizing our lives into a peaceful global family. Kindness as an overarching value-based *practice* would get us out of the fallacy of defining cultural relativity as condoning all cultural beliefs and practices.

Kauri Tree: New Zealand

The Kauri is a very ancient tree in *Aotearoa*, the Land of the Long White Cloud that we call New Zealand. It has a thick, grey-barked trunk and a scraggly top that makes me imagine prehistoric reptiles stomping about among the Kauri trees. My Maori friend Tim and I visit the oldest living Kauri — around 2,000 years old — on our way north to Spirit Bay, the northernmost point of New Zealand where the native Maori do send-off funeral ceremonies for departing spirits.

After a while, we stop to visit the Kauri Museum, which has been built around the upright trunk of a Kauri tree that was buried beneath the last ice age's glaciers some 50,000 years ago by carbon dating, when it was about 1,000 years old. The blackened 140-ton tree trunk had been hauled out of its muddy grave and a floor to ceiling height piece of it was set upright as the centerpiece of the museum, with a stairway to the second floor carved out inside it.

I have been feeling drained all day, by the very demanding speaking schedule I've been on in Australia and continued now in New Zealand — happy to relax in the car on this beautiful drive, but feeling as if my chakras are not even limping in their usual gyrations. As I climb the steps inside the ancient dead Kauri tree, its wood core still its original rose-beige in color around me, tears begin welling up in my eyes as a sudden rush of energy pours through me. Suddenly, all my chakras seem to be whirling at high speed. I'm encompassed or thrillingly possessed by some great being with a massive, palpable spirit. I paste myself against the warm interior wall, not wanting to let go at the top of the stairway. My tears flow in pure joy.

When I walk out into this upstairs hall of the museum, I see it sells all sorts of tourist artifacts made from this precious Kauri's wood. This seems sacrilegious to me. But just as that negative thought forms in my mind, I feel the tree spirit joyously telling me this is its way of spreading itself around the world! So, I buy soap holders and egg cups for myself and to send to Puma and other scattered friends to help with its mission. I am feeling completely alive and very happy.

Outside the museum, this day before Easter is as gray as the past few days have been. Aware that I have only two more days before leaving Aotearoa, I express my wish to see some blue sky and one of its fabled rainbows before departing. No such luck as we continue our journey up to Spirit Bay beach, where many New Zealanders are camping for Easter weekend, though almost none are walking the long curving sand beach. Tim explains that most of them are huddled in their tents, drinking beer, playing cards, and cussing the weather. I wondered if their negative energy is preventing the sun from coming out. Nevertheless, our beach walk in yellow rain suits is glorious, as I am still on my 'Kauri high' walking this snowy white sand, watching glassy breakers along the sweeping curve, with a huge black stone promontory overlooking us and the sea.

Away from the beach of sullen campers, we make our way to the home of a lovely elderly couple, friends of Tim who are seafarers with interesting tales to tell. The next day, as we drive back towards Auckland, the still pervasive gray clouds suddenly lift along the horizon and a gorgeous wide rainbow forms before our eyes. As I exclaim in joy at seeing clear sky *and* the rainbow I wished for before leaving Aotearoa, Tim calls my attention to the fact that we are that very minute passing the Kauri Museum on the opposite side of the road! I am stunned, wondering at the precision timing required to have us see the rainbow at this very moment, so we'd know where the gift comes from. I beam my gratitude to the great Kauri spirit. Within minutes, we are driving straight into a huge double rainbow arc, as if into an even more magical world.

Soon, we arrive to take up the beautiful gift of another overnight in a very special Bed & Breakfast, still being built by friends of Tim's who treat us to an unusually lovely dinner as well. Their large modern Victorian house, with fireplaces in all the guestrooms, overlooks the sea from on high. I am given the one room they have finished, and the attention to the smallest details of comfort is superb — electrical converter, Q-tips in the bathroom, fresh ivy draped along the window sills, roses picked from the garden. Best of all, however, is the bed — a big four-poster made of Kauri wood! So, I go off to dreamland, again encased in the loving arms of a Kauri tree!

Next day, I fly home and, no sooner than I arrive back in California, tree messages come to me. An article in my piled-up mail is about Julia Butterfly, a 24-year-old woman who camped 180 feet up in the arms of a redwood tree she calls Luna continually for two entire years to save it from logging; then a neighbor I have not really spoken to before asks me to defend a large old tree in our neighborhood, threatened with cutting down by developers.

I sit in City Hall through the entire evening hearing, from 7:00 PM to midnight, when I finally have the opportunity to speak on my tree's behalf. I'm the only person who has stayed long enough to defend the tree, as the few others we recruited gave up and left earlier. I try to get attention by arguing that our city officially protects its heritage trees; I bring forth evidence from a builder friend that the tree's roots are not threatening a stone wall as is claimed; I feel like a Luna-tic pointing out that we don't cut down our grandmothers for littering, another crime the tree has been accused of. Nothing seems to be moving the few people still listening.

The Planning Commission decides the developer should redesign the proposed building to make it smaller, but this decision is independent of the one on the tree and another hearing is scheduled to discuss the tree further. I am sure the Kauri tree will help me see this through to a good result.

I think about recruiting a young person to sit in the tree like Julia Butterfly. After my New Zealand experience, I really understand why she became so enamored of her tree that she did not want to come down. So, I contact her and find she will actually be nearby very soon and is willing to come see my tree. Before the next hearing, she is indeed here with me, at my tree and praying for it, yet after two more city hall meetings, the tree is sentenced to death. I continue to pray fervently to the Kauri spirit. Time passes, weeks go by, then months ... and the tree is not cut. I hear that somehow the developers decided to move their project elsewhere. Somehow the tree lives. I do not ask questions. I don't have to. I smile up at my beloved tree and thank Julia for her love and prayers, along with the Kauri spirit, of course.

Living systems in digital and business worlds

One of my most interesting speaking venues is the Digital Earth Society's first conference in the US, on the University of California's Berkeley campus, where my education in global economics and my political activism began so many years ago. The DES came out of Al Gore's dream of collecting all the data we have about our planet Earth in a single computer and finding ways to make it freely accessible to the public. Though he began it with NASA, the Clinton administration crisis followed before it was well developed, and the project was moved to Japan, where the chosen computer is housed, as well as to China, to Europe, and to New Zealand for its conferences, and now at last to the US.

To my delight, my talk is sandwiched between those of my astronaut friend Ed Mitchell and a founder of Google Earth, which is the best public interface the project has developed. Another fascinating presenter is graphical user interface pioneer and inventor of the mouse, nonagenarian Doug Engelbart, who gives me a 3D mouse inscribed "love, Doug" in silver ink. When I ask him. "Now that you've invented the wireless mouse, what will you invent next?" He replies with a coy smile, "I suppose the mouse-less wire."

In my love of all the new technology, I am a *WIRED* magazine subscriber, even winning a contest to get my portrait onto a special edition of its cover. Watching the wildly growing Internet, I have come to see it as the largest self-organizing living system on the planet. The prescient authors of the *Cluetrain Manifesto* recognize its vital importance to the business world, though they see it in terms of reforming capitalism in favor of consumers, unable to predict the ways in which the streaming network of information highways and byways will end up favoring the building of ever bigger and more exploitative enterprises.

Back in Santa Barbara, after my northern intermission years, I again revel in its Spanish architecture of white buildings, arches, red- tiled roofs, and the profusion of flowering trees and shrubs, those very features ever reminding me of my beloved MidEarth Sea. It's great to be in a familiar place again — the first I ever left and then returned to. At least one friend who was not here before has moved here himself. Robert Mueller, the former UN Assistant Secretary General who had called me a visionary prophet, and who had almost miraculously found me in Cusco, Peru while I lived there, and who had sent me to Japan on that ill-fated mission that nevertheless proved to be a fascinating adventure, has by now married Barbara Gaughen, the Santa Barbara friend who gave me the best birthday party I ever had, my 60th. Now they are living on the outskirts of Santa Barbara in easy reach.

Speaking at conference right in Santa Barbara, I meet Rinaldo Brutoco, president of the World Business Academy founded by Bill

Harman and devoted to progressive business practices. Rinaldo feels immediately familiar, karmically reconnected like a re-found brother; I know right away we will be lifelong friends in our mutual interest of changing the economy toward a world that works for all of us and our Earth. He does not live far from Santa Barbara, and we meet often enough, especially in a small Italian restaurant called Via Maestro that is a little European cultural island happily reminding me of my beloved MidEarth Sea years.

After the WBA's journal publishes several of my articles on the Biology of Business, Rinaldo creates a Chair in Living Economies in my name within the WBA. And before long, he and his wife Lalla buy a gorgeous home with a beautiful view, a pool, a guest house, and a huge, canopied terrace for big meetings and parties. It will be a home away from home wherever I land myself in the future.

Shortly before the next phase of my life begins, in 2006, I'm invited to a truly extraordinary event called *Dropping Knowledge*, in Berlin — intentionally held in a main square where books had been burned during the Nazi regime. The organizers had spent two years traversing the world to discover the leading questions people have on any theme of global significance. Then *"112 international artists, philosophers, scientists and human rights activists were invited to simultaneously answer 100 selected questions, recorded by 112 cameras and microphones"*[77] and I was chosen as one of them. Moderators were Hafsat Abiola, daughter of assassinated president of Nigeria, who became a dear friend, actor Willem Defoe, and Bianca Jagger.

We sat around a huge circle of tables, each of us talking straight into a TV camera in our own language, answering each question in turn, in 3 minutes each, from morning to late afternoon, a grueling exercise with just a lunch break. That was followed by a fabulous evening feast inside an abandoned underground train station, at another much smaller circle of tables, so that we sat opposite each other and got to know at least some of the others, as we also had at the lunch break. It was, to say the least, one of the most memorable events ever. The results were published online for many years.

Heading for a Hot Age ... and to Barcelona

I'm writing a lot about global warming, which has only now, in the mid 'Aughts' — as this first decade of the new millennium has been dubbed — gotten the attention of the mainstream press. Jim Lovelock predicted it during our '80s dialogues in Greece and England; now the cooperative efforts of scientists all over Earth are finally amassing the evidence and Al Gore's film and lectures on *An Inconvenient Truth* are circling the globe. In my slideshow talks, I show an astronaut's view of the moon while standing on it, a spinning Earth inserted in the moon's black sky, with the caption: "Watching Earth from the moon, the only evidence of human life over time is expanding deserts."

I see no way of stopping the positive feedback loop: The hotter it gets, the more ice melts; the more ice melts, the hotter it gets. A few technological efforts to stop the process have bombed: iron filings spread over the sea to reflect back heat only kill unsuspecting and innocent plankton; particles released from airplanes over land for the same purpose settle to ground and kill soil microbes.

There are a few other wild schemes of covering polar ice with black blankets or making mylar umbrellas to shoot into space over Earth, but I have become convinced that adaptation is our only option. Thus, I begin researching how people lived well in deserts over thousands of years, and decide to do some research in Morocco, where I know there must be great examples of low-tech solutions that make life comfortable in extreme heat.

Flights to Africa are prohibitive if I have to get there on my own, and though I've been to South Africa twice on invitations, there are no more in sight. Just as I'm checking online for ways to get from Europe to Morocco — I have enough frequent flyer miles to get to anywhere in Europe — someone I don't know contacts me on Skype from southern Spain and asks me for an interview on her international radio show. Leaping on this synchronicity, I ask her whether one can get to Morocco from Spain by ferry and when she says, "Easily, I see Morocco now from my window; come visit me here," I decide instantly to take her up on the invitation.

Thus, I soon find myself once again on a boat traversing a bit of my MidEarth Sea. Morocco's *medinas* — the remainders of its ancient cities — are crammed with mazes of houses hidden behind tall walls flanking streets so narrow the sun only shines down into them for a few minutes a day. They clearly mimic the way narrow mountain ravines preserve their cool depths. The larger houses were built *rhyad* style, centered by inner courtyard atriums with plants and fountains, each story's rooms looking down to them, as well as up to the sky in this architectural design so many contemporary worldwide hotel chains have now copied. When they were first built, wet pads were housed in louvred towers at the top, where breezes blew across them so that cool air dropped down the atrium as rising hot air was allowed to escape through high outer wall clearstory windows.

Long afternoon siestas and flowing white clothing add to the heat-beating desert-dweller solutions, and beneath their cities huge reservoirs collected annual flash flood waters, recycling them through atrium and garden fountains. None of these solutions required modern technology; we forget so easily that humans worked out comfort long ago in countless ways appropriate to their climates.

Back in Spain for the remainder of my visit — a week as a guest in a gorgeous mountain villa owned by a friend of my hostess — I am overcome with the desire to live again by this great MidEarth Sea and decide, sight unseen, on Barcelona as my new destination. It lies on the sea and is convenient to all Europe, so I'll be much closer to venues in Amsterdam, London, and Paris, where I have so many connections. And as I am also a great lover of all things Art Nouveau, such as the Spanish architectural version of it, called *Modernista*, I can immerse myself in that glorious city of Gaudi and other wonderful artists who have left it this unique legacy.

It is also a feeling of impending crisis in the US driving me back to Europe. Hurricane Katrina has demolished New Orleans, and during the ensuing horrors, Senator Ted Kennedy writes a newspaper article headed "Jack-booted Fascism Comes to America." His reference is to the Blackwater mercenaries sent to Louisiana from their Mid-East deployments to 'keep peace,' and permitted to shoot while local police could not. I was recognizing creeping fascism myself and was talking from stage podiums about how we will see it with a 'friendly face' that makes it hard to recognize. The only responses I get are warnings to keep my mouth shut; that there are agents watching me in my audiences. I'm over seventy now and feel too old for a revisit to 1960s and '70s activism; that my energies would be better used in writing and speaking of our human evolution from hostilities to harmonies.

With the new benefit of Google searching and Google Earth maps, I can now arrange my move to Barcelona without having been there, all from my desk in Santa Barbara. Apartment hunting by location, choosing best options, making appointments, booking my flights and a convenient hotel, mapping my way from airport to address through street views, all of this a breeze! The almost thirty years since I'd gone off to Greece has seen an avalanche of new technology. Divesting myself of most possessions once more and packing up yet again has no technology to make it easier but does again give me that sense of being lighter and freer.

Barcelona does not disappoint! The day after my arrival, I sign the lease on a beautiful, online-previewed apartment (flat, in Europe). It is completely refurbished and furnished; from it, I can walk along the broad tree-lined *Avenida Diagonal* that slashes across the otherwise grid-like city, passing dozens of Gaudi and other *modernista* buildings on the way to the central square near the waterfront. Green chattering parrots fly overhead, strutting along sidewalks and eating the flowers in a lovely nearby park; food is spectacular; people are sociable and the abundant sidewalk cafes are always full.

I can take buses easily everywhere and ride them rather than the underground subway to learn my way around where I can see the city layout. I easily get legal residency and even full health coverage on the basis of my Greek citizenship, all making me feel at home. The Spanish I picked up in Peru, rusty as it's gotten, serves me well; I'm delighted all around. My time is devoted to writing, long walks to explore this marvelous city, planning talks for my continuing international travels, and a wonderful new project coming to me from Japan, the far side of the world.

CHAPTER 13

Return to the MidEarth Sea

Shoji and the symposia

Still delighting in being back on the shores of my MidEarth Sea and still getting to know Barcelona, my international travels begin again. The first outside Europe and from Barcelona takes me back to Japan, where I am met and taken directly from the airport to a very lovely boutique hotel. It is early evening and dark outside as I sit up to my neck in the silky hot spring water of a deep wooden tub, looking through plate glass at the stone lantern lighting my room's private garden. The aromatic oils in the warm, moist air surrounding me seem to come from the night jasmine flowering outside.

Wearing the attractive black-on-white print yukata robe and red obi provided for me by the hotel, I have dinner this evening in the suite of my host, Mr. Akio Shoji. Over the many courses of dinner, he explains the program of the obviously spectacular launch he has arranged in honor of the Japanese edition of my *EarthDance* book at his home base on the great northern island of Hokkaido, to which we fly tomorrow.

Mr. Shoji is a businessman dedicated to the mission of feeding the children of Japan the highest quality diet at the lowest possible price. I was prepared before the trip that his two huge organic farms on Hokkaido supply their produce directly to 300 restaurants, which he franchised under the name *Bikkuri Donki* — Donkey Surprise — all family friendly, decorated like old barns, and filled from morning to night as a hugely popular alternative to McDonalds. All 300 franchise holders and their spouses are being flown to Hokkaido for my book launch, along with two university professors of ecology and earth science who will accompany me as speakers at the event.

Before flying me to his Hokkaido home base near Sapporo, we stop in Osaka for a quick tour of a magnificent temple and monastery complex. Then, in Sapporo, we tour his farms, and I am blown away by all I see, including living green-roofed buildings and sculptures amidst vast fields of great plant diversity, fields of medicinal and ornamental plants, as well as food crops, and a most spectacular tomato experiment. For the third year, a single hydroponically grown tomato plant, organically nurtured, has been trained upward and outward over chicken wire topping a steel frame. Thus, the entire patio 'ceiling' is a dense overhead carpet of shining red fruits eased through the wire at just past blossom stage, backed by the greenery of this enormous vine tree. Each year, more tomatoes are harvested and this year's record number is already over 10,000![78]

Shoji-san, as he is widely known, and his lovely wife, who makes a clear tomato wine and jellies from some of the tomato harvest, have a beautiful home on the farm, filled with furniture and décor from around the world, as well as a large guest house in a nearby forest. The farm also houses an art gallery as the Shojis support Japanese artists. School children are bussed to the farms as teaching centers where they learn how their food is grown, how all the chopsticks from all the restaurants are recycled to make charcoal fertilizer and how biogas is made from plant wastes to run the farm machinery. In one teaching room, a glass wall permits them to watch cows being milked in the adjacent barn, after they come in from their green pasture. Their milk is made into puddings, yoghurt drinks, and ice creams that Japanese children can enjoy even though most are unable to digest plain milk.

My book launch is spectacular. Shoji-san proves to be a jazz drummer and composer who has created two new pieces in my honor, played by his jazz orchestra on a stage exquisitely decorated with huge bouquets and strings of mini-lights inside dried orange Japanese lantern flowers. All the performances are duplicated on a giant screen. My previously submitted slideshow has been flawlessly translated into Japanese without altering my compositions or the font colors I matched to my nature photos. Truly a feat! After the program, everyone is invited to a reception room filled with huge tables laden in a profusion of artistically arrayed delicacies.

The following day, I am taken to Shoji-san's forest guest house for media interviews and a gala dinner. The house is an enormous three-story Rocky Mountain log cabin he commissioned to be built in the exact style by a Colorado architect, with all building materials including a center beam pine tree and rocks for a huge fireplace shipped from the US along with all the furnishings from four-poster canopied beds and bathroom fittings to couches, banquet tables, Indian rugs, drums, and other artworks. Staggering to contemplate.

Sitting together in this spectacular guest house after several media interviews, Shoji-san asks me what else I would like to do besides writing books and speaking. None of my ideas about films and other productions excite him until I mention wanting to hold international symposia on the foundations of science to track the ongoing scientific paradigm shift. As he is clearly interested, I explain how the concept of shifting paradigms was introduced by Thomas Kuhn in his 1962 book, *The Structure of Scientific Revolutions*, which became a classic.

I explain paradigm shifting as the change in assumptions about the universe studied by science and *how* it can be studied — that such a revolutionary shift, initiated by highly respected quantum physicists half a century before Kuhn wrote, is making progress now but needs clear documentation to make it more effective. The more I explain, the more he lights up with excitement. When I tell him I tried unsuccessfully to get the president of India — Abdul Kalam, a nuclear physicist — to host such a symposium of paradigm shifting scientists from around the world, Shoji-san responds, *"Then I would like to do it here in Japan."* And so, it came to be.

As we plan the symposium in Hokkaido, including the flights of my chosen participants around the world, I continue enjoying Barcelona on the MidEarth Sea. Only a few days before I am scheduled to fly to Japan for the actual event, Shoji's assistant Elena, who handles all logistics, notifies me that their company CFO is flying to Barcelona to meet with me in advance of the symposium. She asks me to recommend a hotel convenient for me and to meet him there as soon as he arrives as he will be leaving again the following morning. She has already booked an interpreter in Barcelona.

Having no experience with the Japanese world of business, I am caught completely off guard when this senior official from Mr. Shoji's company tells me that my symposium is costing far too much money. As it was Mr. Shoji's decision to house and host it so lavishly — in a splendid hotel overlooking a World Heritage Site lake where the G-7 heads of state have just met — and to fly all my chosen participants from around the world business class, I am hardly at fault. And I cannot help but wonder why this CFO has now used even more funds to come see *me* on the other side of the world at this late hour. Of course, I do not ask him this, but simply listen politely and compassionately as he explains repeatedly, with many bows, that I am being treated like family in this sharing of confidential company matters because of my excellent relationship with his boss. All I can do is to assure him that I will do my best to solve this problem, having no idea how I will do so.

In Hokkaido, as intended, the symposium participants gather to formally document the paradigm shift. My participants are all self-proclaimed paradigm shifters, sampled from around the world: PhD scientists who have changed their fundamental assumptions from those they had been taught to those of the new paradigm they have adopted. The first task assigned the morning after our gala welcome banquet, with Mr. Shoji's jazz ensemble playing for us afterwards, is to begin a dialogue on, and to list, all the assumptions we had been taught when trained as scientists, making a parallel list of the assumptions with which we have replaced them.

When all assumptions are shared, we have lists adding up to hundreds of statements about the nature of the universe studied by science from the two opposing perspectives in our experience. The task of sorting through them to find those most essential and word them to everyone's satisfaction proves formidable, testifying to how little such matters have been brought to light.

Epiphany in Hokkaido

On the second day of the symposium, as I awake to first light, marveling at my panoramic view of the lake with its islands still shrouded in mist as in a huge Japanese painting, I suddenly feel the presence of Giordano Bruno in the room. Bruno, long a hero of mine, was burned at the stake in 1600 for his view of an omni-centric universe. At a time when science was still struggling with Copernicus' revolutionary solar-centered universe in place of the Earth-centered one the Church espoused, Bruno was already ahead of both conceptions.

Somehow Bruno, so very far ahead of his own time, is now with me in this symposium endeavor of moving science ahead in my own time. I am very deeply moved by his presence, my skin alert, tears in my eyes. Musing on all this paradigm shifting through the centuries, I suddenly have an epiphany of realization that paradigm shifting itself is a conquest model — that replacing one set of assumptions with another is like dismantling the stones of a Greek temple to build a Christian church in its place or replacing the governing system in a conquered or colonialized country with that of the conqueror.

In my version of evolution biology, I have identified the repeating maturation cycle in nature whereby species for billions of years have been maturing out of a 'Darwinian' competition mode in their youthful phase into a 'Kropotkinian'[79] cooperative/collaborative mode in their mature phase. This is not a species replacement model, as ecologists have seen it in their typology of ecosystems including highly competitive Type I and interdependent cooperative Type III, but a natural progression into cooperation — not a replacement matter, nor one of conquest, but a learning curve as the advantages of mature collaboration pay off. In my own words: "learning that it is cheaper to feed your enemies than to kill them." A matter of maturation: youth to maturity.

When our group convenes that morning, I explain my epiphany on paradigm shifts as conquests to my participants, proposing that we use our remaining days to continue clarification of the different foundational assumptions of the materialist Western science we have been taught *and* those of the consciousness-based Eastern science assumptions to which we have switched, but to see them not as paradigm shifting within a monolithic science, but as the basis for two valid and co-existing sciences.

I tell the group about my conversations with Willis Harman back in the 1980s when I lived in Greece, when he had asked whether we were talking about expanding the current paradigm or proposing a whole new one. I felt strongly then, as well as when co-writing our book, that it was about fundamental difference. But I have not seen till now that the two could function legitimately in parallel rather than one replacing the other!

After all, I argue, Western science has spawned amazing technologies *because* of its mechanistic universe and the primacy it thus gives to machine metaphors, and no other science could ever do that so well. But that very emphasis on mechanics leaves it lacking in understanding life itself, which is about organism, not mechanism, as I have shown to operate on completely different principles.

Organism is autopoietic, self-creating, while mechanism is allopoietic, literally, in Greek, other-created, therefore requiring an outside inventor or engineer to produce it. Organism has its own inherent rules of operation, while mechanism is given its rules from outside; organisms can self-repair, while mechanisms cannot, except insofar as they are programmed to do so.

Some of the technologies Western science has spawned — such as high-tech agriculture, plastics, and the overuse of fossil fuels — have actually become more life threatening than life enhancing. A science that understands life better might well hold such dangers in check through respectful scientific dialogue.

With this view of things, I propose, we could plan more symposia to uncover the foundations of other valid sciences, with a view to laying the basis for a Global Consortium of Sciences. If religions can respect each other in Parliaments of World Religions, why could science not do something similar?

We are now, after all, a globalized human world, so surely a Global Consortium of Sciences in which there is dialogue to provide mutual fertilization, as well as 'checks & balances,' might solve our most serious global problems. Different sciences could be taught side by side in the same universities in order to foster such dialogues among them up close, thus generating a new kind of richness in global science.

My fellow scientists agree and one of them, an Islamic scientist from Malaysia with his own institute at the University of Malaya, offers to host the next symposium in Kuala Lumpur the following year to focus on Islamic science. Shoji-san is delighted and will be there; I know he will still contribute to my support as co-organizer and feel great relief at having a solution with which to alleviate the CFO's concerns about the expense of a continuing venture. Before leaving Hokkaido, Shoji-san and I talk about other kinds of plans; he especially wants me to help him develop children's education programs, which I would do happily — feeding their minds as he feeds their bodies.

Throughout the symposium, I catch Mr. CFO lurking about with his laptop in hand, though he never speaks to any of us, not even his boss. I ask Shoji-san for a meeting with both of them but get no response. Only after the symposium is over — after a special tour of the farms with a lavish outdoor lunch at the Shojis' home and a side trip to see a special performance by an indigenous family theater group — do I find myself in the car taking me back to the airport with both Shoji-san and his CFO as my escorts!

Mr. CFO is in the front seat with the driver while Shoji-san sits with me in back; thus, they are never face to face and do not address each other. This leaves me as the unskilled, challenged 'diplomat' wracking my brain on how to lower the costs of an event now completed. All I can offer is a serious cut to my own retainer henceforth. It is only after this experience that I learn how Japanese business culture works; that no employee, however high his rank, can challenge his boss.

Kuala Lumpur without Shoji-san

The symposium in Kuala Lumpur draws some thirty participants, scientists, and philosophers of science drawn from various parts of the

Islamic world. It takes a lot of explaining to get them, once assembled, to understand the task of writing out the fundamental assumptions of their science, but the results, once they get into the swing, are truly rewarding.

Islamic science, as it turns out, is deeply rooted in the concept of a living universe with a mandate from its creator, Allah, to study nature from that perspective. That means we now have three sciences studying three fundamentally different universes: a material universe, a conscious universe, and a living universe.

I point out to the Islamic scientists that the science now taught in their universities, in the failure to understand that science is not monolithic, is a Western science, resting on a foundation that is actually a particular worldview disguised as a set of assumptions declared to be universally true. This science will therefore not give Islamic science appropriate recognition or credentials, but Islamic universities could nevertheless teach both sciences side by side, comparing and contrasting them; fostering collaboration between the two.

I also suggest they do something Western science has *not* done to bolster their own Islamic science's stature: develop a real science of economics through the study of nature's living economies. Western science has no science of economics, much less one rooted in nature. Imagine just solving the glaring matter of failure to recycle everything produced by humans that is not consumed, as would a science of economics based on nature's living systems.

The only thing marring my true pleasure with how this symposium unfolded, is the tragic news that Shoji-san suffered a brain hemorrhage en route to Kuala Lumpur and has been taken back to Japan for immediate surgery. After the symposium, I learn from Elena that he fell into a coma after the surgery. My ongoing requests for updates are met again and again with the same report, that his condition remains the same; that he makes no responses whatsoever. I am devastated.

This goes on for 18 long months, at the end of which I receive notice that he has passed away. It is shattering news. He has come to be a treasured friend, as well as a mentor, patron, and brilliant colleague in service to a better world, spectacularly successful in so many ways. I have so looked forward to working more with this amazing renaissance man: highly successful in business, a deep philosopher, practical ecologist, creative musician, generous philanthropist, and visionary educator, all with such great heart.

Mallorca goes green

One of the first people I met after moving from Barcelona to Mallorca is Kerstin, a Swedish artist who has lived in the area for most of her adult life and spent many years restoring and rebuilding a historic olive press farm — *finca* — high above Soller, the nearest large town of around twenty thousand people where I do my supermarket and hardware shopping. Still not owning or driving a car since moving to Greece three decades before coming to Spain, I ride the bus along a breathtakingly beautiful and very curvy coastal mountain road, ever impressed by the patient calm of the bus drivers, utterly unlike the hot-tempered drivers in Greece who would have been disastrous on these roads.

Kerstin is a superb artist, not only in her unique painting and collage technique, but as a chef, and as the designer of her house restoration and architectural additions. She has furnished over a dozen uniquely decorated guest rooms, bathrooms, and an immense living/meeting room in the main part of the rambling house, which she rents out to groups as a retreat center.

In her own wing, the former stables, she has installed a gothic-arched passageway flanked by two 'wing' openings, all lit by a skylight that makes the configuration look like a huge abstract white angel standing between her very large kitchen and her living room. In the middle of the kitchen, a big marble-topped island is always piled high with her fresh garden produce arranged artistically in brief glory before their transformation into her culinary creations.

To my great delight, I manage to make one of the groups who book in at Kerstin's a yoga retreat led by my own dear US friend Rama Vernon, possibly the best yoga teacher in the world. Rama, a founder of *The Yoga Journal*, brought a number of India's gurus to the US where some of them established ashrams with her help. She is an amazing conflict resolution teacher and diplomat who led over forty citizen diplomacy groups to Moscow before and during Gorbachev's late '80s Perestroika years. To have Rama and her darling daughter Mira, whom I've known all her life and who is now an Ayurvedic chef, together in the unrivaled beauty of that glorious mountain setting overlooking the MidEarth Sea is an unforgettable joy.

Kerstin's dinner parties are also unforgettable, ranging from the most elegant formal receptions in the great stone, olive press room with its vast high ceiling and walk-in fireplace to long-table feasts set up in the garden, or indoors at Christmas, for friends and family, with endless Swedish toasting at each successive course.

It is her founding of Mallorca Goes Green that actually led me to Kerstin, and she in turn connected me with Guillem Ferrer, Mallorca's most active native crusader on all green issues. Together, they bring the most amazing people, including Vandana Shiva, India's best green crusader whom I've known for years, Ross and Hildur Jackson, founder/funders of the Global Ecovillage Network, and Satish Kumar, Schumacher College founder, here to Mallorca for annual events. I had first met Satish, born the same year as I was, on an island retreat in Greece where we were both speakers, and I taught a few short courses at his college. Walking with him at the head of a symbolic pilgrimage we green folks had organized on Mallorca was a real treat.

Paradise on Mallorca

Halfway through my first year in Spain, my Paris friend, Jeanne, had come to visit me in Barcelona and together we hopped the twenty-minute flight over to the island of Mallorca to visit mutual friends there for a few days. Robin and Cody Johnson are international conference organizers who'd had me speak at their Bath, England conference a few years earlier, and had moved from the US to the superbly picturesque little village of Deia, nestled below high limestone cliffs in the coastal Mallorca mountains, with spectacular views of the sea below and its own private beach cove — the *Cala* — down a long steeply winding road through long-needled pines and olive groves.

Deia achieved fame worldwide as the home of British poet Robert Graves, known especially for his compendium of Greek mythology, his books *White Goddess* and *I Claudius*, the latter morphing into a popular TV series. Graves raised his children here and loving its wildness, got the town council to rule against the Cala from being excavated to bring yachts into its sweet natural harbor, which still boasts only two hippy-style, '50s restaurants as human additions. He also got a town ordinance passed to outlaw all modern architecture, thus preserving a village that looks like a medieval movie set. Small wonder I fall in love with it myself and jump at a return to island life in my dear sea, however happy I've been in Barcelona.

So, when my year's lease is up, I relocate to Deia, renting a cozy two-story house and quickly adopting two abandoned tabby kittens I call Kusi and Kuri, collectively my Ku's. The house, though relatively new, is medieval style inside and out, as per the ordinance, its thick stone-faced walls beveled around large windows to let in much light, arched connecting passages inside, dark-beamed ceilings, fireplace, tiled floors, and staircase. I fill the large patio with plants and bring a few large ones inside as well, regarding them as friends like the Ku's.

Joining Robin's mat Pilates class — all women and taught by a world class ballerina two years older than I am — puts me quickly into her social circle as we have a long coffee gathering after each Saturday morning session. Within weeks of my arrival, a picture of us on a patio having our coffee appears in *The New York Times*, though we were not even aware of the photographer who shot the photo from the sidewalk below us. I soon learn why so many before me have found this little village of only 750 year-round residents a paradise retreat.

Deia has everything from picturesque roving sheep and donkeys in spectacular settings to very fashionable boutiques. A few self-sufficient farmers still make their own olive oil and wine, grow fruits and vegetables, nuts, meat, eggs, and shear sheep for wool that is spun and knitted or woven into clothing.

In contrast, yet harmonious, the village sports a Michelin restaurant and a five-star hotel. Andrew Lloyd Webber has a home here and Michael Douglas' castle is a very short ride down the coast; many from the London/LA music world come here, especially at New Year's, to sing and play with the local '50s music band that includes two of Grave's sons.

It was Richard Branson, with a German realtor partner, who turned two almost adjoining manor houses into the five-star hotel; Hollywood stars who stay there walk past my house on their way down to swim and lunch in the Cala.

All shopkeepers speak at least enough English to communicate easily, and the village is proud of its three languages: Castillano — as Spanish is called in Spain — Mallorquin, and English, the latter ruled island-wide as an official language taught equally with the other two in schools while I am living there. Mallorquin is a dialect of Catalan, as is Languedoc in southern France, not far to the north of Mallorca. And while my name is Isabel in Castillano, I'm delighted to find it is Elisabet, spelled my way, in Mallorquin!

But there are problems in in this idyllic paradise, too, and while my girlfriends here quickly discourage me from anything remotely bordering on lectures about scientific subjects or politics, my political side cannot resist some, to me, obvious opportunities to make change.

My boutique village has a so-called 'recycling center' that is an utterly disgraceful garbage heap overflowing its bins knee deep onto the floor of its enclosure right next to the public school. When people can no longer wade through the mess to get to the bins, they simply toss their trash outside it into the street right in front of my house.

Being new here, I write the most diplomatic article I can muster for the local news sheet, lauding my adopted village for its exquisite beauty, pointing out the importance of children learning how recycling is the very link that closes a vital economic loop, and describing my vision of the recycling center next to the school being as lovely as Deia's best boutique shop, perhaps with art works on its walls.

I make friends with the young man who is Chief of Police, his only assistant the parking enforcement lady, trying to recruit him to my cause, however skeptical he is. I talk with my neighbors about property values going down in this mess; they shrug their shoulders saying nothing changes in the village. I do research on the house-to-house collection in another village and find it costs less than collection from a center like ours, only to learn that our mayor is closely tied to the island garbage industry — if not mafia — that collects from centers including this one.

Indeed, nothing changes for quite some time, but I keep up my friendly lobbying and gradually the overflow into the street shrinks away as new bins are added. Then, suddenly, when I lose all hope of further improvement, builders arrive and in two weeks have everything cleaned up as they construct what I dub 'the castle wall' around the center, clearly at considerable expense to the Town Hall as it is beautifully stone-faced with a new drive-in door for the collecting trucks. People smile and thank me for my gentle but persistent influence.

One of the wonderful features of the village is its amphitheater, where all manner of festivals, exhibits, and performances are held almost year-round. Other festivals are staged down in the Cala, or around a huge annual bonfire in a mid-village parking lot, where great gnarled roots and twisted bodies of deceased olive trees burn slowly for several days and nights as people party around the fire with food, drink, and music. There is also a large indoor space when winter weather calls people inside for costume balls and concerts.

Such endless traditional festivities clearly bond the villagers as they have through the ages — something vital to living where everyone knows everyone else. A very tall natural pine on the lawn of the grand hotel towers over the village and is lit to its tip over the Christmas holidays;

spectacular fireworks are set off several times a year high in the sky and on one holiday — in true medieval style — on the ground, as well in blazing sprays and red-lit smoke around dragons and shrieking people in devil and bird head masks.

I continued to pursue my work in science via the second symposium in Kuala Lumpur and trips to speak on biological evolution and our human future in Brazil, Chile, New Zealand, Australia, Indonesia, and Africa, as well as in London, Amsterdam, Paris, Munich, Rome, Istanbul, and Oslo. The new wave of TED talks leads to two invitations to give them, one in Hamburg, Germany, the other in Marrakech, Morocco at Richard Branson's sister Vanessa's *Rhyad* hotel, gorgeous with its courtyards of trees, flowers, and fountains.

At home in Deia, I respond to an invitation to host a radio talk-show broadcast from New York City; the title we settle on is "The Oracle of Mallorca." That gives me the opportunity to interview writers and activists around the world who are close to my evolution of humanity cause and to play music of my choice for a far-flung audience.

My social life in Deia becomes increasingly political. I'm recruited to political activity as my young friend Lluis, who house-sits with my Ku's and plants when I travel, decides to become a mayoral candidate. His father was mayor in the past, though conservative, while Lluis is not. My voting rights come with my legal residency, and so Lluis puts me on his progressive party's *Lista*, the ten official party members from which the town council members in his party will be selected if he becomes mayor. I campaign for him through two mayoral elections four years apart, making lots of wonderful plans for Deia with him, should he win. While our efforts fail narrowly both times, Lluis and his supporters will continue to try beyond my sojourn in Deia and will eventually win, to my great delight. But that is still off in the future.

I also join a group of local artists pooling resources for models, hang a few drawings I produce in an exhibit at La Residencia, the Branson hotel, and do some jewelry making to revive that part of my early training. Having a good camera eye, I also revel in taking countless photos to capture scenery, events, and the faces and creatures that are hidden until you spot them in gnarly old olive trees, which are up to a thousand years old here!

Eventually, I even join the drama club, which, unlike my English-speaking Pilates 'club,' is entirely Mallorquin in language and thus a serious challenge. It is the only non-partisan activity in which a recent conservative mayor (not Lluis' father), who still runs things like a mafioso from behind the scenes, acts along with my younger would-be mayor, Lluis, who proves to be a great comic! Mallorquin is just enough like Castillano to make it very confusing and yet so different that I understand little of what our instructors are teaching and have to do a great deal of watching what others do in our various exercises to copy them as best I can.

Translating the plays for myself with help from Google translate is good linguistic exercise, as is learning my lines, which is fun as I've always picked up foreign language pronunciation easily. We perform comedies; my fellow village actors are superb and thus a joy to be among. We design our own costumes, construct and paint our sets, and stage our plays in the amphitheater.

One year, the town hall even comes up with enough funding to set up an amazing framework of rented theater curtains and lighting. In the play we put on during my last year on Mallorca, by then in my late seventies, I play a fat, naïve young blonde in heavily padded traditional Mallorquin dress, love-struck by an impossibly unfaithful pirate. Ah, theater!

Poison in paradise

In my last two years in Deia, I take up another campaign — to rid the village of its toxic Roundup spraying for weed control. What are considered weeds are to me just the lovely natural greenery of a rural village, and I regularly harvest the edible plants I'd learned to identify on Greek islands in the same MidEarth Sea. They are still my favorite veg, raw or boiled and covered in lemon juice and olive oil beaten creamy with a fork, now also going into my green smoothies as my modern conveniences include a blender. I missed such wild greens all my intervening years in America where it is hard to find even a bunch of dandelions in a farmer's market. Because of the Roundup spraying along the roadside, I have to go farther afield to find unpolluted ones, and I cringe watching children trailing their hands through the newly sprayed plants on the way to school.

Armed with lots of research articles I've found online, I write a petition and gather signatures, then get a German doctor friend I met in a retreat in southern France, and who lived in nearby Valldemosa when he was young, to come help me testify before the town councilors. Again, I'm told my campaign is futile as things do not change in Deia. Robert Graves was no doubt told the same thing, yet he got things done, and the recycling center's renewal is evidence of current transformation, so I persist once again.

As politics function in Deia, the mayor's vote makes the decision on issues, as *all* issues are seen and voted on as partisan, and the recent elections were so close that the six other members of the council are evenly split between the two parties. It is thus virtually impossible for anything ever to get done by our progressive opposition party — a microcosm of the macrocosm in Washington DC, where the Republicans are now committed to opposing anything that President Obama proposes on principle. I watched the first Obama election with German cousins in Hamburg, where the whole city flew American flags in celebration of the outcome; by now his second term is well underway.

I get my petition to ban Roundup translated into Mallorquin and read it aloud to the councilors and a sizeable group of villagers who turn up for the hearing, which is lengthy with arguments and deliberations. Our relatively new, but staunchly conservative, mayor — an attractive blonde who wears red heels with her tight jeans — knows me as a *Lista* member of her opposition party. But our arguments are powerful, and she has a son among the village school children. Monsanto's Roundup is thus banned permanently, literally at the stroke of her pen. People comment later that the meeting was the first peaceful cross-party dialogue they had ever witnessed in our Town Hall.

Before I leave Mallorca, I meet the grandson of famed Catalan artist Joan Miro who lives in his grandfather's house overlooking the sea. Almost as soon as we meet, he confesses his antisocial nature, yet he keeps talking and ends up greatly enjoying our conversation, so he invites me to speak at a Miro Foundation garden event, coordinated with Guillem Ferrer. After seeing my slide presentation beamed onto a large wall at the edge of the garden, he gives me an original Miro print in gratitude.

Thus, my years in Deia weave together the three main strands of my life: Science, Spirituality and Political Economy, as well as recovering the artist still in me.

From Istanbul to Oslo

In June of 2013, I am invited to speak in Istanbul at a posh annual event, called The Performance Theatre — known as TPT — and 'staged' by the Xyntéo (said *Zyn*téo) Foundation based in Oslo, Norway. My dream audience turns out to be the most senior people of many of the biggest multinational corporations in the world, along with a few other dignitaries, both Turkish and from elsewhere. Eager to be at my *very* best, I prepared hard for my talk, as usual making beautiful slides to illustrate it, only to be told shortly before the event that I will not have the half hour I was told, but only 15-20 minutes, so possibly even less than a TED talk!

The opening evening reception is dazzling, on a lovely 7-star hotel veranda overlooking the Bosporus, and so flies by too quickly. The morning of my talk, after I've cut out nearly half my beautiful slides, I get further notice that my talk will have to be cut down to *five* minutes! I cannot believe I've been flown to this TPT event, which feels to me like a once-in-a-lifetime opportunity to be heard where it really matters, only to be so crippled as a 'performer' in this 'theatre.' What am I to do but grin and bear it? I decide to scrap the slides altogether and just wing it, not knowing how I can cut them down any further.

Just before I am called to the podium, I flash on one other time when I had a dream audience and only *three* minutes to talk to them! It was in Washington DC during the first Clinton administration in the early '90s when I lived there. I had attended the meetings of the President's Commission on Sustainability with great interest and hope, and at the end of the last one, after a lengthy debate on whether the commission needed to include economics when its mandate was only concern with environmental issues, I was fortunate to be given just three minutes to address the Commission.

The debate had been heavily weighted against including economics, so I pointed out the etymology of the two words, *economy* and *ecology*: that both words come from the ancient Greek word for household: *oikos* (pronounced ee' kos, at least in modern Greek).

The word 'economy' (*oikos+nomos = oikonomia*) means the rule or governance of the household. The word 'ecology' (*oikos+logos = oikologia*) means the creative organization of the household. So, I asked the audience, *"How can we talk about only one of the most important aspects of running our human household without the other? The problem is not whether to integrate economy with ecology, but that we have separated them."*

I added my hope that they invite a child and a Native American grandmother to their future deliberations — the child to remind them for whom they were working; the grandmother to remind them of the need for wisdom, as well as consideration of future generations, preferably seven of them. That completed my three minutes.

Surely, then, I can say something meaningful to these high-ranking executives and board members in Istanbul with five whole minutes at my disposal. And so, I begin by thanking this audience for being true heroes in globalizing our economy through their creative, competitive initiatives, as that was a necessary evolutionary step for humanity. I invited them to shift gears now to become the heroic leaders of a sustainable future based on stabilizing the economy in peaceful cooperation. Apologizing for my field of evolution biology because it only provided economists and business leaders with the Darwinian story that guided them throughout the expansive industrial and globalizing phase, I offered new findings that could provide them with the guidance necessary to implement the next phase, which must now be created with extreme speed if humanity is to survive our current crises in good health.

With half my time used up, I follow this with my elevator pitch on how the mature cooperative phase of Nature's evolution cycle comes about and why we humans can apply its endlessly repeating lessons in order to develop mature living economies.

Apparently, I make a good enough impression to be invited back to next year's TPT. Past ones having been held in more than a dozen cities around the world, this next one will come back to its home base in Oslo. I am not scheduled to speak at all, because of a rotation policy, but they are paying my way to be present and to participate in their workshops, adding my thoughts wherever appropriate.

It is, as expected, another wonderful occasion, staged in the still quite new Oslo City Hall where the Nobel Peace Prize is awarded, and this time 17-year-old Malala Yousafzai, the Pakistani girl who had been shot by the Taliban for promoting girls' education, is the featured guest, as she is shortly to receive this year's Nobel prize in this same venue.

As it happens, on the closing day, I have had little opportunity to share my views, and my raised hand during the final plenary 'roving mic' dialogue has not gotten attention. Time is running out fast and I am frankly disappointed, and also annoyed with myself for that. So, I decide to go into complete surrender and simple presence. It is what it is.

Just as I relax into that state, the mic is suddenly thrust over my shoulder from behind me. I have no idea how it got there as I'd been tracking the mic people and had just seen that both of them were far from me. As I stand up in surprise, I make an instant silent prayer to whatever guidance is with me, asking for the right words to flow through me. I thank a few people for specific contributions, and then say, as I write it out immediately afterwards:

> *We all seem to agree there must be a new narrative. So, when Malala gets all of the world's children into school, what is the story they will learn there to help them build a new way of life for all humanity? The challenge I put out to you all is to create a new story for humanity to live by that is as fascinating and appealing as the adventurous Hero's Journey, the Darwinian economic expansion story we have lived by. How do we make the story of creating a cooperative and peaceful world as exciting and alluring as those wild adventures have been to us? To do that, I propose that the new narrative must somehow include the ecstasy of creating true community!*

This final session is closed immediately after my remarks by its moderator, the senior editor at *Fortune* magazine, then the Xyntéo Foundation's CEO ends the TPT, and Lord John Browne, TPT chairman and former CEO of British Petroleum (BP), makes the final closing remarks, addressing them to Crown Prince Haakon of Norway and all the attendees, ending with the words: *"... and I really liked Elisabet's concept of ecstatic community!"*

I can hardly believe my ears! Having had no formal role at this year's TPT; having given up even the hope of making a single comment to the whole group, I've ended up getting the final word, and through the lips of Lord Browne himself. I could not have gotten a better endorsement in this community!

Even the use of my first name, makes me feel part of this elite 'family.' After that, we all go off to the new Oslo Opera House for a special performance, followed by a boat ride up the fjord and a gala dinner party, all celebrating the 150th Anniversary of Norwegian shipping insurance company Der Norske Veritas, whose founder/CEO is a member of the Xyntéo Foundation.

Having discovered that John Fullerton, founder of the new Capital Institute, was in Oslo to meet with our sponsoring organization on the day after our meeting closed, and as I could bring a guest to this party, I contacted and invited him to join me, which he happily did.

The opera house performance begins with a brief history piece on the Vikings, followed by a lovely, abbreviated performance of the ballet Swan Lake, and then the enormously heavy red velvet curtain begins to rise again for a one-act version of *The Flying Dutchman*. With the full blasting prelude filling the room, a strange loud grating sound makes it suddenly obvious that something is not right with the great curtain. By some magic, the ticket I was issued has me seated front row center, right at the brass rail separating the audience from the orchestra, such that I am almost directly in front of, though higher than, the conductor.

I could not have had a more ringside seat as the left half of the curtain rises, while the right half makes this hideous grating racket as it is only partly dragged up the huge height it is meant to go, while the rest is held firmly to the floor. The part that *has* gone up is now tearing loose from the rest, which then falls in what seems slow motion as I watch the xylophonist just manage to drag his instrument away before it thuds down into the orchestra pit where he has been standing. The conductor stands by, frozen, horrified and helpless opposite me.

Within moments, a crew of black-clad men are wrestling away the fallen ton of drapery as a huge screen appears to show a brief video. In a matter of minutes, the show is back on. There have been no injuries and a minimum of delay! But no drama ensuing can match this finale, which has held the entire audience, including Prince Haakon, spellbound. Perhaps, I reflect when my breath is back, this is an apt metaphor for The Performance Theatre in its dialogues on rescuing a disastrous economy.

Later, we hear that a panel flush with the stage floor intended to flip up the floor lights on its under surface, had caught the great curtain's hem last time it was flipped down. Everything in a new theatre, of course, is electronic, so highly efficient, but not resilient, unable to sense its own failures if its engineers have not foreseen them and programmed in a 'halt' response when things go wrong. Again, of course, I am thinking of our global economy, roaring on with no halt response either.

The boat ride on three large ferries and the evening dinner party proceed without a hitch, the Prime Minister joining Prince Haakon and 1200 guests including our TPT group in an enormous floating arena DNV has built in the fjord fronting its headquarters. The precision and speed of service at dinner is as impressive as the venue, stage, and show, with large screens and gigantic TV cameras on booms. Word is that DNV spent €7 million for this bash, but Norway has zero unemployment and does mostly good deeds around the world with its excess oil money, so I just sit back and enjoy the extravagance. Every time I wake up from now on, to read for a while in the night as is my wont, I will read by the light of my solar-powered 'Little Sun' dinner favor, happy in knowing that someone in an off-grid village somewhere in Africa gets to read by theirs.[80]

Betty Sue Flowers

Otto Scharmer's colleague, Betty Sue Flowers, is someone I've long admired for her work with Joseph Campbell and journalist Bill Moyers, resulting in the televised series and book *The Power of Myth*, and for her work with Joseph Jaworski in producing his business leadership book *Synchronicity: The Inner Path of Leadership*. The more recent book, *Presence*, I mentioned in my Introduction to this book, is a dialogue among herself, Otto, Joseph and Peter Senge, their colleague in the business leadership training world.

Presence has been my favorite word in the English language ever since a dialogue with Puma about the word Pacha in his Runasimi language long ago in Peru, when he was still a kid. Pacha is an inclusive, holarchic word that means Cosmos, Earth, time and space or place, depending on context, and one's orientation within them all. That made me decide on *presence* as the closest word to Pacha in English, as it signifies my aware presence in time, in space, on Earth, and in my Cosmos. Indeed, it is my simultaneous awareness of presence that unites them all in a time-space holarchy.

Betty Sue came to her 'Vista' from a background in literature; I from evolution biology and as a devoted Seth books reader. Both of us were drawn into the business world in the recognition that the stories underpinning its ways are the stories that have the greatest influence on our human future. They are the stories that most need to be acknowledged and the stories for which we most need alternatives to head off disasters, to navigate our way through a perfect storm of crises — from the pollution and destruction of ecosystems to disastrous climate change — our now globalized economy has brought on.

Betty Sue has shown this in her work on scenario building with Royal Dutch Shell, teaching the world that the future is not something we attempt to predict as we wait for it to happen, but something we co-create for better or for worse with our choices. I have meanwhile been trying every way I can to help the business world understand and act in accordance with my evolutionary maturation cycle; to see that Nature is on our side for creating a better future if we only pay attention to her ways.

Three months into our dialogue, Betty Sue forwarded an email she received from Sherra Aguirre, a businesswoman about to retire from a company she had grown from a small home cleaning business to a large enterprise cleaning hospitals and airports. Betty Sue shared Sherra's words with me because they sounded so similar to the way I spoke of things, and promised to introduce me to her when I could get to New York City.

My first actual, rather than virtual, meeting with Betty Sue came to pass in early 2013, in her New York City home. Through my fashion designer Mallorca friend Sybilla Sorondo, I was fortunate to have an invitation to stay with Diandra Douglas in her four-story brownstone near Central Park, just a short walk around its corner from Betty Sue's on Central Park south. Diandra grew up in Deia and was Michael Douglas' first wife, for whom he bought that castle on the coast near Deia. Now divorced, New York City is her home, with a farm upstate.

Winter snows always make the city magical, all grime hidden briefly as sooty greys become white with the same fresh crystalline paint that turns trees into Christmas cards by day and even more so along lamplit streets by night.

Time always races too quickly through the events you most enjoy, and so our meetings overlooking the park from Betty Sue's picture window were suddenly a memory interwoven with the dream of 'next time.' And that next time, little more than a year later on my trek to Hawai'i, proves as delectable and passes equally fast. In the lunch she arranges with Sherra, that anticipated friendship pops into bloom as well.

Storytelling in Findhorn

During these last Mallorca years — never dreaming they are to *be* my last — I am called to Scotland for a gathering of all the Findhorn Foundation Fellows scattered around the world. The foundation's park itself looks much the same as it did when I was last here in the 1980s — winding paths through gardens and wood-frame buildings, the fanciful art of its great meeting hall; grass-topped hobbit houses, the half dozen giant whiskey-barrel homes — my old friend Roger Doudna still in his — the original 'caravan' trailer still preserved as a relic. Very few new buildings have been added on its grounds, but a windmill towers over it all. And, as the founders had predicted long ago to their airmen neighbors, the Findhorn Foundation has outlasted their Kinloss Airforce Base across the road, now closed down.

Many people, even if not members of the foundation, have moved onto the land surrounding the park, in the dunes by the sea, building sizeable new homes, mostly of natural materials and supplied by clean, green wind and solar energy, like the park itself. I cannot help but wonder how long it will take the sea level to rise around them.

It is lovely to be part of this international assembly of my fellow 'cultural creatives.' I propose that since we humans all live by our stories, and as our evolution is being held up by adhering to an outdated story, and as Joseph Campbell called for a New Story for all cultures before he died, we might organize an event to bring together the best storytellers of the future we can find, not as talking heads in a conference, but to share their stories with each other and anyone who wants to come to learn from them to hone their own stories.

This idea is welcomed and Richard Olivier — son of actor movie stars Sir Lawrence Olivier and Dame Joan Plowright — jumps in by volunteering to head the organizing committee for the event. Richard's London company, Olivier Associates, trains business leadership through Shakespeare, one of the best storytellers of all time, and one who, like the ancient Greek playwrights, taught humanity a lot about coping with the consequences of bad decisions on the part of leaders. Great insight on Richard's part to recognize them as good teaching stories for our times.

The Summit takes two whole years to design and implement as this is a new concept for the Findhorn Foundation and takes an immense amount of dialogue in a gradually expanding committee. Findhorn is deeply rooted in the values of consensus building, and like the foundation itself, our Summit is an exercise in transitioning from top-down management to self-organization, from lectures to open space technology, from usual financing to a gifting economy. In the end, we are able, with some generous gifts, to pay the expenses of fifty indigenous storytellers and fifty youth, along with a few hundred other accomplished or budding storytellers from all over the world who kick in theirs.

I love personally inviting some of the best storytellers I know and am able to get my Peruvian son Puma there after years of not seeing him. It is a delight to see him as an adult spiritual leader, experienced tour operator, husband and father, yet still with his boyish bounce, as happy in an apron playing at kitchen volunteer as in front of the mic, standing with me in the lovely intricately patterned matching poncho and shawl his wife has woven for us from the silkiest baby alpaca wool. My gratitude overflows at having this opportunity to catch up with him in person, rather than only through email and online videos.

The Summit is life-changing for many of the participants, from the anguished real-life stories of people from war-torn parts of the world to the deeply healing ceremonies brought to us by indigenous people including my Puma, from the riveting rapper poetry of young people to the sagely reflective stories of elders. Our shared intention, despite our apparent differences, is to weave a better world by rooting our stories for the future we hope to create in ancient knowledge and wisdom. We search for the best content, images, and metaphors to make new and inspirational stories to guide our world in its metamorphosis.

On just the second day of the Summit, a sudden spirit call appears loud and clear in my mind: *"Go to Hawai'i!"* I'm shocked. I know immediately that it is not telling me to go to Hawai'i for another visit, but to actually go there to live. I was last there a few years ago to speak at a conference in Honolulu called Voyage of Aloha, co-sponsored by my dear friend and chosen 'brother' Rinaldo Brutoco's World Business Academy and the Joseph Campbell Foundation, the great mythologer having lived out the latter part of his life in Hawai'i. For that conference, I invited Apela Colorado, my WISN friend, to come over from neighboring island Maui, where she was living, to share the speaker stage with me.

I had first touched foot in Hawai'i on my trip to China in the early '70s and had visited a few times in the '90s for speaking engagements on different islands, becoming enamored of the reclamation of sovereignty movement there, once I learned Hawai'i's history. But the thought of living there had never once crossed my mind and is a shock now that I'm well established and happy on Mallorca.

My roommate, Stephanie Tolan, is a longtime friend who has come to Findhorn at my invitation. Stef is an award-winning author of novels for young people, each of her stories taking on some important social issue, and of a whole book called *Change Your Story; Change Your Life*, a theme we have talked a lot about over many years. When we meet in our room after supper, I tell her of the spirit call, and in doing so remember that we have a Hawai'ian storyteller here at the summit — long white hair, a staff like Moses. I have noticed him but have not heard of him before and have not yet spoken to him.

"I've got to find ... Kalani? Is that his name?" I say to Stef, and decide to go out right now to see if I can find him. I walk out into the dark, cross the parking lot, and head up the barely lit path to the Great Hall at my usual fast walking pace, hoping someone still up there might know him. Hurrying along, engrossed in my intention, I smack straight into a man coming down the same path. It is Kalani!

First confirmation. I make a date with him for the next day to talk about this call. He is gracious and encouraging, immediately inviting me to come to his community on the Big Island, where he is sure I would enjoy the matriarchy in which he lives happily himself. In talking with him, the idea of an actual move begins to come into focus, and my mind moves into sorting through past experiences and people in Hawai'i; whom could I contact? What might develop there? Rinaldo had introduced me to Roger Epstein, a Honolulu attorney, another co-sponsor of the Voyage of Aloha conference. So, I sent an email to him along with my other Hawai'ian island contacts, to begin exploring possibilities for settling there, and he quickly and graciously offered his home as my landing deck.

CHAPTER 14

Hawai'i

Settling in

In the midst of my six-week stay with Roger, when he's kindly let me move from the guest room to his master bedroom to enjoy that view while he's off on a short trip, I wake to his indeed panoramic view of the Honolulu coast below. I listen to sweet morning bird calls, trying to interpret them. Ha! They are clearly calling back and forth to each other, *"sagaPO, sagaPO."* "I love you; I love *you*" in Greek. Reminds me of the sheep I heard speaking their *bleeeeuugh* French when I first found myself in Greece.

So delicious to reflect on the continuing magic of my life, my few material possessions stashed in cardboard boxes had arrived in Honolulu just a perfect 24 hours before me, without my awareness of the shipping schedule and, also unbeknownst to me, on the same airline. Roger could thus come to the airport using his pickup truck to get me and my boxes at once. No hitch at customs.

Immersed in books on Hawai'ian history and culture, I watch a public TV drama on the overthrow of Queen Liliuokalani, seemingly programmed for my arrival, making the details of the American takeover so real. I'm quickly entranced by the flowing harmonics of Hawai'ian music and dance and delighted by the ubiquitous flowering trees and shrubs.

Because women calling themselves The Outdoor Circle a century ago had planted trees along all Honolulu's avenues, and had gotten all outdoor advertising banned city wide, there are no neon signs, billboards, or other signs anywhere. Even the buses I ride have only public notices posted inside, in many languages, mostly Asian, the Asian population here exceeding 60 percent. All this, along with its parks and beaches, makes for an exceedingly unique and beautiful city.

Roger and Rinaldo have me writing proposals for projects they've dreamed up. One is aimed at getting Hawai'i's billionaires, including

Mark Zuckerberg, Jeff Bezos, Larry Ellison, Pierre Omidyar, and Oprah Winfrey to care about community and fund its development inclusively, rather than building walled enclaves against intrusion in a very possible difficult future of climate change, given Hawai'i's dependence on massive food and energy imports.

Another is building a 'lifeboat' intentional community practicing self-organization and sustainable self-sufficiency on the Big Island, where Rinaldo has his eye on a suitable, high coastal cliff site. Roger becomes my second mutually-agreed-on brother, a *hanai* relative, as this is widely practiced in Hawai'i. They have me on just enough of a retainer to allow me to house hunt for my own digs.

I look all over the city for a studio apartment, not wanting a bigger space than that, to avoid accumulation of stuff and because I simply do not need it. Nothing I find seems quite right, until one day I find the perfect perch on the 18th floor of a mid-city building. Five other people have seen and loved it before me, yet, again magically, I win the lease.

The building is a round twenty-story tower, with elevator and stairs at its core, and twelve faces on the outside, for each studio with its 18-foot-wide glass wall, floor to ceiling. A sliding door lets onto a narrow lanai (Hawai'ian for balcony), all along it; both far-side glass panels louvered for perfect airflow control.

The studio is thus shaped like a wedge — think pizza with the point of each slice cut off for a hallway around the elevator core — with an entry thus facing that huge glass wall. Bathroom and kitchen back-to-back along the entry way, then a wide-open space that feels like one big lanai to live on, so I make my bed low and get lanai/patio table and chairs, and a garden recliner chair along with my requisite desk and bookcases, leaving a wide-open space in the middle with just an area rug on which to practice my Pilates centered on the lovely hardwood floor. The entire unit has been newly refurbished with new floor, cabinets, bathroom, and kitchen fixtures. I build my color scheme on the wine-red, purple and teal of my Moroccan wall hanging, now on the wall behind my bed.

Not long after settling in, I discover that Helen Stewart, an old friend from Seth conferences who is an intuition specialist and author, moved to Honolulu not long before me. She quickly invites me to a meeting of local Seth followers in her home; I'm amazed that there are over 20 people on the invitee list. One of them, Grace Lin, works with a doctor in Taiwan who has built a large Seth following there, too. Another, Richard Dickison, becomes a great friend who helps me enormously with computer issues. We begin holding regular meetings in the Pagoda Hotel garden so close to my new home.

My hanai Samoan family

Little children in a Samoan family sit at my feet singing welcoming greetings to me as a new 'Auntie' coming into their family. The term 'hanai' refers to adoption into a non-biologically related family. The head of this family, Dr. Failatusi Avegalio, is Samoan royalty and a revered and much-loved professor at the University of Hawai'i where he is director of its Pacific Business Center. Known widely as Doc Tusi, he signs his emails to me humbly, '2c.'

My first connection with Doc Tusi had come about through Ramsay Taum, a native Hawai'ian I'd met at the Voyage of Aloha conference, who lives here in Honolulu. Ramsay suggested I contact Doc Tusi for some information I was seeking. We soon meet in person, to his delight, as he had read my *EarthDance: Living Systems in Evolution* book almost twenty years ago and had been amazed, as he told me, that a scientist could be so deeply in touch with indigenous cultures. He said it had changed his life, as he had long thought he'd have to give up his traditional knowledge in favor of modern science; that I had shown him this was not so. He had even felt that our paths would cross eventually and had recognized my name at once on the email I sent him at Ramsay's suggestion.

Tusi met his wife Linda in Kansas, on his first education venture away from Samoa, and now they are grandparents. Her sister, who has Down's syndrome and erratic behavioral challenges that require full-time wheelchair care, lives with them and, however difficult her care, she is considered a blessing for the children as they learn to lovingly care for her. This is indicative of the deeply loving and service-oriented values I watch this family put into daily practice.

Just inside the front door of their bustling, happy wood-frame home high above the ocean is a framed photo of Tusi at his son's age, showing the traditional tattoo that fully covers his skin from waist to knees. Prince Philip had his photographer take it when visiting Samoa. Three copies were made — one still hangs on the royal yacht Britannia, one is in an English palace, the third was given to Tusi, who had lost it for years when it surfaced magically, returned to him by someone who had found it in a flea market and recognized him in it.

His son Talavou has the same traditional tattoo, made on a trip back to Samoa with his father at only sixteen, as great a test of pain endurance as any rite of passage can be.[81] To wear such a tattoo is to be committed for life to the well-being of your people and all others.

Now, for another family occasion, Tusi has driven an hour and a half down the coast of this beautiful island of O'ahu to fetch me in Honolulu for a very special gathering, the send-off for Talavou, who is being deployed to the Middle East as a Black Hawk helicopter pilot.

A long table is laden with home-cooked food on a broad wooden lanai as Talavou's parents, aunts and uncles, siblings, their offspring, and a few close family friends gather here for this lavish feast in his honor. We are perched over a long green slope of tropical greenery peppered with other well-worn, wood-frame houses descending to the ocean, watching the slowly setting sun as one after another family teenager stands to pay tribute to their uncle Talavou, thanking him for the values and life-lessons he has taught them. I feel deeply privileged to witness this profound evidence that so ancient and beautiful, so ethical and loving a culture, survives in our world of blindingly hi-tech consumerism amidst ecological and political turmoil. The strapping, yet gentle young warrior we celebrate is clearly already a proven teacher; he is also a beekeeper, nurturing creatures facing extinction at human hands to help them make honey while they still can.

My send-off gift to Talavou is a Maori design sea-turtle pendant of silver and gemstones I was gifted in Aotearoa years ago and have never worn as it felt too masculine for me. I knew I would one day find the right man to whom I could pass it on. I had also saved a lovely artist's card made from a painting of sea turtles and pasted this message I wrote onto its back as my wish for his safe return from his military deployment:

> *In a story that circulates in Greece, a student of Socrates visited him in prison shortly before he was put to death and asked: "Master, how did you see the path of your life so clearly that you could follow it so faithfully?" Socrates replied, "I never saw the path ahead, but I could always sense when I was off my path, and so I could correct my course and stay on it." Like Socrates, sea turtles may not 'know' where they are headed, but they correct their course continually by their inner compass and so stay on their trajectory. We can all perfect our inner compass in this way.*

After I'm an established auntie in his family, Tusi asks me to speak at a conference he is organizing — a whole conference devoted to Ulu, the breadfruit tree that has always provided sustenance to Polynesians as a staple food, and which they took on their oceanwide canoe travels, thus spreading it even to the Caribbean, where many a family has an ulu tree in their yard.

Ulu growing is amazing no-work agriculture and an almost miraculously versatile staple food, thus both an agricultural delight and blessing. You can sleep under an ulu tree till it drops its versatile fruit on your head. It is an extremely prolific tree, infant trees sprouting all over its branches and roots, making sure you and your progeny will not run out of ulu fruit. Definitely should be part of agroforestry wherever climate permits.

Before it is ripe, you can make anything out of ulu's pale flesh you could make with potato; dried and ground it is even more versatile as flour. When it is deep orange, ripe and soft, just plopping spoonfuls of the flesh into hot coconut oil fries you the most delicious patties. Trouble is, the Big Food industry has caught onto its enormous nutritional benefits for its increasingly diet conscious, wheat-intolerant global customers and wants to patent this Polynesian food that has been honored and gifted by its natural human caretakers for thousands of years. More on this later.

Sister Saint Joan

While still at Roger's, I had met Sister Joan Chatfield at the conversation circle meetings he holds regularly in his home. Having heard of her as a widely known peace activist, I'm delighted at getting to know this feisty, fearless nun and hear of her adventures here. While she became a dean at Chaminade University, the largest private university in the state, her staunch activism and insistence on speaking truth to power got her fired as dean for insubordination. Simply ignoring the punishment of demotion, she continued her work there.

As we become friends, she introduces me to the new Pope Francis' *Laudato Si'* encyclical which thrills me with its profound concern at the widespread human destruction of ecosystems, so very consistent with my own work. To quote it just very briefly in lines that themselves quote his predecessor John Paul II:

> *Once the human being declares independence from reality and behaves with absolute dominion, the very foundations of our life begin to crumble, for, "instead of carrying out his role as cooperator with God in the work of creation, man sets himself up in place of God and thus ends up provoking a rebellion on the part of nature."*

Sister Joan decides I should give a series of lectures at Chaminade — a Catholic university, and me not even a Christian, lecturing there on this Pope's encyclical! She takes me to the Chaminade campus and I am entranced by the lovely architecture of its chapel: a round building, like the one I live in, also with huge glass windows all around its single spacious story, topped by a great dome, all surfaces white inside and out, with spectacular views of lush flowering greenery and ocean from its high campus perch. I'm entranced and ask if I could give my lectures in this amazing chapel. She likes the idea and somehow gets us the permission to do it. We make a publicity brochure and I get to work studying the 163-page book that is the full encyclical 'letter' and making three beautiful hour-long slide shows, with lots of photos illustrating the parallels in Pope Francis' work and my own.

A few weeks after my series of three presentations, I meet the president of the university, a priest himself, at a public event. He confides in me that he actually read the *Laudato Si'* encyclical only after my presentations! Yet another interesting experience for me, to find myself teaching such religious professionals.

Joan lives in a house of half a dozen nuns, the oldest almost a hundred years old and a founder of their order in the Hudson Valley where I grew up. Joan herself is mid-'80s and I only a few years her junior. It is apparent that she has difficulties walking, as I notice her chronically swollen legs and ankles below her skirts.

She regularly nods off during events we attend together, but only gradually, as my own hips begin to cause me pain, do I realize how much more serious pain she must be in. Sitting in her car driving lots of carless people, including myself, on our errands all over Honolulu is the most comfortable she can be. Never once, however, does she mention her pain. Rather, she is endlessly cheerful in her service to God however she can carry it out.

Several more years pass before her sudden death. Right in her shared home, she trips on a small step from one part of the house to the other, a step she has navigated thousands of times, now falling so hard her head hits the floor and knocks her out. Her sisters call an ambulance that takes her to the hospital, but she never regains consciousness, and her heart soon stops, as I am sure hosts of angels have carried her joyfully onward. Joan is and always will be a saint and a role model to me, as well as a cherished friend.

Professor back to business

After avoiding academia for over forty years since MIT in the early '70s,

I am recruited unexpectedly as a professor in residence at my already familiar Chaminade University, but now in its School of Business and Communications MBA program. Its dean knew of my earlier work on living economies in the progressive, experimental Bainbridge Institute MBA program, which he later headed. He discovered my move to Honolulu through Roger.

Again, I am drawn into the business world as an educator, as I had been in the USA and Brazil, then Europe, especially London and Amsterdam. The dean has me very happily working with himself and two Native Hawai'ians, Ramsay Taum and Kauila Clark, both of whom I'd met at the Voyage of Aloha conference. Now, I am truly delighted to work on this project with them: a four-course concentration on Business in Island Economies, based on the living economies of nature and traditional Hawai'ian values and practices of living in harmony with Nature and each other, each of us teaching one of them. Such a perfect way to continue blending my understanding of biological evolution with the worldviews and practices of indigenous cultures.

My course is called Aina, Hawai'ian for Earth: She who Nurtures; the other three are Maka'ainana (Community), Kuleana (Responsibility), and Po'okela (Leadership). All the important aspects of business; all rooted in the traditional practices of Hawai'i as a Constitutional Monarchy.

Hawai'i's economy was set up as what we now call *bioregionalism*, a sustainable economy, appropriate to the region in which it operates, in terms of its natural resources and carrying capacity. The most natural boundaries on Earth are local watersheds, and on relatively small islands these are easy to see as streams run down from the highest locations to surrounding sea, so can be used to delineate the borders of farms between them. And so, in Hawai'i, every farm included the land lying between streams, thus having timber and tree fruits in upper forests, fields cleared for planting below, constructed fishponds at low flats, and finally, the sea itself with its natural harvest. Each farm was thus self-sufficient and equitable in relation to others.

This 'bioregional' *Ahupua'a* system, along with Hawai'i's constitutional monarchy, and its diplomatic and trade relationships with Japan, England, and other countries, was destroyed heedlessly and recklessly by the American men who took over with their interests missionizing the population, establishing a military base, and planting the profitable monocultured crops of sugarcane and pineapple. When Queen Liliuokalani was put under house arrest in her palace in 1893 and wanted to call the US president on her phone, she discovered the White House did not even have telephone service yet!

From my first speaker trips to Hawai'i, with never a thought of coming here to live, I had been drawn to people working actively on Hawai'ian independence and the restoration of constitutional monarchy. The first of these was Poka Laenui, whose wife Puanani was one of the founding members of WISN, our Worldwide Indigenous Science Network. Poka had a radio show in Honolulu, on which I spoke several times in support of this campaign during the '90s. Working now with Ramsay on the Island Economies concentration soon leads to a revival of this interest.

Hawai'i's population at the time of its overthrow was the same size as it is today, about one million, and its food supply was clearly sustainable. But as the land was taken over, fishponds were in the way of developing coastal lands for quickly popular tourism, and so were filled in to provide more ground for development, especially of hotels. Farm boundaries went unrecognized as forests were cut, huge fields were planted with sugar cane or pineapple, and construction proceeded heavily along the coast and climbing ever higher up the valleys.

Plunging my first Aina course MBA students into on-the-ground realities, after a few sessions on such history in relation to the living economies of nature, I take them to community organizing meetings in Kaka'ako, a coastal part of Honolulu, close to my home, where local people are trying to preserve some semblance of community based on traditional values and practices in the face of development overrunning them. Here, the students get a sense of the economic challenges up close, how businesses operate, how people's lives are directly affected and how community power can self-organize to solve problems, even by forming new business enterprises.

As classes are scheduled from 6 to 9 PM, whenever we meet in our university classroom, the students and I take turns bringing food. We push tables together, eat on a tablecloth like a family. Students are in their 20s and 30s, some with children, most subsidized for military service, some working a job while getting this degree.

The second time I teach the same course, the students compare the current economic/business situation on our island with visions of what they would like it to be in the future. They research what local projects exist in food, housing, waste, community initiatives, etc. and organize field trips to visit them. As a final class project, they write and perform a retrospective radio show on how the transition to the better future they envision in their own old age actually came about.

The third class focuses on island business in the face of climate change and designs a board game played on a map of Honolulu showing sea-level rise and playing out various challenges and solutions. The game, structured somewhat like Monopoly, is actually produced with board, player pieces, printed money bills, cards, and instruction manual. Thus, I maintain my own interest, by varying each round of this Aina course, always staying in touch with Scott, the dean, Ramsay, and Kauila to ensure coherence.

Making sense of a fast-changing world

Mid-February 2017 and I wake with a smile on my face remembering how I spent the middle of the night in and out of dreams in which I ruminate endlessly over how to get more information on artificial snow-making machines. Just what questions should I ask in an email? "I'm a high school student studying snowmaking and would like to know in what areas of the US they operate?" "What must the ambient temperature be for the snow to last?" "How much snow can they generate per hour?"

And so, on and on, over and over, I ponder the questions relentlessly up to wondering whether they work better in indoor arenas or outdoors, as I recall learning about the artificial ski run in a Dubai shopping center years ago. Then, suddenly, I am wide awake, when I thought I'd been awake all through the whole dream ruminations.

Waking up around 4:00AM is pretty usual at my advanced age, and I've learned to use it to advantage as an undisturbed time to meditate, so I ask myself, "Okay, Elisabet, don't try to analyze this trivial, if rather annoying, dream for meaning; just drop down out of your head and into your heart."

No sooner had I done that than I laughed out loud as my snow-making machine unveiled itself suddenly as the metaphor it was. Just before going to bed, I'd emailed a friend the link to a long, detailed article on how fake news is generated and then distributed through millions of individually tailored messages based on people's detailed online profiles — a technique perfected by a research company in England called Cambridge Analytica, hired by the Trump election campaign. A huge technologically engineered 'snow-making machine' that won Trump the US presidential election because Hillary Clinton was still mired in using older, far less effective, mass polling profile categories such as women, blacks, professionals, etc.

Donald Trump is in the White House, to the horror or glee of a divided world that is universally fascinated by him, both sides watching his every move with baited breath. Indeed, never in my now long lifetime — having become an octogenarian in Hawai'I — have politics been more gripping, more vital.

I read Shoshanna Zuboff's *Surveillance Capitalism: The Fight for a Human Future at the New Frontier of Power*, a deeply researched book by a Harvard professor on the global architecture of behavior modification from the Korean War to the present. Having experienced the beginnings of behavior modification with B.F. Skinner in my university years, and tracked some of it, Zuboff's book is an eye-opener on just how such mass manipulation goes hi tech.

The Guardian, which became my go-to news source living in Europe, reviews it saying *"Tech companies want to control every aspect of what we do, for profit. A bold, important book identifies our new era of capitalism"* and continues: *"While insisting their technology is too complex to be legislated, companies spend billions lobbying against oversight."*

The review continues:

> *"Originally intent on organizing all human knowledge, Google ended up controlling all access to it; we do the searching, and are searched in turn. Setting out merely to connect us, Facebook found itself in possession of our deepest secrets. And in seeking to survive commercially beyond their initial goals, these companies realized they were sitting on a new kind of asset: our "behavioral surplus," the totality of information about our every thought, word, and deed, which could be traded for profit in new markets based on predicting our every need — or producing it.*[82]

Thus, the book describes the insidious way we learn to live with such utterly undemocratic exploitation of ourselves without our awareness at any but the most superficial level. I spend hours every day researching how this oligarchy so cleverly stays in power in this last gasp of empire building I see as our human evolutionary adolescent crisis, calling ever more strongly for our maturation. I am the inveterate cosmic snoop and must know how it all works.

The intentions of those who currently control our global economic and political reality are far from some deep hidden conspiracy; it is more the case that they are hidden in plain sight. Only our lack of attention conceals them.

WEF, The World Economic Forum,[83] has glitzy annual meetings in the Swiss Alps village of Davos every January, and they are widely reported in the mainstream news. *Forbes* reported 119 billionaires in attendance in 2020. WEF founder, Klaus Schwab, an economist who, with his wife Hilde, created the Schwab Foundation for Social Entrepreneurship in 1998, implemented a brilliant strategy: Invite all global leaders of nations, multinational corporations, and banks to a posh holiday week on a remote and pristine mountain retreat once a year, to hobnob with each other and collaborate to strengthen their individual strategies.[84]

Schwab has been training Young Global Leaders for 40 years, including Angela Merkel, Emmanuel Macron, Bill Gates, Justin Trudeau, Jacinda Ardern. He currently has 1,400 YGLs working in community with each other around the world.[85]

On the surface, reading WEF literature, it all seems very benign. It purports to support the UN Development Goals but has its own versions of how to implement them, proud that the UN in turn supports the WEF. In other words, they are deeply in cahoots, as we say. The problem lies in *how* the WEF "Great Reset" plan for the world, including development of poor nations, is to be implemented — *how* the global elite will control global health, food, housing, business, education, media, and more.

Take Bill Gates' endeavors in food and health as one example. He is now the largest farmable land holder in the US and exerts major influence on farming in sub-Saharan Africa and Asia. He is heavily invested in both hi-tech agriculture and in biotechnical food production. As of this writing, $3 trillion of investment is projected to meet 60 percent of the world's food needs by synthetic food production within the next few years.

Why run foul and expensive CAFOs (concentrated animal feeding operations) when you can make fake meat in vats. Gates is also heavily invested in new mRNA vaccines and synthetic drugs as the sole solution to global health problems. In short, small farmers growing healthy non-toxic, non-monocultured food that might keep us healthy are to be eliminated, as are all natural medicines.

WEF's success is in integrating extremes of both the political Left and Right, finding the control strategies that meet in what is technically, by Mussolini's definition, fascist management by a corporatocracy. A Klaus Schwab video that went viral shows him saying: "You will own nothing, and you will be happy" while a drone delivers an Amazon package to your doorstep. So many people on social media were riled by this, seeing that if the people own nothing, then the corporatocracy must own everything, that Schwab scrubbed the statement from the WEF site. It is one thing to be open about your intentions, but it is also crucial to keep them looking benign. He had goofed.

It is mind boggling to see my world struggling with this necessary transition into human maturity — the lengths to which those running the global economy will go to hold on to their ruthlessly undemocratic power. Never have I had a greater need to see the world from a higher spiritual perspective, to discern what is happening without judgment, but with carefully deliberated action. I began Chapter 5 of this book, on weaving my reality back in 1980's Greece, with these words:

> *The three streams of science, society, and spirit were running through me with interesting meanderings, impeded at times by turbulence or obstacles that only the years of deep reflection upon the MidEarth Sea brought to a steady, coherent flow.*

Now, here in Hawai'i, in all my talks these decades later, I tell the story taught to me by Polynesian navigators, about how to "stand tall in your canoe until you see your destination" — how to raise your consciousness high enough to see your destination when all other means fail. I remind people how they have played on Hawai'ian beaches or other fun places in their minds during dull lectures, or while waiting for a scheduled appointment; how easy it is for your consciousness to roam. So, I invite them to lift off till they are high above the human drama, as if it plays out on a vast stage far below. "Discern the patterns in that vast scenario of our human drama; looking at it from above so you can see it in a Big Picture perspective."

This helps people see where they could take their lives, "how to stop beating your head against walls in trying to do things that don't work; finding instead, something you love doing that can be done with others in a way that helps build a better world as the status quo dissolves around you; see like-minded people already doing it; find a way to join them."

I then quote the ancient Sufi poet Rumi: *"There are a thousand ways to kneel and kiss the ground,"* and give them all the best examples of grassroots people power growing in pockets around the world.

Food

Among my examples of positive developments around the world is Allan Savory's restoration of desertified grasslands by restoring their missing hooved animals, which are needed by healthy grassland ecosystems to keep the land fertilized in the dry season and to break up the natural way in which grass clumps and chokes itself without them.

He learned from nature how wrong it is to pen cattle densely into unhealthy feedlots and feed them on soy they cannot readily digest and which is what turns their breath and farts into dangerous gas.[86] I meet Allan at a conference where he asks if he may use one of my slides: that depicting man on the moon looking back at Earth, where the only sign of human presence, if it could be seen over time, is the growth of deserts. Its caption is: *Humans, biologically, are a desert-making species*. We have deforested massively along with destroying grasslands.

This disastrous separation of plants and animals to produce our food, monoculturing both and feeding both artificially, has created two problems where there were none, all in the search for profits. Sludge waste ponds on pig farms, disgustingly cruel and dirty chicken warehousing, stinking cow manure pile up, all turn many people to become animal rights crusaders and vegans.

Because animals have faces and very cute babies, people identify with them in deep concern, which they do not feel for plants. Yet plants are equally, if not even more, sentient than animals. Their sensory organs are invisibly distributed throughout their roots, stems and leaves, and so go unrecognized by everyone except plant research scientists.[87] In fact, plants are equally mistreated by the depletion of healthy soils as their animal partners are removed in favor of toxic chemical pesticides and fertilizers.

As the vegan movement grows, the food industry, quick to spot new markets, begins to 'support' it by creating artificial vegan 'fake meat.' As I write, a $3 trillion market, supplying 60% of food worldwide, is projected for 'vat food' as producers realize it is cheaper to manufacture than to grow live food.

The fake food manufacturers benefit hugely from the burgeoning vegan propaganda that vegan food saves us from illness, climate change, and cruelty, though no food has ever been healthier or better for the planet and us people than that of old integrated and chemical-free family farms such as those on which I was raised. I write an article called "Ending the Food Wars," published on my website, to plead with everyone fighting for healthy food, no matter which healthy food diets they choose, to recognize this insane exploitation we all suffer in common and stop telling each other what to eat, joining forces instead against all unhealthy food production.

AI, an oxymoron

SO much coming out now on AI — Artificial Intelligence, which I consider an oxymoron, as the real thing, intelligence throughout Nature, will never be copyable in mechanical models. That said, I'm glad AI is now under such scrutiny, because this manmade 'intelligence' has, indeed, become a dangerously unmanageable behemoth of bots their designers let loose without seeing the danger they unleashed.

As I am finishing up this book, the beast has gotten fatter, faster, and even more far reaching in the form of chatbots that steal from anything ever published or posted online, in print or in sound, to regurgitate essays, stories, and even poems slickly assembled and, on demand, in the voice of any author. Gone are the fought-for authors' copyrights, as well as all privacy, not to mention the creative thinking that up to now was considered important for each of us to learn as participants in this creative universe.

AI designers and other insiders, themselves, are warning that the near insane race of massive businesses for the best new chatbots — Google and Microsoft to wit — are getting so out of hand that their programmers have lost control and humanity at large may be in danger of robots taking over the world. In one such article, repeating lines express this concern: "It's that culturally we lack a story as to why values even matter to begin with."

I wish I could give them the story they seek, as I have it. Nature, including our bodies, are highly ethical systems in which individuals, from cells to organisms, and their communities are ever in dialogue to reach balanced harmonies in which both can flourish. You would die were your body not run this way. Ah, I could go on. And I wish I still had a voice in the tech community, but I've become old and obsolete it seems.

No one writing such articles ever thinks of questioning the very concept of AI ... what is "artificial intelligence"? Do any of its practitioners ask what "real intelligence" is? None of them question the arrogant pursuit of control that leads to attempts to outsmart nature in a youthful expansion economy phase that has become unsustainable.

Now the latest competition is to create the best artificial intelligence before studying the real thing. None look to indigenous cultures that understood humility and learned from Nature and could thus take their consciousness deep into Earth and out to stars, heal illnesses, and so much more for which we rely on technology. We have virtually no survival skills for facing a future in which most of our technology will be useless because we have no means to repair and rebuild it.

My point is that arrogance on the part of these competitors for outdoing Nature never see themselves within a larger picture in which their chase after profits is the last gasp of the empire building that has proved unsustainable and calls for us humans to mature into destined cooperation.

After I write this, I discover a wonderful book by James Bridle: *Ways of Being: Animals, Plants, Machines: The Search for a Planetary Intelligence*. Bridle is a remarkable AI techie, who also explored Nature's living systems in the greatest detail, coming to see the "more than human world" as excluded from all we understand as our knowledge of the world. The passages I so resonated with are from chapters 5 & 6:

> ... *written language, in superseding oral culture, has been responsible in part for our increased estrangement from the more-than-human world ... technological implementations of language — in the form of mostly English code, and ultimately in 1s and 0s — exacerbates this estrangement still further.*

Here Bridle came to what I call communion (direct transmission), as opposed to communication (all the languages used to transmit). Communion is what my cells do to be in constant touch with each other; what trees and other plants do; what Strongheart taught J. Allen Boone to do in the book *Kinship with All Life*, as I spoke of in Chapter 8. Bridle goes on to say, about Alan Turing, who invented computers in the 1930s:

> ... *Turing had a very clear idea of what computers would be and what they could do. 'Electronic computers', he wrote, 'are intended to carry out any definite rule-of-thumb process which could have been done by a human operator working in a disciplined but unintelligent manner.' ... That is, Turing's a-machines, the computers we would all inherit, would do what human computers had done before them, only faster. The limits of these computers would be the limits of human thinking. Indeed, they would come to define it.* [my underline for emphasis]

> *... Ever since the development of digital computers, we have shaped the world in their image. In particular, they have shaped our idea of truth and knowledge as being that which is calculable. Only that which is calculable is knowable, and so our ability to think with machines beyond our own experience, to imagine other ways of being with and alongside them, is desperately limited. This fundamentalist faith in computability is both violent and destructive: it bullies into little boxes what it can and erases what it can't. In economics, it attributes value only to what it can count; in the social sciences it recognizes only what it can map and represent; in psychology it gives meaning only to our own experience and denies that of unknowable, incalculable others. It brutalizes the world, while blinding us to what we don't even realize we don't know.*

This is, to me, a supremely important insight because of my passionate advocacy of indigenous ways of knowing, as well as that of the non-human beings of Nature we have trampled so recklessly. Every being in Nature alive today has the same length evolutionary trajectory, so all are equally 'highly' evolved. But only humans squeeze ourselves into knowing only what can be calculated, measured with instruments.

CHAPTER 15

Final Insights

Political economy and democracy in Nature

Part of my personal Big Picture perspective is my belief in reincarnation, shared by half the human population[88] and as I've mentioned here in chapters 4 and 11. I see my past lives as all present in the non-linear, non-spacetime NOWness of deep reality. In exploring some of them, I've noted a pattern of getting myself into serious trouble by speaking truth to power, confirmed more recently in a reading by astrologer Heather Ensworth, who bestowed it on me for letting her interview me and is rapidly becoming a dear friend.

It dawns on me now that I have discovered a way to do this without being burned at the stake or meeting some other such end. For so many years I've been revealing another secret kept hidden in plain sight: that Nature has been doing economics and politics as long as life has existed. I just had not recognized that as the safe way to speak truth to power! When I use my body economics model to show the clear unsustainability of our economic system, no one ever challenges me on its cooperative and ethical nature.

The divisions we impose in our political world are disastrous. Nature is profoundly conservative with what works, and radically changes what does not. That is how it keeps living systems healthy. There is no antagonism between these modes; Nature simply makes the appropriate response in every situation. This is how our two-party political system *should* work; people choosing whether they prefer being protectors or change agents and acting so in cooperation with each other. To vote to do one or the other every few years makes no sense at all. The top leadership should always include both modes, the public voting on the best people to serve in each capacity and in partnership. Surely, that would be a feature of a mature democracy.

When I show how democratically our 50 trillion or so cells live to keep us healthy and compare that with how we as citizens live in our political system, it never invites argument, but rather gives people pause for thought. We simply cannot deny that Nature has evolved a maturation cycle that passes from creative youthful expansion and the competitive hostilities it engenders, to the mature, cooperative harmonies of creature bodies, and of well-balanced mature ecosystems such as prairies, rain forests, and coral reefs. We recognize it in our individual maturation through adolescence.

Many analysts of our political and economic crises are pointing out that our proclaimed democracy has again become an oligarchy, as it was when the 'Robber Barons' of the late 19th century empowered themselves. Oligarchy is a matter of "those who have the gold rule," and it should not surprise us that it rears its head repeatedly when our economy has so long run on growth, using a monetary debt system based on usury, which was designed thousands of years ago to concentrate wealth. Indeed, it was warned against by Jesus according to the Bible, and outlawed by Islam, while Judaism forgave all debt regularly, yet we continue to generate money as debt.[89]

Wealth has always bestowed political power. Our US Constitution was written by socially prominent men of considerable means. Through Benjamin Franklin's association with the Haudenosaunee 'Indians,' his fellow founding fathers saw the possibility of democratic governance — just democratic enough to prevent insurrections against that wealth. They included the separation of powers Franklin learned from the Haudenosaunee, but they left out the enfranchisement of women, children, and Nature that was so endemic to those 'Indians' on whose land they wrote their constitution that it did not have to be named in *their* constitution, their Great Law of Peace.

Called the Iroquois by French setters, the Haudenosaunee were a League of Nations formed under this Great Law of Peace and actually practiced what we called democracy, as it included women, children, and Nature herself in all their deliberations and made themselves consider the projected effect of their choices six generations into the future.

No one owned pieces of Nature; no one went homeless or hungry, women had equal status with men, but played different roles. For example, men tamed wild animals and hunted for food, while women grew gardens. Clan councils of grandmothers chose male chiefs, but then warned those who did not serve their people, taking them out of power if they did not heed such warnings.

Through the reports of missionaries and traders to Europe, the New World native 'Indians' came to be seen there as 'noble savages' whose ways of life actually inspired the European Enlightenment[90] and through that the European revolutions, as there were, then, no role-model democracies other than the ancient Greek original. The latter had been attractive to the founding fathers for enfranchising only propertied men, and in the slave-owning South for including that institutionalized practice.

Still, the Constitution was a noble experiment, with enough sense of fairness eventually to end slavery and an ever-increasing enfranchisement of non-landholding men, then former slaves, and finally women. The two-party system made it possible to rein in oligarchs when their rule became widely enough recognized, as in the case of the Robber Barons, when they caused economic depression.

Under Franklin Roosevelt, we got a New Deal making economics considerably fairer, and now we see new politicians calling for a Green New Deal and even questioning capitalism itself, proposing some debt forgiveness, advocating minimum wage raises, etc. while working to regenerate the ecosystems we have damaged.

The fundamental question we must ask ourselves now is whether it is possible to have a political democracy using a wealth-concentrating monetary system, which demands a growth model economy measured by its money flow, even as we see it has been turned into a global casino impervious to real human needs.

My dear friend Hazel Henderson[91] showed so clearly the fallacy of the money-flow measure of an economy wherein expensive oil spills, lucrative illness, and other costly disasters make the economy look good. Her alternative, the measure of well-being using the Calvert-Henderson Quality of Life Indicators,[92] has influenced such wonderful developments as the very similar Bhutan Gross National Happiness Index.[93]

It becomes ever more obvious that the transition to a better future will not be a reformation of the corporatocracy, or techno-feudalism, as Jem Bendell calls it,[94] nor a Phoenix rising from its ashes, but rather its replacement, just as the butterfly replaces the chrysalized caterpillar as imaginal cells do the work of building a butterfly. In all my talks and interviews, I cite examples of what is going right in our messy world.

Among my favorite examples are the Mondragon Cooperatives in Basque Spain,[95] begun by a Catholic priest who enlisted young people in designing a society that was neither capitalist nor communist but based on loving human relationships. It grew to large industries co-owned in equal shares by all who worked in them, with no salaries more than six times the lowest. They built schools, a university, health centers, a world-renowned art museum, and the largest research center in Europe.

Another favorite example is the vast rural Sarvodaya project in Sri Lanka,[96] founded by Dr. A.T. Ariaratne, whom I'd met at the first organizational meeting of the United Religions Initiative in Stanford, California and, years later, visited in his Sri Lanka home. Sarvodaya has united 15,000 villages and hamlets in bootstrapping their development, everything based on just two principles children are taught to meditate on when very small: inner peace and generosity. Imagine a world where everyone is peaceful and focused on what they can do for others.

Vandana Shiva's Navdanya project brings women from all over the globe together in building regeneration and biodiversity projects to preserve healthy food wherever possible,[97] and Allan Savory's Holistic Management of desertified land[98] has restored grasslands all over the world.

The Global Ecovillage Network (GEN), and the Business Alliance for Local Living Economies (BALLE) I helped initiate while a Fellow of the Social Venture Network, John Fullerton's Capital Institute,[99] are further examples. Endeavors all over the world include the Donut Economics of Kate Raworth,[100] the many alternative currencies running in parallel to official money, along with countless umbrella organizations and conferences, both on the ground and online, devoted to establishing caring and sharing communities.

People all over the world recognize that the empire building era is over, that growth capitalism is not a mature economic system. They see that a new world must come from grassroots initiatives that link together in ever more complex networks, just as the earliest cells of Earth pioneered so long ago, and just as ecosystems revive after enormous disasters — many new organisms popping up and linking cooperatively; no one of them in charge.

My own voice from the past

My old friend Ellie Goldberg, who has devoted much of her life to fighting against the lead poisoning to which children are still now exposed, suddenly surfaces after many years in which we lost contact. She sends me a treasure trove of the long letters I sent her from my Greek island all through the 1980s, all single-space typed on vellum paper to save on airmail costs. Among them is this report I wrote right after my ten-day visit from Jim Lovelock of Gaia fame — the visit I wrote of in Chapter 5, before this letter surfaced.

Dear Ellie,

Thanks so much for the lovely long letter, the WP book, and Globe article. Nice night to answer ... rainy, the cats and I packed indoors, my fisherman not home, and me filled with an incredible glow piled up over the past ten days by Jim Lovelock's visit — the man I think of as discovering that Earth was alive while looking for life on other planets. Ten days that may change my life ... or lead to the fulfillment of effort I've hoped would someday be possible.

I hardly know where to begin. The man? His effect on me? The ideas discussed? His amazing inventions and theoretical breakthroughs? Well ... let me start by saying that I'd foreseen the visit as one of a great scientist coming by some miracle to see the girl dropout amusing herself in the woods, probably just because she happens to live somewhere he wanted to go, and he was a warm person touched by the invitation.

The latter contains a touch of reality, but the first part he quickly dispelled, welcoming me immediately as a valued colleague. He thinks my book MidEarth *is a really fine piece of work, and we discussed a chapter a day in detail as he read it. Much of his advice has to do with encouraging me to state my views boldly, with passion, poetry, courage in my convictions (which doesn't exclude humility) — in short, in any way except the academic way I tend to slip into. "Don't put yourself in the category of the Capra types," he said, "with all the quotes and academic trappings (even where their information is false), because you have more important things than they to say and a better way of saying them; don't date yourself by referring to the 'new wave,' your book may be valid for a very long time."*

Such comments were fascinating to me. He's right that I've tried to please academics in this book and that I don't have to and shouldn't. His opinion is that academia is the worst environment possible in which to do good science; that my coming here to the remote woods/sea was the most sensible and courageous thing to do toward real progress in thinking. In many more or less subtle ways, he let me know that he considers my thoughts on the cosmos, world, and humanity, science included, as valid as any he's

> *encountered. I know he will promote my work, tell the members of the UN University (a self-appointed traveling body working on global environmental problems) about me, quote me in his own work, and continue our relationship. And on top of that, he's going to send me a computer!*

How delightful to reread this now in old age. He did send that first computer I hauled up the hill to my island home on a donkey! And as it turns out, my *EarthDance: Living Systems in Evolution* book, written back then in the 1980s, on that computer he sent me, with little later updating is indeed still valid — the very book Doc Tusi had read and which he claims changed his life.

In Chapter 12 of *this* book, I spoke of Jim as a superb climatologist warning of disaster. He suggested we had better pray for the ice age we are now more or less due for, as it looked more like we humans were driving Earth into a hot age. With every passing day now, his prediction is confirmed. The US is blanketed in smog from wildfires burning for months now across Canada and all the southern states, not to mention several other countries, are suffering unprecedented heat waves.

Dreaming and Waking Realities

In these Hawai'i years, I take a dream course taught by Seth network teachers, and report this dream in my course journal, after asking for a dream that would harmonize the aspects of my being:

> *Have been trying to find myself as some kind of decision needs to be made. As I'm looking for myself, I'm aware that there are two possibilities: either I will be squishing together elements of the past, which I see symbolically as my hands mixing cooked, mashed red yams and white potatoes, or I will be trying new things. When I finally find myself, I am doing the former. Am disappointed, but only mildly.*

My journal continues:

> *Although there were two of me, one observing the other, this was not a lucid dream as that duality seemed entirely normal; I did not know I was dreaming. The potato symbolism clearly came from my Thanksgiving meal shopping when I found the store had run out of the red yams I wanted. The only alternative was the pale cream-colored Okinawan kind I'd never tried. As it happened, I was surprised at the beautiful lavender and purple mandala-like*

> *designs on the creamy white of their insides, only revealed as I cut them. Seemed like a reward for trying something new.*
>
> *Also, before sleep, I had read the J. Gary Sparks book by Carl Jung and Arnold Toynbee,* The Social Meaning of Inner Work, *comparing the two men's dreams and visions of how individuals interact with their societies during the rise and decline of civilizations, identifying myself, as I read, with the creative individuals of past and present times. Both authors — one focused on the inner life, the other on the outer — wrote about how the creatives who become role models during the rise of societies are unheard or actually silenced during their decline, and that they must therefore lead the way to a new society through their inner work. To me, that work is why I enrolled in this course, and I take this dream as encouragement that I'm on the right path.*

As I reread these journal notes, I realize deeply that the following two paragraphs tell the most important, even life-changing, insights the course led me to:

> *Interesting that this book came to me after I enrolled. The message is not to choose between inner and outer work, but to recognize, as Seth so insistently does, that they are never separate; to develop and harmonize them both in balanced relation to each other, as aspects of ourselves. In following up every Seth book reference, even going beyond the reading assignments, I had a kind of epiphany.*
>
> *Last week I'd really gotten it that dream reality and waking reality were equally real, running in parallel, actually never separate; that our challenge was to develop and harmonize them both in balanced relation to each other, as aspects of ourselves. This week, the emphasis was on how our beliefs and expectations create our dream realities as much as our waking realities.*
>
> *Being a Seth reader from the get-go, I have long assumed I create both my dreams and my waking reality, and yet, I now see something in their — what shall I call it? — interface. I have long attributed all the best and clearly 'magical' events in my life — and there have been so many — not to my own intentions, but to following clear instructions from some cosmic caregiver entity I called HP (for Higher Power) that kept the 'magic' going in the most amazing ways as long as I stayed faithfully on the path 'instructed,' usually by a clairaudient voice. As after its instruction to move to Hawai'i, I had to stay in total trust for it to work out no matter how unlikely that seemed.*

> *Point is that I ascribed the 'magic' to a rather remote or cosmic outside entity, while seeing my actions toward fulfilling the instruction as unflinching obedience to this HP voice. This was somehow different from believing I created all the other aspects of my reality, including the things that were not going so well — everything I did other than by following instructions from that HP outside myself.*
>
> *So, the epiphany during this dream course is that there never was a remote HP; that my own multidimensional self, includes its soul aspect, which is what I was 'obedient' to in creating all those instances of waking world 'magic.' They happened because I was 100% obedient to my own soul's stated direction!*

This, of course, is exactly the 100% belief phenomenon that I described in Chapter 11 in regard to Walter Russell and Joseph Chilton Pearce. I just had not seen it that way as long as the orders seemed to come from a remote HP when I immediately began to take steps to follow each such order, despite having no means to do so. And always it had worked out 'magically' as I never wavered from the designated path.

Physical challenges become challenges to belief

The most recent instance of such 'HP magic' was a trip to Florida from here in Hawai'i at a very desperate time of intense chronic pain, before I took this dream course and had my profound insight. After one hip replacement, the increasing pain in my other hip was misdiagnosed as being due to spinal stenosis and so I continued to hobble about for almost four years, grinding down what was left of any cartilage in the second hip.

I had connected my condition with the statue of Atlas crushed under the weight of the world, forever unable to rise to his feet. Had I, too, crippled myself by taking on the weight of the world, endlessly researching its condition and seeking ways to heal its ills? The thought of death as a release from acute pain was becoming ever more inviting, when suddenly I was offered a free month in a healing center in Florida.

It felt like an HP mandate I must take up, however impossible getting there appeared to be, as I could not even get across a room without a walker. But I 'knew' I must go, and, as in the past, everything I needed came: air ticket, wheelchair service, rides, a dear friend in Florida volunteering to drive hundreds of miles to pick me up and get me to my destination, and later coming all the way again to reverse the journey. In retrospect, I marvel that I was able to endure any of that trip as every part of it was seemingly impossible for me to have done. It is clear that only because I had taken it as an HP mandate was I able to follow through.

On arrival at the center, a wheelchair magically appeared when I was told there were none, along with a new unconditionally loving friend who got me through what turned out to be more like a nightmare than a healing journey, as the director/owner insisted I walk more and faster daily, while also trying all sorts of healing modalities on me, some of which increased the pain, but he allowed no argument about whether any of this might not be so good for me.

As my pain got even worse, my dear new friend Mitchell Rabin, who was teaching a Qi Gong class, hauled me around tirelessly in the wheelchair over cobblestones and very bumpy fields to widespread classes and meetings. He also did much to comfort me in our off-work time, keeping me from utter despair as the owner grew ever more bullying, even demanding we (there were other guests) stop talking with staff and each other. A few other staff members were also compassionate and readily helpful as they broke the restrictive rules on the sly, such bright notes in a sadly dark time.

It was the chiropractor who proved diagnostically helpful, not only insisting I go straight back home to have a second hip replacement, but identifying another anomaly, telling me I must also get a chiropractor to work on my Atlas, as it was seriously out of line. My Atlas?? How could he have known of my self-image? "What Atlas?" I queried in confusion.

He had to explain that the C1 vertebra in my neck was formally known as the Atlas, upon which the skull rests. Quite the surprise. Without completing the month, I changed the date of my return air ticket to leave quickly after his diagnosis, and immediately scheduled the second hip replacement on my return to Honolulu. I also found the most wonderful hands-on chiropractor here, who continues to work on my neck to this day.

As I was recuperating, PBS aired a wonderful new version of *Around the World in 80 Days*, in which the balloon gave me a new metaphor: turning the world globe resting on my shoulders into a hot air balloon, I could try getting it to lift me rather than crushing me under its weight! A day after I told an East Coast friend, Valerie Vandermeer, this in a Zoom call, she sent me an image of myself (from an Internet photo she found) in the basket of an Earth balloon flying through white clouds in a blue sky peppered with the repeated word JOY!

Valerie and her daughter Caelyn, have brilliantly taken the "16 Features of Healthy Living Systems"[101] I used for years in teaching businesses to become more like living systems, streamlining them into 12 skills anyone can learn to do the same both personally and in their organizations.[102]

Much to my surprise, there was to be yet another insight into my condition very recently. Despite all efforts to focus on balloon lift, walking regularly as much as possible while religiously doing daily and nightly exercises, I was still in considerable pain. One day, in a group dialogue on Zoom led by chiropractor Chad Sato, he spoke about the relationship between words and health — especially the words by which we describe our feelings and experiences. At one point, he asked us to take seven deep breaths and then go back to identify what was going on in our lives when some physical ailment began.

I went straight to my chronic joint issues, and instead of the old Atlas image, something entirely different popped up: My loss of Shoji-San, the wonderful Japanese businessman who had brought me to Japan several times after reading my *EarthDance* book, treating me like a Queen and eventually funding my international symposia on foundations of science, in Japan and then in Malaysia — all described in Chapter 13.

He had been paying me considerably more than I needed to live on for several years when he collapsed from a brain tumor en route to the second symposium and fell into a lasting coma after emergency surgery, his death reported six months later. My sudden new insight now was that his funding had become the 'structural support' of my life, and then it was GONE! It was just as I ran out of the money I'd saved from what he paid me that I realized I would not be able to climb the steep hill in Deia (Mallorca) daily for another winter.

I had not yet identified my joints' deterioration but was feeling its pain. I just knew I would have had to leave, and then, 'magically,' I got that HP (Higher Power) 'order' to move to Hawai'i. No resources, but to say it once again, the 'order' threw me into the 100% belief required for me to 'obey.' So, I did get to Hawai'i, complete with all the 'magic' as described earlier.

Now that I can see my internal structural support issues as a response to losing my external structural support, I'm faced with what to do next. Looking inward, I am unable to envision complete healing. I believe in a physical world as a very real part of the keyboard of vibrations we all are, and which I mentioned several times in Chapter 11. I also believe in the wonderful line of ancient Greek philosopher Anaximander I cited in

Chapter 5: *Everything that forms in nature incurs a debt, which it must repay by dissolving so that other things may form.* Evolution through recycling! And I'm definitely a believer in recycling, as well as in reincarnation.

In other words, our physical bodies are not intended to last beyond their fair term; no one reaches old age with the body of an adolescent. Even the best of health measures cannot create physical immortality. I am hugely grateful that I can continue to do interviews and presentations online at my now advanced age, the massive expansion of Zoom a gift of the COVID years that allows real elders to continue beyond physical limits. That said, I am about to embark on my first international travel since COVID as soon as I complete this book. And I have set my mind to see this trip as just the level of exercise I need right now to keep my joints functioning optimally. Thus, I make it my intention to practice zero doubt for one adventure at a time.

Crisis as Opportunity; Celebrating Crises

These are two titles I have often used for my presentations over the years. As you know, dear reader, they reflect my belief that humanity — or more accurately, those who have wrestled dominant power to control our globalized human civilization — have brought us to the adolescent crisis phase of a maturation process pervasive in Nature; a process for which the metamorphosis of the insatiable and destructive caterpillar giving way to its lighter-on-Earth butterfly is an apt metaphor.

Many now see it as breakdown to breakthrough. In the first section of this chapter, I mentioned the name Jem Bendell, whose new book *Breaking Together* tells the reality of the breakdown of our globalized civilization in greater detail than I've seen elsewhere. He argues persuasively that we can no longer stop the breakdown caused by our mismanagement of ecosystem exploitation, pollution, species extinctions, chemically dependent agricultural monocultures, economies driven by expansion, etc., regardless of all the greenwashing we are told can still stall true disaster. He pleads with us to accept the consequences while doing everything in our power to survive as best we can by building sharing and caring communities.

Discussion vs Dialogue

I just watched a live debate at Oxford University online. The topic was whether the Savory Institute's regeneration of desertified grasslands case was effective in climate mitigation, the debaters George Monbiot and Allen Savory. Allen's work was described in the previous chapter. As I watched/listened, I was constantly reminded of my distinction between debate or discussion and dialogue. Allen was trying to dialogue, respecting George's positions as he felt them, while George was persistently hostile, simply trying to negate whatever Allen said.

Discussion is the method of debate, and is a word coming from the Latin *discutere*, meaning to strike asunder, break up. The discussion of a debate is pointedly analytic and different from dialogue. Dialogue is a lovely word, from the Greek *dia-logos*, meaning through the word, one reaches harmony. Agreement is not the aim.

In dialogue, the participants seek some kind of harmony, as in the different notes of that chord which plays the role of resolution at the end of a musical piece. Its harmonious difference contrasts with the antagonistic difference of debate, which pits participants against each other, analyzing each other's positions to oppose them, with a winner and a loser as its result. I have often used the word dialogue in this book very intentionally, as I am a great believer in the need for much more of its harmony seeking in our world.

In the 1980s, when I was living in Greece, the Athens pollution cloud was a serious plague and hotly debated with various government agencies accusing each other of inaction and each pleading their own need for more research that gave more accurate numbers on how bad it was. In frustration at the ever-worsening cloud, I wished I could just get the contestants in this endless debate to take a simple average of their opposing figures and get on with *doing* something with obvious causes in traffic exhausts and other known emissions.

In the Oxford debate, while Monbiot persistently drilled for precise numerical evidence of carbon sequestering or storage, Savory just wanted to tell how to re-green desertified grasslands and show how well that worked. Almost countless farmers, by now, would have testified on his behalf with their own visible evidence.

It all made me think of how I learned from both the Western science I was taught, and the Indigenous science I learned later. The latter had plenty of evidence for remarkable achievements in medicine, astronomy, agriculture, navigation, and other categories of Western science, but numbers were rarely any part of such evidence.

Again and again, in this world of ever sharper divisions that destroy our natural community, I remind my audiences to explore loving diversity while deploring divisiveness. We must work relentlessly to build caring and sharing community as the techno-feudal world isolating us from one another collapses.

The H2 Clipper[103]

In my search for best green energy and technology solutions, I never found anything more amazing than the spectacular hydrogen dirigible and pipe-in-a-pipe technology invented by my dear friend and unofficial brother Rinaldo Brutoco.

As you will see from the site, the Clipper is both filled with compartmented hydrogen for its immense lifting capacity and uses hydrogen to fuel the four small jet engines that drive this marvelously aerodynamic craft laterally at speeds never before seen in hydrogen aircraft. The flight deck in its nose cone permits an almost 360-degree view.

So many people still have concerns about the safety of hydrogen, given almost a century of the Hindenburg disaster stories blaming it, that this is addressed in the last of the FAQ section on the website. Or check Toyota's hydrogen car test.[104]

I have my own special dream for these 'sky canoes' as I see them from my Polynesian vantage point, but first, this hydrogen matter, because a very recent 2023 PBS documentary on the Hindenburg disaster still reached no clear conclusion on what caused it. This surprised me because, during the COVID lockdown, when there was such ample time for research, I looked very deeply into that fiery Hindenburg crash in May 1937, the year after I was born, just 650 feet above the landing pad on its Lakehurst, New Jersey airfield, during a thunderstorm.

It was fascinating to watch early film footage of this zeppelin's building in Germany, to learn of its many successful trips on a triangle from Germany to South America to the USA, and why a lightning strike to its explosive skin set the entire zeppelin instantly afire, while the hydrogen inside it escaped harmlessly into the sky once the skin was punctured. It is now one of my very favorite sleuthing results, as my immense curiosity was validated when I finally figured out which German company had produced the 'doping' or 'shellac' or 'paint' that turned out on analysis to be explosive rocket fuel.

I could not find the name of that company anywhere, but I had found *"a 1937 letter from the Zeppelin company to the paint manufacturer expressed concerns, noting that tests showed the covering was 'readily ignited by an electrostatic discharge.'"* Hunting further, I found *"the German paint company went on to make rocket fuel of a similar composition for the V2 rockets."*[105]

That's when my own lightning struck me. The German word for paint is *farben*. And the German company then making V2 rockets was I.G. Farben, a company so vital to Germany's fighting WWII it had to be protected from identification with this international disaster. And, indeed, it was a company whose facilities were spared Allied bombing because the US wanted its facility, production, and scientists after the war for its own rocket and nuclear development.

Now back to my own interest in the wonderful H2 Clipper, its virtual testing by French aerospace company Dassault now complete and the prototype to begin construction in a Spanish airfield next year. I am not likely to live long enough to fulfill my dream of flying in one, but I can dream of these sky canoes sailing the skies of the Blue Continent called the Pacific.[106]

Look up into the sky and see these slim, needle-nosed sky canoes, with their four small jet engines suggesting paddles, soaring overhead. Maori/Maoli Sky Canoes, a native-owned company as one of the many flying these craft around Earth. These fly from the Maori land of Aotearoa we call New Zealand to the land of the Maoli, a word for Native Hawai'ians, and to other Pacific destinations.

Clean and green, they link the people of this Blue Continent as they can land anywhere, keeping our human community together when coastal piers and airports have been washed away. Canoes have always been central to Maori, Maoli, and other island nations, as the recent global circumnavigation by the traditional canoe Hokule'a exemplified in its *Malama Honua* journey.[107]

Peak experiences

Asked recently what were the peak experiences of my life, I immediately recalled Jean Houston's question, when I was visiting in New York while still living in Greece. Jean had asked me what I would most love to do in life, and I had replied, without reflection, "Dialogue with the finest minds on the planet."

As I told in Chapter 10, this had also occurred to me again when sitting with astronaut Ed Mitchell in a Brazilian garden party where we two 'speakers' were to address the other guests. After all, there I was with one of the finest minds on the planet, which is why I looked at Ed and asked, "Why don't we just have an impromptu dialogue?" He agreed happily, so we did that for our rapt audience, rather than giving a little speech each. Ed, of course, sitting under that full moon, recounted his own peak experience on the way home from his moon-walking Apollo 14 mission, as he had written about:

> *In my cockpit window every two minutes, Earth, the moon, the sun, and the whole 360-degree panorama of the heavens ... and suddenly I realized that the molecules of my body, and the molecules of the spacecraft, and the molecules in the bodies of my partners were prototyped and manufactured in some ancient generation of stars.... that was an overwhelming sense of oneness, of connectedness, it wasn't them and us, it was that's me, that's all of it, it's one thing. It was as though my awareness reached out to touch the farthest star, and I was aware of being an integral part of the entire universe. And it was accompanied by an ecstasy, or a sense of, Oh my God, wow, yes, an insight, an epiphany.*[108]

Now I was having a peak experience in this dialogue with Ed, bolstered by more conversation with him during our helicopter ride and on other occasions.

Many years before that, as recounted at the beginning of this book, my conversations with Henry Miller in his Malibu home in the '70s was also a peak experience, as were my dialogues with Jim Lovelock those ten days in Greece in the '80s, my conversations with Thomas Berry on his Hudson River bank lawn in 1991, and those with Jean Houston herself, with UN Sec'y General Robert Mueller, and with Rodrigo Carazo, president of Costa Rica and founder of the University for Peace, with Leon Shenandoah and Oren Lyons, with Deepak Chopra and Bruce Lipton, David Lorimer of the Scientific & Medical Network and more.

In short, that intention that had burst unthinking from my mouth in response to Jean's question, has held up to this day, and my favorite speaking is in dialogue with a continuing stream of wonderful hosts.

Discoveries and contributions

Asked for my best discoveries and contributions, I would begin with my insight that Nature is our greatest role model for economics and politics, as can be shown through ecosystems and our own bodies. It also shows the way to a wise society, or Ecosophy[109] by making our economy subservient to Nature's ecology, rather than making Nature subservient to human economy as presently practiced so unsustainably.

Then I would add: Simplifying the complexities of evolution biology by choosing good metaphors such as the maturation cycle from youthful to mature modes, a body economics model that shows why our human economics cannot work in a living system, and my Keyboard model showing how cosmos, planet, and person are all composed of the vibrations of matter, energy, and mind/spirit.[110]

Lastly, I would add my insight that the Western science I was taught is not the only possible science as it rests on a particular foundational worldview without which it could not exist. One cannot make scientific theories about how the Cosmos or Nature work without concepts of what Cosmos and Nature are. I showed, in my international symposia in Japan and Kuala Lumpur, as well as all my work with indigenous people, that other global sciences exist, with demonstrably different foundational worldviews. I pray someone will take up my intention to develop a Global Consortium of Sciences to parallel the Parliament of World Religions, and to provide checks and balances among them, as described in Chapter 13.

We explorers and discoverers, all stand on the shoulders of those before us, and I see gratefully from countless references to my work and responses to interviews and presentations that I am now part of the evolutionary chain of understanding this human condition as a scientist with the deepest respects for all the arts, all the other ways of knowing.

EPILOGUE

Looking back on my intellectual and spiritual life, which is what this book recounts, I feel very privileged to have learned from indigenous peoples what I could not learn in universities — the diverse ways of sensing, knowing, and understanding Nature and human life within it, so far from the worldview of the now dominant culture in which I was raised. Two Living Treasure awards from WISN and my Stars of Oceania award for work with Pacific Nations on Ulu (Breadfruit) as food security, are truly treasures.

The greatest influence on the foundations of my overall worldview — what I call my VISTA — is Seth, the discarnate entity for which Jane Roberts acted as conduit; to wit my many references to it.

Then there are my wonderful mentors from those I never got to meet in person (though I have letters from some), including V. I. Vernadsky, Erich Jantsch, David Bohm, Walter Pankow, George Wald, Francisco Varela and Humberto Maturana, Thomas Kuhn, Lyall Watson, J. Allen Boone, and those I did get to meet, most of whom became friends, including Henry Miller, Jim Lovelock and Lynn Margulis, Teddy Goldsmith, Ralph Abraham, Fritjof Capra, Thomas Berry, Jean Houston, Hazel Henderson, Barbara Marx Hubbard, Vandana Shiva, Robert Mueller, Rodrigo Carazo, Bruce Lipton and Steve Bhaerman, and more that will continue to come to mind.

It is also among my blessings to have gained a working knowledge or better of German, French, Greek and Spanish languages, as languages are so closely related to worldviews.

Worldviews — VISTAs — as my passion led me to the discovery of multiple sciences in our world, and thus to holding the Symposia on Foundations of Science. I pray there will be scientists who pursue those symposia I did not get to convene and build that Global Consortium of Sciences I have so dreamed of, to parallel the Parliament of World Religions.

It has also been my privilege to visit so many countries and cultures leaving their imprints on those ecosystems of our awesome planet Earth. I am always aware of how national boundaries were scratched across the surface of Earth — so 'unnaturally' — and of how our now-globalized 'post-modern' humanity has spread its dazzling technological prowess, however unevenly, among these nations.

Let me count those countries now, as I have never actually taken their tally: In the Americas I count Canada, US, Mexico, Guatemala, Costa Rica, Venezuela, Brazil, Argentina, Chile, and Peru. Then on to South Africa, Morrocco, Egypt, Israel, Bahrain, India, Sri Lanka, Turkey, Greece, Italy, Portugal, Spain, France, Germany, Belgium, Netherlands, Ireland, Scotland, England, Estonia, Norway. Around the Pacific: New Zealand, Australia, Indonesia, Malaysia, China, Taiwan, South Korea, Japan.

Thirty-nine countries, all continents. I think of Hawai'i as the fortieth, as I've been a strong supporter of its regaining sovereignty. In the COVID years, when travel came to a sudden halt, I had a virtual new country, with a virtual consultancy with futurists in Dubai, the United Arab Emirates. Physically, I walked in the snowy mountains of the Chilean Cordillera and in the deserts of Bahrain, China, Egypt, California, and the Andean altiplano. I visited the deep rainforest jungles of Brazil and Indonesia and the majestic northern forests of Canada and Russia.

But even better than the geographic tally is the enormously wide variety of the venues into which I was called to speak and do workshops and consultations. In addition to my many gatherings of indigenous people, there were national government agencies in several countries, the United Nations headquarters in NYC, as well as its Rio '92 and Indigenous Nations Agency conferences in South America.

Then, because of my work in the Biology of Business, there were business schools and multinational businesses and future societies concerned with economics. In the field of religions, I found myself speaking to Christian Catholics, Episcopalians, New Thought and Interfaith churches, Theosophists, Anthroposophists, Buddhists, and Taoists. Then the many conferences on Science & Spirit or Consciousness, on women's empowerment, on peace, and on climate change.

Some of my favorite unique ones were a Goi Peace Initiative in Japan, where Gorbachev was a fellow speaker, an International Planetarium Directors Conference in Athens, Greece, a Conscious Clothing Convention in Sri Lanka and the first Disclosure Conference on UFOs in Washington DC. At my symposium in Kuala Lumpur, mostly men participated, and they gave me more respect than I've felt from male colleagues in the US.

In Berlin, I was one of the 'voices' at the Round Table of Free Voices from all over the world. Then there were my TED talk in Richard Branson's sister Vanessa's Morocco mansion, the founding meeting of the United Religions Initiative in Palo Alto, CA, the founding meeting of Rising Women, Rising Word in the House of Lords, London, a Convention of Russian Indigenous Peoples in Moscow, and, of course, the meetings with the Dalai Lama in Dharamsala and in the Pope's Summer Palace in Rome.

Somehow my work, as an evolution biologist and futurist, on this Perfect Storm of Crises and ways through to a better future, found resonance in this great and cherished variety of gatherings.

My daughter Johara, my grandchildren, and great grandchildren through her, should any of them read this book, may wonder why they have so little mention. As I said in the Preface, this book is not an autobiography, but just about my intellectual and spiritual development. Only my son Philip avidly followed this intellectual trajectory of mine from the time he was still a teenager, when I brought him to Greece. There, as reported, he read my writings as they evolved, making a great sounding board, and much later built my beautiful website, where he will post this book as it becomes available. I am deeply grateful for all his support.

Besides my global family, to which I put myself in lifelong service, I was also aware of other incarnations, and therefore interested in my karmic lineage, so to speak. In no few of my very large number of other Earth lives, my soul purpose was dominated by speaking truth to power and that did not go so well. Having learned in this life to get my politics and economics from Nature's most mature bodies and ecosystems, I believe I have finally gotten it right. Citing Nature as source for my concepts has proven the most effective, powerful, and harmless way of showing what is not right in our world and how we can do better despite all the challenges we now face.

I pray humanity will get through the bottleneck I see from my perspective, but of which I will not experience the greatest challenges. I believe we humans will pass through it in far fewer numbers, but with the survivors as true pioneers once again; pioneers with the heart, knowledge, and will to make it into the caring and sharing maturity that is in harmony with all the rest of Nature, as is our true destiny.

References

1   Taken up later by Rupert Sheldrake.

2   Expanded later by Bruce Lipton.

3   Fuzzy logic is a form of many-valued logic; it deals with reasoning that is approximate rather than fixed and exact.

4   An etymological clarification I owe to the evolutionist, Erich Jantsch.

5   See Bohm's *Wholeness and the Implicate Order*, Routledge, 2002, for example.

6   James Lovelock's *Gaia: A New Look at Life on Earth*, Oxford University Press, 2000; first published in1979.

7   Much later, in 2004 (20 years after it was begun), John Perkins' *Confessions of an Economic Hit Man*, as described on Amazon.com "reveals a game that, according to John Perkins, is "as old as Empire" but has taken on new and terrifying dimensions in an era of globalization. And Perkins should know. For many years he worked for an international consulting firm where his main job was to convince LDCs (less developed countries) around the world to accept multibillion-dollar loans for infrastructure projects and to see to it that most of this money ended up at Halliburton, Bechtel, Brown and Root, and other United States engineering and construction companies. This book, which many people warned Perkins not to write, is a blistering attack on a little-known phenomenon that has had dire consequences on both the victimized countries and the U.S."

8   These became the first two chapters of David Bohm's book *Wholeness and the Implicate Order*, published by Routledge, Great Britain in 1980.

9   Campbell, Joseph, edit., *The Portable Jung*, "The Difference between Eastern sad Western Thinking," p. 481, Viking Press, NY 1971

10   *Cash and Violence in Laos and Viet Nam* by Anna Louise Strongwas published by New York: Mainstream Publishers in 1962.

11   Erich Jantsch, *The Self-Organizing Universe: Scientific and Human Implications of the Emerging Paradigm of Evolution*, Pergamon Press,1980.

12   Searching the Internet today, you will see images of Red Flag Canal along a completely green mountainside that was still utterly barren when I was there. The canal has become a proud national monument with big hotels and an endless stream of visitors, while the entire valley is fertile and productive.

13   This was scarcely acknowledged before the late 1970s and is detailed in Lyons, Oren. et al. *Exiled in the Land of the Free*. Democracy, Indian Nations and the United States Constitution. Santa Fe, NM: Clear Light, 1992.

14   The Standard Model in physics is the paradigm of quantum field theory and describes subatomic particles and their interactions via basic forces. It is often used more loosely to describe Big Bang universe physics.

15   *The Tao of Physics: An Exploration of the Parallels Between Modern Physics and Eastern Mysticism* by Fritjof Capra was published in 1975 by Shambhala Publications of Berkeley, California. Capra was a member of the Fundamental Fysiks Group that explored the philosophical implications of quantum theory. It was founded in San Francisco by two physicists, Elizabeth Rauscher and George Weissmann, and included Fritjof Capra, John Clauser, Philippe Eberhard, Nick Herbert, Jack Sarfatti, Saul-Paul Sirag, Henry Stapp, and Fred Alan Wolf. Of these ten members listed in Wikipedia, I met seven of them over the years both personally and in several leading edge science groups in which I was involved. Capra's later books were *The Turning Point* (1982), *Uncommon Wisdom* (1988), *The Web of Life* (1996) and *The Hidden Connections* (2002).

16   In Walter Russell's book The Secret of Light (1947) he captions his dually spiraling universe illustrations with "The creating universe appears from the One and disappears back into the One."

17   In *Cosmic Catastrophes*, by Gerrit Verschuur, Addison-Wesley 1978.

18   When the film *Hidden Figures*, about the amazing Black women at NASA came out in 2017 I felt certain that Shirley had helped in their career advancement.

19   Many later channelers were highly influenced by Jane's material (some having attended regular live sessions held in her home for years), but, for me, none could add anything significant to Jane/Seth's original works.

20   Watch a live amoeba here: http://www.youtube.com/watch?v=7pR7TNzJ_pA

21   http://en.wikipedia.org/wiki/Lynn_Margulis

22   From the first of Lewis Thomas' fascinating and pithy essays in his book, *The Lives of a Cell: Notes of a Biology Watcher*, Bantam Books, Viking, NY 1974.

23   These were called The Camelford Conferences on the Implications of the Gaia Thesis and resulted in several pubications under that name.

24   Goldsmith,Edward. Blueprint for Survival Penguin Books Ltd; Revised edition (June 28, 1973) Also available online at http://www.edwardgoldsmith.org/books/a-blueprint-for-survival/

25   http://www.edwardgoldsmith.org/49/thermodynamics-or-ecodynamics. This critique of entropy was also noted by another favorite writer of mine, Arthur Koestler, who also limited entropy to the description of closed systems.

26   Vernadsky, Vladimir. 1926,1986. The Biosphere. Published originally in 1926; reprinted U.S. edition 1986. Oracle, AZ: Synergistic Press.

27   Bateson, G. (1979). *Mind and Nature: A Necessary Unity (Advances in Systems Theory, Complexity, and the Human Sciences)*. Hampton Press.

28   Maturana, Humberto, with Francisco Varela. *Autopoiesis and Cognition: The Realization of the Living*. Boston Studies in the Philosophy of Science. Paperback, 1991.

29   It was only after I 'coined' *allopoietic* on my own that I discovered Maturana and Varela had been using it themselves, but differently. While I was distinguishing mechanical from living entities, they defined allopoietic as: "The state or character of systems whose operation results in something other than the maintenance of their defining organization . This term is mainly invoked to establish a contrastive alternative to the autonomy and autopoiesis evidenced by living systems (the primary focus of Maturana and Varela's work)." This made them include a car factory as allopoietic because it did nit produce other car factories, but cars.

30   Koestler, Arthur, *Janus: A Summing Up*. Picador Books 1979

31   Seeking the True Meaning of Peace Conference in San Jose, Costa Rica 1987

32   Jantsch, Erich and Waddington, Conrad H. *Evolution and Consciousness: Human Systems in Transition*, Addison-Wesley, 1976.

33   *The Heart of The World: Elder Brother's Warning* was made by Alan Ereira for the British Broadcasting Corporation and released in 1990.

34   http://www.ratical.org/radiation/UraniumInNavLand.html "the Indians dug the ore that started the United States' stockpile of nuclear weapons. For thirty years after the first atomic explosions in New Mexico, uranium was mined much like any other mineral. More than 99 percent of the product of the mines was waste, cast aside as tailings near mine sites after the uranium had been extracted. One of the mesa-like waste piles grew to be a mile long and 70 feet high. On windy days, dust from the tailings blew into local communities, filling the air and settling on the water supplies. The Atomic Energy Commission assured worried local residents that the dust was harmless. ...The biggest expulsion of radioactive material in the United States occurred July 16, 1979, at 5 a.m. on the Navajo Nation, less than 12 hours after President Carter had proposed plans to use more nuclear power and fossil fuels. On that morning, more than 1,100 tons of uranium mining wastes — tailings — gushed through a packed-mud dam near Church Rock, N.M. With the tailings, 100 million gallons of radioactive water gushed through the dam before the crack was repaired.

By 8 a.m., radioactivity was monitored in Gallup, N.M., nearly 50 miles away. The contaminated river, the Rio Puerco, showed 7,000 times the allowable standard of radioactivity for drinking water below the broken dam shortly after the breach was repaired, according to the Nuclear Regulatory Commission. The few newspaper stories about the spill outside of the immediate area noted that the area was "sparsely populated" and that the spill "poses no immediate health hazard."

35   A natural chalk, the hard version of which is Andean lapis lazuli.

36   Kari Oca Village Declaration of the World Conference of Indigenous Peoples on Territory, Environment and Development, May 1992.

Preamble:

The Indigenous Peoples of the Americas, Asia, Africa, Australia, Europe and the Pacific, united in one voice at Kari Oca Village, express our collective gratitude to the Indigenous Peoples of Brazil. Inspired by this historical meeting, we celebrate the spiritual unity of the Indigenous Peoples with the land and ourselves. We continue building and formulating our united commitment to save our Mother the Earth. We, the Indigenous Peoples, endorse the following declaration as our collective responsibility to carry our indigenous minds and voices into the future.

Declaration:

We, the indigenous people, walk to the future in the footprints of our ancestors.

From the smallest to the largest living being, from the four directions, from the air, the land and the mountains, the Creator has placed us, the Indigenous Peoples, upon our Mother, the Earth.

The footprints of our ancestors are permanently etched upon the lands of our peoples.

We, the Indigenous Peoples, maintain our inherent rights to self determination. We have always had the right to determine our own forms of government, to use our own laws, to raise and educate our children, to our own cultural identity without interference.

We continue to maintain our rights as peoples despite centuries of deprivation, assimilation and genocide.

We maintain our inalienable rights to our lands and territories, to all our resources — above and below — and to our waters. We assert our ongoing responsibility to pass these on to future generations.

We cannot be removed from our lands. We, the Indigenous Peoples are connected by the circle of life to our lands and environments.

We, the Indigenous Peoples, walk to the future in the footprints of our ancestors.

Signed at Kari Oca, Brazil on the 30th day of May, 1992.

37   Adnan Sarhan founded the Sufi Foundation of America Retreat

Center near Torreon, New Mexico. http://www.sufifoundation.org/

38   See http://www.oneprayer.org/ for a photo history of the Vigil from 1993 to 2012, which gradually included many of the world's faiths as well as native people.

39   From her NYT obituary at in 2013/09/20, which credits her with the discovery of opiate receptors in cells although: "The discovery of the opioid receptor would, in 1978, earn the coveted Albert Lasker Award, often a precursor to the Nobel Prize. The award went to Solomon H. Snyder, who headed the lab. Neither Dr. Pert nor any of the other lab assistants was cited. Such omissions are common in the world of science.... She became a leading proponent of the unity of mind and body, and the ability of emotions to affect health. When Bill Moyers, in a 1993 PBS special, "Healing and the Mind," asked her, "Are you saying that the mind talks to the body, so to speak, through these neuropeptides?" she answered, "Why are you making the mind outside of the body?" She was also featured prominently in the 2004 film *What the #$*! Do We Know!?*, which attempted to bridge science and spirituality."

40   My article was called "The Evolution of Governance," *In Context* magazine, Fall/Winter 1993/4. *In Context* later morphed into *YES* magazine.

41   *The Unfolding Story*, Video, Foundation for Global Community, Palo Alto, repeated aired on PBS.

42   J. Allen Boone, *Kinship with All Life*, Harper & Row, 1954. Several more paperback editions keep this one in print.

43   J. Allen Boone, *You Are the Adventure*. Prentice-Hall, Inc. 1943 (another edition from Robert H. Sommer, New Jersey 1977.

44   St. Exupery is best known for his classic children's book *The Little Prince*. He was an aviator that took mail across the Andes from Buenos Aires to Santiago de Chile in the 1920s.

45   See my article "Journey to Hapu" at http://www.ratical.org/LifeWeb/Articles/hapu.html

46   *Web Without a Weaver: How the Internet is Shaping Our Future* by Victor Grey was published not long after, with cover blurb: "In a non-technical, articulate voice, Internet historian and strategist Victor Grey weaves diverse information into an easily understandable and revealing picture of the global future being shaped by the Internet." My review of it was published: Evolution biologist Dr. Elisabet Sahtouris says of Victor Grey, "I really love that he wrote the book I hoped someone would write about the Internet. The Internet from the start has interested me as the biggest and most impressive self-organizing system in human history, forming with lightning speed to save us on the brink of disaster, and he says it all so eloquently, elegantly and readably. I am most impressed!"

47   See, for example, *Stone Age Economics* by M. Sahlins, 1968, and

"Notes on the Original Affluent Society", *Man the Hunter*. R.B. Lee and I. DeVore. New York: Aldine Publishing Company) pp. 85-89. Also: Sahlins, M. 2005. The Original Affluent Society [Online] in M. Sahlins, *Stone Age Economics*.

48   Prologue to *Genesis de la Cultura Andina* by Carlos Milla Villena, Lima 1983.

49   *Wings of Courage*, an IMAX film by French director Jean-Jacques Annaud.

50   As I write this, I have just spent a week with Puma, now 34, married to his local sweetheart and father of two boys, at the New Story Summit hosted by the Findhorn Foundation in Scotland. The bouncy, bright-eyed boy with the loving heart and huge smile is still there in the powerfully built man who heals everyone coming into his presence.

51   I later met another woman, in a high government position in a European country, who also willingly donated her eggs for alien breeding and told me she had been taken onto a spaceship to see her offspring.

52   Erich Jantsch. *The Self-organizing Universe: scientific and human implications of the emerging paradigm of evolution*. Pergamon Press, 1980.

53   Simon & Schuster had published it under their title *Gaia: The Human Journey from Chaos to Cosmos*, my agent not even informing me until it had alreadly been rushed into print as a hot title. In my view, Gaia is not a Human Journey, but a name for Earth as a living planet giving rise to humans in its evolution.

54   Harman, Willis & Sahtouris, Elisabet. *Biology Revisioned*, North Atlantic Books, Berkeley 1998, p. 123.

55   Looking though a series of dictionaries, one finds both consciousness defined in terms of awareness, and awareness defined in terms of consciousness, yet none make them identical. Clearly the matter of definition remains unclear.

56   *Biology Revisioned*, North Atlantic Books, Berkeley, 1998, by Willis W. Harman and Elisabet Sahtouris. p. 223.

57   These were eventually published as "Prologue to a New Model of a Living Universe," chapter in *Mind Before Matter: Visions of a New Science of Consciousness*, O Books, 2007, and "Towards a Future Global Science: Axioms for Modeling a Living Universe," *World Future Review*, Dec. 2008.

58   *Biology Revisioned*, p217-18.

59   He had actually read it in its original version, *Gaia*, as published by Simon & Schuster.

60   *A Walk Through Time*, Wiley & Sons, 1998. Sid Liebes and Brian Swimme, who wrote the Preface and Prologue were given equal billing as authors.

61   *The Reflexive Universe: Evolution of Consciousness*, 1976, New York: Delacorte Press, ISBN 0-440-05925-9, corrected ed. with introduction by Huston Smith, 1976, Anodos Foundation.

62   See https://www.resonancescience.org/blog/The-Rotating-Universe for Haramein and Rauscher's work.

63   I have never been able to find Wald's reference for that extraordinary statement — that it had been realized that radiation and gravity were in perfect balance in our universe — which was remarkable at the time he wrote it, even contacting his son for suggestions to follow up.

64   *The Man Who Tapped the Secrets of the Universe*, by Glenn Clark is a wonderful small book account of this extraordinary man.

65   Joseph Chilton Pierce writes of similar impossible but doubt-free achievements while he was young in the first chapter of his book *Biology Transcended*.

66   The largest growth in Seth readers is now in Asia, through the work of Taiwanese medical doctor and psychiatrist Dr. Tien-Shen Hsu. See https://sethcenter.com/products/the-secret-to-healing-cancer-dr-tien-sheng-hsu

67   Indeed, exactly this model is called by Dr. and Master Zhi Gang Sha, in his many books, including *Soul Over Matter and Soul Mind Body Science System*, the grand unification physics model of the ancient Taoists.

68   Watson, Lyall, *Beyond Supernature: A New Natural History of the Supernatural*, Bantam, New York 1988 has a chapter on Society including Eugene Marais' work on termite mound building and ant societies, William Wheeler's (Woods Hole) "an organism is not a thing but a process" and "one of the fundamental tendencies of life is sociogenic" and English naturalist Edmund Selous who spoke of thought transference in bird flocks in 1931.

69   See my website for the list. http://sahtouris.com

70   The Itaipu dam hit the world records in energy production in 2012 and 2013, and produces entirely clean electricity-saving one hundred million tons of carbon dioxide emissions compared with coal power plants.

71   Dalai Lama Renaissance and Dalai Lama Awakening, narrated by Harrison Ford, Wakan Films http://www.dalailamafilm.com/

72   Kiuchi, Takashi and Shireman, Bill (2001), *What We Learned in the Rainforest: Business Lessons from Nature*; Berrett-Koehler: San Francisco.

73   Teilhard de Chardin is best known for his book *The Phenomenon of Man*, and together with V.I. Vernadsky had coined the terms Biosphere and Noosphere.

74   Considering this letter an unpublished article called "A Scientist's Thoughts about Redefining our Concept of God," I posted it on my website www.sahtouris.com under articles: cosmology/science evolving.

75   Research now shows that six-month-old babies prefer helper figures in a visually presented story to competitors, but shift to the opposite preference by the age of one! https://www.youtube.com/watch?v=gefVcVMah5c&feature=youtu.be

76   Paul Ray and Sherry Anderson, *The Cultural Creatives: How 50 Million People are Changing the World*, Harmony Books, 2000, pp 21-2.

77   https://en.wikipedia.org/wiki/Dropping_knowledge

78   According to Wikipedia: In 2006, an agricultural theme park called Ecorin Village was built in Eniwa. At the gardening center of the theme park is a greenhouse housing *Tomato no Mori* (とまとの森) "Tomato Forest"), which in November 2013 was awarded the Guinness World Records award for the largest tomato plant in the world, measuring 85.46m2 at the time.

79   In the Soviet Union, evolution biology was taught as cooperative through Petr Kropotkin's seminal 1902 collection of essays, *Mutual Aid*.

80   Little Sun is a solar-powered LED lamp developed by artist Olafur Eliasson and solar engineer Frederik Ottesen, designed to deliver clean, affordable, reliable light to the 1.6 billion people worldwide without access to the electrical grid. Five hours of charging produces up to three hours of bright light (plus additional hours of lower light). Every purchase makes it possible for Little Suns to be sold in off-grid communities at locally affordable prices. Olafur Eliasson has work in MoMA's collection.

81   The public TV series *Skindigenous* is a wondrous trip through different indigenous cultures' tattoo traditions.

82   https://www.theguardian.com/books/2019/feb/02/age-of-surveillance-capitalism-shoshana-zuboff-review

83   https://www.weforum.org. Anyone can join the WEF's global network on that website.

84   Schwab's latest book on the world's future is called *The Great Narrative (The Great Reset)*. https://www.amazon.com/Great-Narrative-Reset/dp/2940631301

85   https://www.younggloballeaders.org/people

86   https://savory.global/

87   For example, the book *Brilliant Green*, by Stefano Mancuso shows trees having at least a dozen senses in addition to our human five of sight, hearing, touch, smell, and taste.

88   https://www.britannica.com/topic/reincarnation, 2023.

89   See, for example *The End of Money and the Future of Civilization*, 2010, by Thomas H. Greco, Jr.

90   *The Dawn of Everything: A New History of Humanity* by David Graeber and David Wengrow. A dramatically new understanding of human

history, challenging our most fundamental assumptions about social evolution — from the development of agriculture and cities to the origins of the state, democracy, and inequality — and revealing new https://www.ethicalmarkets.com/possibilities for human emancipation.

91   https://www.ethicalmarkets.com/

92   https://www.environmentandurbanization.org/calvert-henderson-quality-life-indicators-new-tool-assessing-national-trends

93   https://ophi.org.uk/policy/gross-national-happiness-index/

94   *Breaking Together*, by Jem Bendell, 2023.

95   https://www.mondragon-corporation.com/en/

96   https://www.sarvodaya.org/

97   See the film at https://www.youtube.com/watch?v=MM1D_syZOM0

98   https://savory.global/

99   https://capitalinstitute.org/director/john-fullerton/

100   https://doughnuteconomics.org/about-doughnut-economics

101   http://sahtouris.com/#8_2,0

102   https://www.4evlutn.com/

103   https://www.h2clipper.com/

104   https://www.youtube.com/watch?v=jVeagFmmwA0

105   http://www.rebresearch.com/blog/the-hindenburg-disaster/

106   I read that young Native Hawai'ians designed a digital game about sailing a sky canoe through the Cosmos to learn wisdom in visiting other worlds but have lost its traces.

107   See short video at https://youtu.be/LOWjsoyAXVY

108   *The Way of the Explorer: An Apollo Astronaut's Journey Through the Material and Mystical Worlds*, by Edgar D. Mitchell and Dwight Williams | May 7, 1996. *From Outer Space to Inner Space: An Apollo Astronaut's Journey Through the Material and Mystical Worlds*, by Edgar Mitchell, Avi Loeb, et al. | Jan 1, 2023.

109   https://www.kosmosjournal.org/article/ecosophy-natures-guide-to-a-better-world/

110   http://www.sahtouris.com/docs/Keyboard.pdf

A Note from the Author

What legacy can a dedicated adventurer, a cosmic snoop, a deep pastist, and futurist leave to her world at the end of a long life? For well over half my 88 Earth turnings, I've been dedicated to the age-old questions of who we humans are, where we've come from, and where we seem to be headed. As an evolution biologist (deep pastist) I eventually realized my science was only one of many sciences we humans developed to answer such questions, each based on a particular worldview, actually on a particular story of *How Things Are* from microcosm to macrocosm.

Story used to be called fiction, but recently, our rigid boundary between fiction and fact has become very fuzzy and storytelling has gained ground as what distinguishes us from other creatures. It is our way of exchanging our experiences, of forming our realities.

All of us go through life molding our experiences into such stories. This book, then, is the legacy I leave you all, dear readers, a compilation of the experiential stories, many quite magical, which formed my evolving worldview, my VISTA. I wish you all good fortune in evolving yours.

Dr. Elisabet Sahtouris is a globally known evolution biologist and futurist. Her other books are *EarthDance: Living Systems in Evolution*, *A Walk Through Time: from Stardust to Us*, *Biology Revisioned* (with Willis Harman, *Gaia's Dance: the story of Earth & Us*, and *Bacteria Я Us*.

www.ingramcontent.com/pod-product-compliance
Lightning Source LLC
Chambersburg PA
CBHW070638050426
42451CB00008B/203